PRAISE FOR

ORGANIC DISCIPLEMAKING

"The organic disciplemaking teachings and practices laid out in this book have transformed the lives and ministries of my two children who became part of Xenos while attending university. Both have blossomed into effect disciples, disciplemakers and godly leaders. The many Xenos workers who have joined World Team for cross cultural church planting often have a distinct advantage over other workers who have learned about discipleship but have not experienced it. I encourage you to read this book with thoughtful reflection and critique so that you can apply it as you and your church disciple others to follow Jesus."

ALBERT EHMANN
Executive Director of World Team

"Dennis and Jessica are a master disciple-makers. Dennis has personally mentored more people into spiritual maturity and leadership than anyone I know. *Organic Disciplemaking* is a new classic on the details of *what*, *why*, and *how* to make disciples in the 21st century. It is Biblically solid, theologically sound, and practically effective. Buy it. Read it. Do it."

DR. DAVE EARLEY
Director for the Center for Ministry Training
Liberty Theological Seminary

"Christ's last command was to make disciples (Matthew 28:18). But what does that look like in the 21st century? *Organic Disciplemaking* offers Biblical, practical, and insightful steps to make disciples. Don't expect extra-Biblical formulas or quick-growth strategies. Discipleship takes work and sacrifice, and the authors honestly share their failures and what they learned from them. I had the privilege of visiting the McCallum's home in June 2005. I experienced what takes place regularly at their house—a group of University students (both Christian and non-Christian) crowding into the living room to ask questions and explore the Christian faith. The McCallums, like hundreds of others at Xenos, open their homes to make disciples who make more disciples. Xenos Christian Fellowship, in fact, has more than a thousand people meeting weekly with their disciples. Pay careful attention to what these authors say about organic disciple-making!"

DR. JOEL COMISKEY
Author and President, Cell Church Solutions

"Read this ministry lifting book! Dennis and Jessica invite you walk with them into a practical, balanced, and detailed "how" book of tested ministry. I was refreshed with insights on transmitting vision, coaching, discipline, endurance, and evangelism. In every strata of training there is the passion stream of "multiply"! You'll get fine tuning that will help produce disciplemakers. God uses all kinds of people to make their growing leadership base. They, in turn, model Christ and multiply home groups with fresh new leadership—and on a church base."

DR. WAYLON B. MOORE
Missions Unlimited

ORGANIC DISCIPLEMAKING

ORGANIC DISCIPLEMAKING

MENTORING OTHERS
INTO SPIRITUAL MATURITY
AND LEADERSHIP

Dennis McCallum
Jessica Lowery

TOUCH PUBLICATIONS

Houston, Texas, U.S.A.

Published by TOUCH Publications
P.O. Box 7847
Houston, Texas, 77270, U.S.A.
800-735-5865

Cover design by Don Bleyl & Associates

International Standard Book Number: 0-9752896-9-1

TOUCH Publications is the book-publishing division
of TOUCH Outreach Ministries, a resource, consulting, and
training ministry for churches with a vision for
cell-based ministry.

Find us on the World Wide Web at:
http://www.touchusa.org

Visit Xenos Christian Fellowship's web site at:
http://www.xenos.org

CONTENTS

SECTION TWO — KEY COMPONENTS IN DISCIPLESHIP

SECTION THREE — COACHING

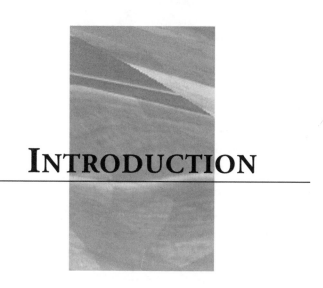

INTRODUCTION

or•gan•ic _r-_ga-nik\ *adjective*
1. of, relating to, or derived from living organisms

When we entrust our lives to Jesus, we are joined to him in an organic way. Paul says, "He who unites himself with the Lord is one with him in spirit" (1 Cor. 5:17). This is not an institutional or a legal linkage. When God joins us to Christ, our life becomes so entwined with his, it can only be considered a living, organic link.

Likewise, our connection to one another in the body of Christ is organic. In another passage Paul says, "We, who are many, are one body in Christ, and individually members one of another" (Rom. 12:5 NASB). Here we learn that the body of Christ is not an institution but a living organism. When we understand our mystical union with Jesus and each other, we also quickly realize cascading implications for other areas of life and ministry.

The church today is reawakening to the power of an organic approach to ministry. An organic approach focuses less on positions in the church and more on relationships. Instead of seeing God moving out to people mainly through church programs, organic ministers envision God moving from person to person creating direct spiritual impact through relational love. Modernists may see the church as rows of listening people. But God reveals a community where his life flows through people like blood vessels or nerve cells (Eph. 4:16; Col. 2:19).

Growth in the church changes under the organic approach as well. Instead of linear approaches limited by schools, degrees, and buildings, organic growth takes the form of dynamic, multiplying cells. Just as living cells duplicate themselves exponentially, the body of Christ explodes in every direction under the organic model.

Nothing is more organic than making disciples. Disciple-making depends more on high quality relationships than any other ministry. As you will see, making disciples is the most natural and organic way to expand and deepen the body of Christ. Indeed, all our aspirations to see God's church living out our organic union with Jesus will break down if our disciple-making ministry fails. Making real disciples is our only hope for seeing authentic organic ministry maximized in the church today.

For fifty combined years, God has been teaching the two of us about this marvelous approach to expanding the kingdom of God. He began thirty-five years ago.

Dennis: When I was 19 years old, I had just begun my walk with the Lord, trying to serve him with everything within me. Shortly after my commitment to Christ, I went to a three-day conference in Columbus, Ohio where Dr. Howard Hendricks spoke on personal discipleship. I felt my heart deeply stirred by his stories of multiplication and fruitfulness through discipleship. Somehow, I was able to attend a lunch with Dr. Hendricks. I told him I had never heard the concept of discipleship taught before, and how excited I was about it.

He leaned toward me. "The question is, Dennis, if I come back to Columbus in a couple of years, will there be any little Dennis' running around?"

I shrugged sheepishly. Then, after thinking about it for a moment, I smiled, "Yeah. I think there might be."

That was the day I began praying that God would let me find someone I could disciple.

While listening to Dr. Hendricks speak, I sensed that discipleship might be something I could do, unlike more public types of ministry. My friends and I had started a small home Bible study that was growing, but none of us knew where it was headed in the long run. What were young guys like us, whose hearts burned at times with a desire to serve God, to do? Hendricks' stories of how a godly man named "Walt" had duplicated himself through a Sunday school class of teenagers, and the dozens of well-known Christian leaders generated thereby, fired my imagination. What if I could raise up a few disciples, and they did likewise? Maybe a process of duplication could break loose and sweep up huge numbers for Christ? Isn't that what Jesus did?

I approached several guys I knew, but none seemed very interested. Then I found another guy named Gary who had recently come to Christ. He was showing signs of excitement about his faith, so I pointed out that I had been studying this notion of discipleship, where you meet and study with someone, and that I was looking for someone who was interested in trying it with me. He said yes.

Gary and I started hanging out several times a week, and since I had no car, he drove me to some Bible study groups where I was giving my testimony or teaching. At these meetings we often had the chance to witness and counsel young Christians, which we found terribly exciting. We read books, discussed Bible passages, prayed together often, and grew increasingly close as friends.

Later that year, I launched my first high school Bible study group, and it grew rapidly. Gary helped me with the group, and the following year, I found a way to have Gary take over a student Bible study of his own. We constantly shared what we were teaching and consulted on how we should handle situations in our groups. He learned to teach and lead groups during that year.

In the decades since then, Gary has become one of the most respected Bible teachers and leaders in central Ohio. He has led hundreds of people to Christ, and has taught the word of God to thousands. Even more importantly, he has discipled other men. Men discipled by Gary are teaching and leading groups all over our area and overseas. Those men have discipled many others. Today, dozens of groups involving well over a thousand people are in fellowship in our church alone because of his ministry. Many more serve in other churches.

This was my first experience with discipleship. Although it didn't look like much at the time, today I look back and realize that at nineteen years of age, and with little expertise, God used me to do something that has impacted the lives of thousands since. Looking ahead, I realize the process has only begun. Dozens of men in the discipleship generations after Gary are still busily multiplying themselves and reaching non-Christians for God. Gary is discipling several more guys today. Who knows where this process will lead?

Gary and I are ministry colleagues today. I stopped discipling him about the time he came to know as much as I did, which didn't take long. Later, he and I both went to seminary and I've moved on to disciple dozens of other men in the years since. Those men, and the men they discipled, form the bulk of the workforce for our church, other churches, and in our mission efforts around the world.

Not all my discipleship efforts in the years since have been as successful as the effort with Gary. But by God's grace I have been enabled to raise up numerous other disciples, some of whom are promising leaders for God. Only time will tell how fruitful these young leaders will be as their ministries continue to develop. I don't need anyone else to tell me something my own experience confirms: Personal discipleship works!

In the years since I started with Gary, our little Bible study has grown into a sizeable community with over two hundred house churches in our city. That has led to important changes in our approach to making disciples. No longer is it the individual out on his own trying to accomplish an improbable task. Now people make disciples within the framework of the body of Christ. The organic dimension of disciple-making is seen in the community of God. Working in community opens doors we never would have seen open if we were on our own.

Jessica: A few years ago a young believer in my home church named Amira approached me. She asked if I would meet with her and help her grow spiritually. I was thrilled! This rarely happens. As it turned out, she and her older sister had talked about it beforehand, and her sister had suggested this course of action to Amira.

We began meeting and studying weekly. After a few short studies on the basics of Christianity, I asked Amira what she would really love to learn.

"I want to learn the Old Testament." She said.

"The whole thing?" I was surprised.

"Yes." She said.

"Ok," I mused. "It may take a few weeks for me to prepare that kind of study, but we can start as soon as I'm ready." I got to work. In a few days, I had planned a cooperative, survey-style study of the Old Testament. I was really excited about this study! I had never put so much work into preparing a discipleship study plan.

Meanwhile, I invited a grade-school friend named Buddy to come to our home group. Though he had been far away from the Lord for a number of years, when he came back he loved our home group and brought his girlfriend, Lindsay along. Lindsay and Amira hit it off right away and became close friends.

One day, while Buddy was at my house talking to my husband, he mentioned that Lindsay was looking for someone to help her understand the Bible. I told Buddy that I was studying with Amira, and that I could invite Lindsay to join us.

That week at home group, I told Lindsay about the exciting Old Testament study that Amira and I were about to begin the following week. My enthusiasm for it was completely genuine, and Lindsay became excited about it too. The three of us began our study that weekend.

Even though Lindsay and I had not established a relationship before this, the fact that Amira was involved made the whole arrangement natural and fun. These two girls continue to be best friends to this day, almost five years later. In organic disciple-making, I strive to work within relationships. The fact that we were in the same community made it easy to achieve closeness and trust in a short time. At least five different members in the body were involved in this short story: Amira, Lindsay, Buddy, my husband Ryan, and me. We all worked together as a living unit.

It was just as natural for these two to help each other spread the word of God to others. As they won other friends to Christ they began making disciples in their own right. Today, both of them lead their own home churches.

Some people shy away from an organic approach to ministry. After all, investing in relationships over a period of years is costly, and friends can let you down. But we both believe the biblical pattern is still the best. Our experience in our home church, Xenos Christian Fellowship, confirms the power of disciple-making. Visitors to our church often comment on the remarkable level of commitment and learning they see in our members. God has used the concept of making disciples to develop a wonderful community of eager Christian workers.

Xenos is a local church that grew up spontaneously beginning in 1970, during the Jesus Movement. Since the second year of our existence, personal discipleship has been at the center of our philosophy and practice in ministry. For the first decade, Xenos had no paid staff of any kind. Volunteer leaders, raised up through personal discipleship, carried out all the ministries in the church. As numbers increased, we moved to a paid staff, but have never lost the ethos of volunteer house church leadership and personal discipleship. In spite of a devastating division in the early 90's that set our church back ten years, Xenos has grown today to 5,000 in attendance.

Xenos is organized around home churches. Each home church has 15 to 40 members. Home churches meet either weekly or bi-weekly in the evening. We have large corporate gatherings like other churches where clusters of home churches come together for learning and celebration. However, attendance in home churches is far greater than at our large corporate gatherings (what we call *Central Teaching*). Home churches also conduct cell groups made up of either men or women. The cells gather weekly for in-depth Bible study, discipleship, transparent sharing, and prayer. We currently have over 500 cell groups meeting and training members. Members can also take a series of ten-week classes that fill in knowledge across the whole span of the Bible and practical theology.

Personal discipleship is widely practiced at Xenos. Leaders are not recognized unless they are truly making disciples. With over 250 student and adult home churches, each lead by a team of three to six leaders, the church has over 500 recognized leaders and around 900 "servant team" members. All servant team members must show they are working with disciples before being accepted to the team. Throughout the church, most people are either being discipled or are discipling others. Because of this high involvement in personal disci-pleship, the community is close-knit. Members tend to grow and mature more than they would if the church met mainly in large worship services. Most people in Xenos actively look for opportunities to build their own ministries with the help of their friends. This is how organic ministry flourishes.

Xenos is unusual in one other way: The church deliberately targets the most anti-Christian part of our community. Church growth experts have determined that more than 80% of church growth in America is the result of people transferring membership from other evangelical churches. But Xenos members are just the opposite: 82% of our people were "unchurched" at the time they came to Xenos, and over 60% of all Xenos members were non-Christians when they came.[1] The high percentage of converts means our assumptions about discipleship may be somewhat different from what most churches would adopt.

For example, Greg Ogden suggests leaders begin discipleship with the most mature members of the church, and that they use a disciple-ship covenant.[2] These are good suggestions in churches where leaders are just introducing discipleship. But such people were discipled long ago at Xenos. We are left today mostly using one-on-one or one-on-two relationships to help people who have only recently met Christ and need help at a rudimentary level. If Xenos members want to try making a disciple, they know they will probably have to lead someone to Christ first. This difference, like others, demonstrates why each church community has to develop approaches to disciple-making that fit their context. If your experience or situation is different than ours, you will have to adapt our discipleship model to your own situation.

Each home church in Xenos seeks to replicate itself within one to three years, depending on the type of group. To succeed, the home church must raise up a new team of leaders at the same time they double the size of the group. Leaders who know they must raise up and train new leaders rapidly are highly motivated to excel in their personal discipleship work.

This is our ministry environment. We are excited about what God has done here, and we want to share some of the conclusions that make up Xenos' view of discipleship, not because we believe these conclusions are the only valid ones, but because they affect some of our arguments in later chapters. We also believe today's Christian leaders are interested in models that have actually worked in a western, urban environment. We are aware that other churches have different approaches to discipleship that may be just as valid as ours.[3]

We think it's important to know that the picture of disciple-making taught in scripture and modeled in the early church still works in the real world today, both with students and adults. In this book, we will share both theory and practical ideas for developing a disciple-making ministry the organic way. We believe if you study this book and take the time and the risk to invest your life into others in life-giving discipleship, you will never regret the effort.

DISCIPLEMAKING
SECTION ONE

WHAT IS DISCIPLESHIP?

DISCIPLESHIP IN THE NEW TESTAMENT

The word "disciple" comes from the Greek word, *mathetes* – a student, or learner. The concept of discipleship was widespread in the Greco-Roman world, and sophists and philosophers in Greece had their disciples. The New Testament notion of discipleship was probably colored more by Jewish rabbinic training at that time. Jesus was not the first rabbi to have disciples. It was already a common means of training long before Jesus. John the Baptist had disciples before Jesus did (Mat. 11:2; 14:12; Mk. 2:18), as did the Pharisees (Mat. 22:16). Paul himself had been discipled by Gamaliel, one of the most prominent rabbis of his day (Acts 22:3).[1]

Ancient rabbis spent years with their disciples, teaching their way of life, their understanding of scripture, and how to teach it to others.[2] Like Jesus, they often lived with their disciples for extended periods.

The process of discipleship was a complete shaping of a new rabbi—a passing on of everything the rabbi had; his character, his knowledge, his values, and his wisdom. Ancient Jewish discipleship was an educational process, but it contained much more than our modern concept of education. Rabbis transmitted biblical knowledge, but the close association in daily life also transmitted elements not found in books. The rabbi sought to transmit his outlook, wisdom, and character. This was personalized education where two men formed a close, trusting relationship. Within that relationship, the rabbi could sense inner spiritual needs in his disciple and minister to those. The idea was to produce a certain kind of person. The intensive personal attention in this style of training dictated that a rabbi focus on only a few disciples at a time.

Jesus apparently took this model and used it fully, even expanding on the norm. He lived and traveled with the twelve, and seems to have focused even more on the top three: James, John, and Peter. Although some New Testament authors refer to all Christians as disciples (in the sense that they are all followers of Christ), the majority use refers to those who were trainees of a specific teacher.[3]

The same seems to be true of Paul, the only apostle for whom we have extensive biographical information. Right from the beginning, Paul worked at discipleship. After his three-year stay in Damascus, he had to escape by being lowered from the city walls. According to Acts 9:25, it was "his disciples" who lowered him in a basket.

Later, Paul lived and traveled with numerous young men and at least one married couple, teaching them his extraordinary body of knowledge, both in the Old Testament scriptures (where he was an expert) but also from the amazing revelations he had been given by God. They also got the chance to see Paul at work in the field, and no doubt participated with him in actual ministry situations. This kind of field training could develop skills and understanding in a way no classroom could. Paul was in a position to see with his own eyes how younger workers ministered. That would lead to the best kind of coaching and feedback.

More than 30 men and women are mentioned by name as fellow-workers with Paul. It seems likely that many of these were discipled by Paul, and there may have been others not mentioned. In a ministry spanning roughly 30 years, Paul could easily have raised up 30 or more disciples.

In one famous passage, Paul instructs his favorite disciple, Timothy, to carry on the work of discipleship:

> *"And the things you have heard me say in the presence of many witnesses entrust to reliable men who will also be qualified to teach others"* (2 Tim. 2:2).

Paul was concerned with duplicating disciples down through four generations: 1) himself 2) Timothy 3) "reliable men" and 4) "others." From this single verse, we clearly see that Paul used personal discipleship as a conscious strategy for developing leadership in the early church. He also urged women to disciple other women (Tit. 2:3), a practice unknown in Judaism.

In the New Testament church, where there were no seminaries or graduate schools of theology, the church's leadership was apparently raised up by a process of personal discipleship. In the absence of any mention of other means for raising up leadership, one can only assume that such discipleship was likely not just the main means, but the *only* means used. Apparently, most Christians (not only leaders) were discipled at some level in the early church. Paul says, "We proclaim Him, admonishing every man and teaching every man with all wisdom, so that we may present every man complete in Christ" (Col. 1:28). This general description of his ministry strategy suggests

Paul was not satisfied with gathering a large group of converts. He was intent on delivering each Christian to a significant level of maturity through a process of admonition and teaching. We think the evidence suggests that personal mentoring was widespread in the New Testament church, not just for an elite of prospective rabbis, as in Judaism. The idea that every Christian should be a disciple of Jesus probably contributed to the move toward universal discipleship.

DISCIPLESHIP AND MULTIPLICATION

The period from the death of Christ until the end of the first century was the most fruitful in the history of the church. During these few decades, Christianity spread clear across the Roman Empire and even penetrated deeper into Africa, the Parthian Empire, and India. The best estimates put the number of Christians at the end of the first century at around 1 million.[4] That's an increase of 2000 times the number of Christians before Pentecost (perhaps 500). And all of this growth was facilitated by the process of discipleship. Without mass media, advertising, church buildings or seminaries, the primitive church expanded at a rate never equaled in the nineteen centuries since.[5]

Both Christian and secular observers recognize the New Testament church as a perfect example of a church planting movement.[6] In this type of movement, local house churches each strive to replicate themselves by planting additional churches. The result can be exponential growth.

To understand the power of exponential growth, consider the following scenario: No one would feel bad about a church that could win fifty thousand people in two years. In fact, we know of no church that has done so well. And if they won an additional fifty thousand each two years thereafter, such a church could win 1.5 million people during a sixty-year period. Remarkable indeed! This would truly be a super church.

On the other hand, a single house church of thirty people, where the average member did nothing but win and disciple one other person during a two-year period would seem rather unremarkable. They would have a mere sixty people after two years, and would become two home churches. But if the original group and the new group both did the same thing during the following two years, and this process continued for the next sixty years, the result would be far more remarkable than that of the super church. In fact the duplicating group would have won 16 million people! They would, in fact have out-performed the super church by more than *ten times!* Not only that, but within another twenty-five years, this duplicating group would have won every person on earth.

We are not suggesting these numbers are realistic, but they do illustrate the power of exponential growth. However, notice two important points about these calculations.

1. To achieve true multiplication growth, the duplication of individuals and churches must go forward without degradation. If the quality of disciples or churches declines at all with each duplication event, the whole process breaks down very quickly. Quality is one key to ongoing duplication. Historians have noted that church planting movements tend to fizzle out after a number of years. Why? Probably some movements compromise on quality for the sake of quantity. Others may grow so concerned about quality that they cease duplicating and become saddled with too many rules and restrictions.

2. In the duplication model, results are very small during the early years, compared with the super church. By year 10, for example, the duplicating group would have only 480 members in sixteen house

churches, while the super church would already have a quarter million members. Can you imagine these two groups looking over at each other? How inferior the duplicating group would feel with less than five hundred members to show for ten years hard work, seeing a super church nearby that had reached a quarter million people during the same period! At this stage the super church would be more than five hundred times larger than the duplicating group. Surely, it would seem, God's blessing rests on the super church, and not on the duplicating church. (Although we know the duplicating church is actually doing ten times better than the super church, even though it doesn't show yet). It would take a powerful act of faith to continue using the duplication approach. Anyone impatient for quick results will abandon duplication.

Organic growth is biblical and powerful.

In advocating multiplication growth, we are not suggesting that classroom instruction is wrong. Paul used it in Ephesus (Acts 19:9; 20:20), and we use it extensively in our church. But we see classroom instruction as useful to *supplement* personal discipleship, not to *replace* it. Most local churches in the New Testament probably had no access to classroom teaching. In order for such small house churches to become self-replicating, they had to be able to raise up new leadership from within their own ranks.

Here, then, we see the intimate connection between discipleship and church planting movements. Discipleship is a means of leadership development that permits multiplication because it doesn't require feeding leaders through a central hub, like a seminary or Bible school. We like the idea of a primary dependence on personal discipleship, with supplemental classes where motivated learners can quickly add to their objective knowledge of the Bible, ministry theory, and theology.

We're not saying seminaries are harmful or wrong. Most of our top leaders are seminary graduates, and the scholarship we gain from a seminary can greatly enhance the teaching ministry in any church. Our church even hosts an extension campus for a major seminary. It makes sense to send key people to seminary so they can gather up the scholarship there and bring it back to the church. However, for most leaders in the church, personal discipleship (possibly supplemented by periodic church-based classes) is a fully adequate, in fact, superior means of training.

We argue—just as the key to church planting movements is that churches duplicate themselves—the key to church duplication is that individuals duplicate themselves. And individual duplication is the process of personal discipleship. This is why, before any church planting movement can reappear, discipleship must precede it.

Even in churches committed to more traditional forms of growth, good discipleship will greatly enhance the quality of church life. Churches that disciple large numbers of members have no shortage of volunteers for ministry. Such churches retain more of their new people, and the level of commitment is higher. In a word, when people in the church are growing spiritually, everyone is happier. Nothing is better for spiritual growth than personal discipleship.

AFTER THE NEW TESTAMENT

In the years following the writing of the New Testament, the notion of personal discipleship gradually went into eclipse. During following centuries church leaders began to emphasize the higher position of clergy, who had special prerogatives to lead the church and serve even as mediators between the members and God. This shift apparently began partly because of a good-hearted effort to stem the rising tide of false teaching threatening the church during this period. Very soon, however, the clergy's position expanded to unimagined extremes, eventually reserving the right to read and interpret the Bible. Even translating the Bible into local languages eventually became illegal. When church leaders excluded lay people from reading and learning the Bible, the basis for personal discipleship was shattered. In this setting, traces of discipleship in the New Testament sense gradually diminished to the vanishing point.[7]

The clergy-laity distinction removed personal discipleship from the hands of common Christians. From the time common Christians were banned from major areas of ministry in the church, personal discipleship became meaningless and indeed forgotten to most Christians. The idea that someone could help develop a normal Christian like Timothy into a powerful leader for God was replaced by the idea that the church hierarchy creates priesthood through its training facilities and the ritual of ordination.

The Reformation did little to change the church's thinking in this particular area. They continued to advance, in practice, if not in theory, the notion of clergy as completely distinct from lay people.[8] Clergymen learned the languages and read the manuscripts of church fathers and the scriptures during a several yearlong rigorous process of education. Lay people were not trained to teach the Bible or to do other significant ministry, such as counseling or leading groups.

Certain movements during the past millennium have resorted to personal discipleship as their key ministry method. These make for interesting study, because several of them experienced remarkable results. But they have tended to revert to traditional, western approaches to leadership training, or have been stamped out by persecution.[9]

THE 20TH CENTURY TO THE PRESENT

Then, in the 20th century, discipleship reappeared with significant vigor. Dawson Trotman was an important voice bringing the notion of personal discipleship to the attention of the larger Christian world. He was the founder of the Navigators, a ministry based mainly on personal discipleship. This group has enjoyed immense success worldwide. But it sees itself as a para-church organization, and therefore has not engaged in church planting in America. Trotman and those he influenced have had extensive impact in other groups as well. Campus Crusade for Christ leader Bill Bright adopted a form of discipleship under the influence of Trotman and Henerietta Mears. But again, Campus Crusade took a stand as a para-church group rather than a church planting group. Similarly, Trotman is credited with influencing Billy Graham to introduce a simple type of discipleship in his crusades. Once again, the Graham organization sees itself supporting existing churches rather than planting churches. Although none of these organizations has engaged in church planting, they have had incredible impact in western Christianity.

Books advancing the idea of discipleship have received a wide reading during this period. In the 1960's author Robert Coleman wrote a very influential book, *The Master Plan of Evangelism*, where he advocated a return to the biblical pattern of discipleship.[10] Similar arguments were advanced by numerous evangelical leaders, including Howard Hendricks, Walter Hendrickson, Leroy Eims, Waylon Moore, Bill Hull, and others.[11]

But discipleship has suffered reversals during the past century as well. During the late 60's and 70's the idea of discipleship was discredited in America by the so-called "shepherding movement." This movement advanced a mistaken, hyper-controlling discipleship theory, rather than a facilitating theory. They argued that learning to obey a human authority is a good way to learn how to obey God. In this movement, your discipler, or "shepherd" would be encouraged to oversee almost everything, including your personal finances, dating choices, and every other significant decision in your life. Predictably, the movement became increasingly authoritarian and controlling. In the end, the church and the press pounded the movement into non-existence. But the whole experience left a lingering suspicion hanging over the notion of discipleship. Still today, some church leaders view discipleship as cultic, mainly because of the bad fruit produced in this movement.

Throughout the 20th century, discipleship has been adopted far more widely in missions circles rather than in the western church. Numerous fields around the world practice personal disciple-making as the primary way to raise up leadership in the local church. Partly because of the lack of available seminaries and partly because of a desire to imitate the primitive church, a number of fields in Latin America, Africa, and Asia have systematically pursued personal discipleship and self-replicating church planting. As a result, mission experts are aware of a number of incredibly vigorous church planting movements around the world today.[12]

But as a rule, the western church has never fully returned to the New Testament pattern of personal discipleship. George Barna documents the sad fact that the church in America talks a great deal about discipleship, but does not practice it very often.[13] The result of this omission is that church-going Christians today often manifest shallow commitment, biblical ignorance, and inability to do advanced Christian ministry. Even though the concept of lay ministry has risen in popularity in the modern church, without discipleship it runs into trouble. How can lay people be trusted to do complex types of ministry if they are almost completely untrained? Many churches try offering training classes, but these cannot accomplish much in terms of real character change and mastery of advanced ministry skills during their five or ten week curriculum.

Now in recent years, we see signs that western evangelical churches may be embracing discipleship as never before. In a recent survey, George Barna asked senior pastors to name their top priorities in ministry. He reports, "The most frequently mentioned priorities were discipleship and spiritual development (47%); evangelism and outreach (46%); and preaching (35%)." These easily outranked priorities held higher in earlier surveys, like worship and pastoral care.[14] The western church as a whole may be embracing personal discipleship as its philosophy of ministry, but still struggles to see it as its practice in ministry.

Some churches and individual Christians do practice discipleship faithfully, as Barna also documents.[15] In fact, a growing number of churches have established discipleship as the center of their ministry. The cell church model, which has caught on in many American churches, calls for each group leader to mentor an assistant leader in preparation for planting a new cell group. Famous churches like Willow Creek and Saddleback have given far greater attention to their small groups as a missional thrust of the church, and they are steadily turning their members' attention to personal discipleship.

Whether or not your church embraces discipleship as the primary way to train up Christians, anyone can embark on a disciple-making project. In this study we hope to supply a framework and practical ideas for discipleship that can get even beginners started on a fruitful life of disciple-making.

2

ORGANIC DISCIPLESHIP:
AN OVERVIEW

CREATIVITY AND DISCIPLESHIP

Making disciples is an intensely creative process, and God is able to use all kinds of people for this task. Organic discipleship is creative discipleship. In organic styles of ministry, lists of procedures are off-target. A disciple-maker is one who takes existing concepts and situations and creatively combines them into ever-changing new ways to build up believers. The intention of this study is not to map out a formula for disciple-making, but to stimulate the creative process. By suggesting ideas in a variety of areas, our hope is to spark you, the reader, to create similar or related ideas that fit your setting.

No two disciples are alike. And no two disciple-makers are alike. Therefore, any attempt to describe the "right" way to make disciples is pointless. Because discipleship is creative, we will not offer a curriculum or lesson plan in this book. Instead, we offer goals and examples that should stimulate your creativity. As you read our ideas and experiences, pray that God will spark new ideas you can use in your situation. Your ideas may well be quite different than what we suggest.

Although disciple-making is a creative process, some principles are universal. Try to sort out those parts of our account that apply in most or all situations from other parts that could be changed to fit with your ministry environment.

WHAT ARE THE GOALS OF DISCIPLESHIP?

One of the main goals of discipleship is to provide the body of Christ with leaders and role models who can teach others and lead Bible studies, ministry teams, or home groups. We would definitely want our disciples to reach a point where they can raise up additional disciples, and that implies a level of maturity sufficient to teach and model true Christian living and ministry. If we have any criticism of the popular literature on discipleship during the past few decades, it would be this: The recommendations are solid and needed, but they often don't go far enough. The themes of many popular books on discipleship center on basic grounding of new believers, more than on raising up Christian leaders. We agree with Thomas Graham, who says, "The evangelical church stresses discipleship. The focus is on becoming a self-feeding Christian, encouraging holy living, an effective prayer life and sharing one's faith. But discipling people to become mature leaders in ministry is often overlooked."[1] To reach the point where our disciples can lead for God requires significantly more progress in several key areas. But the results of such a job well done are exciting and will likely last a lifetime.

We have distilled a suggested list of discipleship goals to nine areas of growth. We won't cover these goals here in detail, but you can read a detailed explanation with an assessment worksheet in Appendix 1. As you read that description, think about whether you feel our description is too exacting, or whether we are missing significant factors.

To summarize, the goals for discipleship include radical change in:

- *Character* — having a good personal walk with God, becoming a loving person with successful relationships, exchanging selfishness for other-centeredness, freedom from discrediting sin, manifesting the fruit of the Spirit, a relatively stable emotional life, etc.
- *Understanding* — a thoroughly developed Christian worldview, good theology, knowledge of the Bible, and ability to use the Bible in ministry, wisdom, discernment, resistant to false teaching, etc.
- *Ministry capability* — evangelism, pastoring others, personal discipleship, teaching or discussion leading, etc. (Spiritual growth is never complete when it only benefits ourselves. We are created to give love through serving others.)

Together, these constitute a person who is "complete in him," as Paul puts it (Col. 1:28). Many of the changes will be very difficult and involve many months of struggle.

Does helping a young believer move from immaturity and self-centeredness to full maturity seem daunting to you? It is daunting! In truth, you will probably never see full attainment of even the limited list included in Appendix 1 in the life of any of your disciples. But you are looking for *relative* advancement, not perfection. (How many of us can claim that even we, as disciple-makers, have grown to the extent described in every area?) As you continue to grow, and patiently convey what you know of God, your disciples will make surprising progress over the course of several years. The closer you come to this ideal description, the better off your disciples will be. Your goal should be to see some progress in all the areas listed rather than great progress in some, but missing one or more completely. Missing any one of the areas could short-circuit the discipling process.

God is surprisingly merciful and He makes a job that seems impossible happen more often than you would ever expect. On the other hand, the sheer magnitude of the changes needed in order to help a person become "complete in him" suggests you should probably work with more than one disciple at a time. Some disciples will find this road too long to travel, and give up. If you lose one disciple, you may still be able to deliver others.

WHAT ABOUT CORPORATE DISCIPLESHIP?

A number of authors and leaders have recently argued that the concept of individual discipleship is unbiblical. They point out that most advocates for personal disciple-making base their teachings on the ministry of Jesus, which occurred before the body of Christ came into being. They argue that Jesus discipled his guys by himself because he had no choice but to do so. They also point to the abuses in groups like the shepherding movement to show that any time people begin to see another person as their disciple, possessiveness and abuse is likely to follow.

Instead, they feel everyone is a disciple of Jesus, not of another person. They also claim the body of Christ can disciple its members corporately as different people's gifts operate, resulting in a more balanced result—the cream rises to the surface as the community of God interacts. Some have claimed that one-on-one, or one-on-two models are a western, individualistic approach to spiritual nurture.

We believe this position is unnecessarily narrow. Yes, the body of Christ should nurture growth as a community. Disciples can benefit from differently gifted members, receiving things they could not get from a single individual. But do these facts overthrow the notion of individual discipleship? We don't think so.

First, the New Testament does affirm individual discipleship other than the ministry of Jesus, as seen in Chapter 1. For example, Paul's "disciples" let him down in a basket while in Damascus (Acts 9:25). More importantly, the function of discipleship is carried out with Paul's missionary bands and elsewhere, including urging Timothy to disciple others (2 Tim. 2:2). Paul didn't use the term "discipleship," but he definitely used personal mentoring to develop leaders.

A key reason to reject the purely corporate vision of discipleship is pragmatic. Consider the saying, "Everybody's job is nobody's job." Our studies show that in churches where the corporate vision for discipleship is advanced over against the idea individual discipleship, people are simply not being discipled. Those same churches complain that their people are immature, ineffective in ministry, and too busy for the things of God. When these churches need leaders, they have to hire them away from other churches.

On the other hand, churches that are successfully pursuing a cell or house church replication approach nearly always embrace the notion of personal discipleship. The same is true in mission fields we have visited in other countries. Those with replicating church planting movements always believe strongly in personal discipleship. Indeed, it would be hard to imagine a self-replicating home group movement unless group leaders take it upon themselves to help others grow into leadership. Experienced church planters don't just hope new leaders will appear when the time comes. They take positive measures to raise up the needed leadership.

We certainly believe Christians can grow and mature in a corporate setting without anyone viewing them as disciples. However, they grow far more rapidly in an environment where discipleship is affirmed and practiced. This is particularly true in churches where the leadership teaches clearly against possessive and controlling versions of discipleship. In our church people may be discipled by more than one person during different times in their Christian life, or even at the same time, and we see nothing wrong with that. Further, anyone who reflected a possessive or exclusive view of discipleship would be quickly admonished and corrected. Just because immature Christians have misused the concept of discipleship is no reason to throw out the baby with the bath water.

DISCIPLESHIP AND LEADERSHIP

Being a mature Christian isn't enough. The church also needs leaders. On one level, every Christian should be a leader. Every time you influence a friend, you are leading. And every Christian should be an influence for God. If you have a family, you are expected to lead in that role. So it's safe to assume that God wants disciples to learn how to lead others. But what about formal leadership roles? When a person leads a group, this represents a higher level of leadership. Such leaders are typically recognized by the body of Christ as formal leaders. We suggest that if you are successful as a disciple-maker at least some (if not most) of your disciples should become formal leaders.

We will discuss leadership development later. But for now, if your disciples are to become true spiritual leaders, rather than leaders in name only, they will need to learn how to serve and influence others for God. They will also have to learn how to teach or lead discussion in a group; work with ministry colleagues in a team; assess their groups; give their groups vision and motivation; and release disciples to form new groups. If you are intent on multiplying both disciples and groups within the church, developing qualified leaders becomes an urgent goal.

We advocate an "organic" approach to leadership development. In an organic approach, it is assumed that God will move people into leadership naturally as the result of their loving service inside and outside the body of Christ. In this approach, human colleagues *recognize* someone as a leader, rather than *appointing* someone a leader. By recognizing leaders, one can discern who God wants to lead his church. Anyone who has not developed a sufficiently godly character can safely be eliminated. Scripture advances godly character as the first priority in choosing leaders. Therefore, this book will focus most on character development.

When God chooses a person for leadership, the marks of his blessing should be evident. God will move others to respond to your disciple's witness, and to look to your disciple for guidance and training. Signs like these show that God is moving your disciple toward leadership. Notice that Paul says servants should "first be tested; and then if there is nothing against them, let them serve as deacons [or *ministers*]" (1 Tim. 3:10). This suggests he wanted to see evidence that God was using the person, and that the person could handle the rigors of ministry.[2]

DISCIPLESHIP VERSUS GROUNDING

Grounding new Christians means giving them a basic orientation to the Christian life. When people meet Christ, your first concern is to see them "rooted and built up in him," as Paul puts it (Col. 2:7). But is this all you hope to see in discipleship?

If you accept discipleship goals like those described above, you must realize that much of what passes as discipleship today is relatively low-level. A discipleship process that results in people learning how to read and memorize scripture, pray, and witness is a good start. But you need to go much deeper if you plan on developing leaders and role models in the church who can be trusted to care for groups of people. We suggest that your first year with disciples—if they have recently met Christ—should be focused on grounding them in the faith. But we also suggest that you invest an additional one or more years to develop mature character and advanced ministry capability so they can become leaders.

In a church like Xenos, with rapidly multiplying home groups, we pursue some of this development after the person is already leading a group. But unless we see believers developing into "the whole measure of the fullness of Christ," they will continue to be "infants, tossed back and forth by the waves, and blown here and there by every wind of teaching" (Eph. 4:13, 14).

3

GETTING STARTED

To begin the discipling process, two things are required: A disciple-maker and a disciple. In this chapter we will consider the qualifications for both.

WHO SHOULD DISCIPLE OTHERS?

Considering how difficult the task of discipleship is, some wonder whether it would be arrogant to think they are qualified to disciple others. What criteria should a person meet in order to qualify for this ministry?

When we look at the Bible, we find silence on this subject. The examples we have of disciple-makers are highly qualified, like Jesus, Timothy, and Paul. However, this doesn't prove that such high qualifications are necessary. Examples only tell us what was, not what should be. We think the Bible's silence on qualifications for disciple-makers suggests a great deal of freedom in this area. We must assume that the elders appointed by Paul discipled people in the churches in Galatia (Acts 14:23). Yet these men would have been recognized as elders only weeks after meeting Christ. Clearly, it would be nice if the discipler has made more progress than the disciple. But even this is open to question. We have seen spiritual peers disciple each other, like "iron sharpening iron."

Most of the time, we would like a discipler to be a Christian who has made significant progress in his or her walk. We generally feel uncomfortable when brand-new Christians try to disciple. But we have seen Christians only months or a year old in the Lord do good discipling work with new believers, especially if they have good coaching. In fact, having a disciple is a great motivation to grow. We love to see believers take on a disciple as soon as they are able, because we know both the disciple and the discipler will do better as a result. However, believers who have not yet overcome flagrant problems in their own lives, such as sexual immorality or drug use, should seek to be discipled before trying to disciple others.

Dennis: Most people had no idea how immature I was when I won my first disciple. As a year-old Christian, my knowledge level was dirt low. I still had not completely broken away from some very bad sin habits that had controlled my life as a non-Christian. Although I was advancing spiritually, there were periodic relapses into drug use and extreme make-out sessions with my girlfriend. My prayer life was anemic. I had no regular habit of spending time in God's word. But from the time I won a disciple on, my behavior and spirituality both improved dramatically and rapidly. I realized I couldn't afford to indulge the flesh, and my new Christian partner helped keep me accountable. In fact, he was so spiritually responsive that I quickly realized I needed to get a whole lot more serious with God or he would soon pass me by. Within six months, my life was unrecogniz-able compared to where I was when I began discipling. Today, it's embarrassing to admit some of the antics I engaged in at the time, but I'm glad no one told me I was not qualified to disciple.

From a church leader's perspective, several factors may shift your judgment regarding who should disciple. First, if your group has high availability of Christians needing to be discipled, that should make you more open to younger Christians discipling. Second, the best choice for who young Christians should disciple is someone of the same sex they have led to Christ. Paul mentions the concept of spiritual parenthood. "Even though you have ten thousand guardians in Christ, you do not have many fathers, for in Christ Jesus I became your father through the Gospel" (1 Cor. 4:15). We would hardly expect natural parents to leave their infant child on the sidewalk somewhere, assuming someone will take care of him. We like to see believers take the natural step of discipling those they lead to Christ if they are at all able. If we doubt a young Christian's ability to disciple effectively, it will often be possible to come alongside and help them in a three-way discipling arrangement, as we discuss later.

Discipling work is quiet, slow, and often thankless labor. We would much rather see young Christians doing this kind of work than public teaching, preaching, or leading. Public ministry roles have appeal, not only because they can accomplish a lot, but also because people may be drawn to self-glorification. Not so with discipleship. Building a friendship and trying to influence and instruct another within that friendship is exactly the kind of ministry best suited to young Christians (although our most experienced leaders should also disciple, both as an example to the church, and because they are usually most effective). Through discipling, young Christians can learn all the skills needed in larger, more public ministries, but without the public acclaim that poses such a temptation to the immature. At the same time, we find that those who are successful in discipleship are the best candidates for public ministry later.

When young Christians try to disciple, they are far more likely to succeed if they are receiving coaching from an older, more experienced discipler. If you succeed in discipleship, your disciples will win others they can disciple, because part of discipling is helping disciples win their own disciples. And you should stay with them while they do this for a good length of time. (Coaching is discussed in a later chapter).

Some Christians feel unqualified to disciple because they were never discipled. This is wrong. Many of us (including myself—Dennis) were never formally discipled, and have been able to do quite well. The difference between believers who were discipled and those who were not is often how long it took to mature. Those of us who didn't benefit from discipleship may have grown much slower than we would have if a good disciple-maker had helped us. Our spiritual growth, however, is just a valid.

We conclude that the vast majority of believers in any local body are qualified to disciple. Of course those who are more mature and experienced might do a better job than the inexperienced. But to a new Christian, receiving help from a less experienced discipler is way better than receiving no help at all.

WHO SHOULD YOU TRY TO WIN INTO DISCIPLESHIP?

Perhaps no question is more important than whom you decide to disciple. A discipleship ministry involves investing hundreds of hours, possibly over several years. Experience shows that you may end up spending huge amounts of time and effort to no effect if the person you choose is unwilling. Most of us who practice discipleship have had the experience of heartbreaking failure when we are eventually forced to admit that no amount of love and effort will ever move a fundamentally unwilling person beyond a rudimentary level. Some disciples actually walk away from God in favor of a life of sin.

You can never eliminate the risk that your efforts might end in failure. But you can minimize the risk if you are careful to whom you commit yourself in the first place. Some Christians are troubled by the idea of selectivity in ministry. Is this partiality?

You could never justify being selective about who you witness to. Likewise, you should be willing to extend general pastoral help and friendship to all members of the body of Christ. But when it comes to a commitment like discipleship, selection is essential. Selection is necessary for more than one reason. The most obvious is stewardship: you don't want to expend huge amounts of your limited time and energy on a lost cause. But another compelling reason is that the church needs mature leaders and role models, and you can't justify wasting years doing pointless work when other people's spiritual lives are at stake. You also have the examples of Jesus and Paul who both selected disciples from a larger following. Finally, the disciple you select mistakenly will suffer unnecessarily. Nobody is happy when discipleship fails, and this includes the disciple.

When trying to discern who to disciple, you should be praying for a period of weeks or even months before committing to a weekly meeting with someone. Ask the Lord to reveal his will on this highly strategic decision, because once you begin meeting with a person, you will find it difficult to stop. And if you do change your mind and end the discipleship part of a friendship, it will probably result in hurt feelings. If you are apprehensive about your selection choice, it might be wise to engage in a short-term study (four to six weeks) to gauge the person's interest. By stating in advance that the study series is limited in duration, the person won't feel disappointed when it comes to an end. But if, during that time, you become convinced that the person would make a good disciple, they rarely complain about continuing the study indefinitely.

Preconditions

Discipleship, as we are using the term, refers to a training and facilitating process aimed at helping Christians reach maturity and fruitfulness. This implies certain conditions should be present before you enter into a disciple-making relationship.

1. Those you seek to disciple should be authentic Christians. This may seem too obvious to state, but we have seen Christians try to use disciple-making approaches with non-Christians. The results are usually poor. Non-Christians cannot understand what we are doing because, "The man without the Spirit does not accept the things that come from the Spirit of God, for they are foolishness to him, and he cannot understand them, because they are spiritually discerned" (1 Cor. 2:14). Friendship-building with non-Christians is good, but discipleship should be reserved for those with a clear testimony and convincing evidence that they are Christians.

2. You should only disciple those who are fully involved in Christian fellowship. We have had believers ask to be discipled even though they are only sporadically involved in church life, or not involved at all. We believe discipleship is a further source of nurture for those already drawing life from the body of Christ. Too often, believers who agree to disciple someone who does not understand the value of body life find that their disciples never develops this value. In such a relationship, the disciple's needs are being substantially met by their discipler . . . If you're providing room-service, she won't bother to go out to a restaurant! The Bible teaches that "The eye cannot say to the hand, 'I don't need you!' " (1 Cor. 12:21). Christian fellowship, including sharing of spiritual gifts and giving and receiving Christian love, is essential for healthy spiritual growth,

and therefore for discipleship. We urge our disciple-makers to work with friends in a more general way until they grasp the value of fellowship, including not only large worship meetings, but also involvement in a home group where the needed relationships can be built.

By only agreeing to enter into disciple-making relationships with believers walking in fellowship, you give yourself and your disciples a reasonable chance of success.

Features To Look For

Paul urges Timothy to give his time "to reliable men" (2 Tim. 2:2). But how do we know who will be reliable? Whenever trying to discern a person's reliability, consider this rule of thumb: The best predictor of future behavior is past behavior. If you have access to information about a person's past, this should be carefully considered. You aren't necessarily looking for a person who never gets into any trouble. The more critical question is: What was their response when they got into trouble? A person who has repented from the heart and admitted fault in the past is showing you something good. Anyone who has a history of pursuing God in the past is also a good bet as a disciple.

Robert Coleman argues that a willing heart, or loyalty to Christ, is the premiere feature to look for in a prospective disciple.[1] This may well be true. But willingness should not always be interpreted as compliance. Sometimes ornery people make good disciples, and they may become entrepreneurial leaders, capable of feats that compliant people will never achieve. We would not avoid discipling someone just because he argues or seems hard to persuade at times. And at the other extreme, a man-pleaser can be very problematic as a disciple.

In our opinion, you should look for one key feature: that the person is a "doer." James mentions the difference between forgetful hearers and effectual doers (James 1:22, 23). Whenever you see young

Christians who are trying to serve God and others (whether or not they are effective) you should mark that person for possible discipleship. A young believer who voluntarily, on his own, takes some measure to overcome sin is also a doer. Christians who read scripture or related books on their own are doers. Those who bring non-Christian friends into fellowship are doers. Christians who give money to the Lord's work are doers. In many different areas, but especially in areas where others probably won't notice (i.e. things not done for attention), you should recognize doers as those who actually take action, rather than simply talk about spiritual things.

Jesus told a story about two boys who were asked by their dad to mow a field. One immediately said he would, but he never did. The other refused, but later felt bad and did mow the field (Mat. 21:28-31). In analyzing this story, Jesus asked the pertinent question, "Which of the two did the will of his father?" That's what you should ask as well. Young Christians who argue and fight against the truth, but later go ahead and do the right thing are to be preferred over those who always say the right thing, but are not doers.

Misleading Features

Several features can be misleading when choosing a disciple.

A person who is highly gifted may seem like a natural choice. But experience doesn't always bear this out. This is not to say you should avoid gifted people. If all other factors are equal, we would personally prefer the more gifted person. But this is a strictly secondary consideration, far less important than the attitude issues discussed earlier.

Well-educated or highly successful people may again seem like natural choices, because they seem like they will be very influential. But this criteria is really worthless. Highly educated or successful people are just as likely to be distracted by their worldly opportunities and unable or unwilling to devote themselves to spiritual growth.

Jesus warned that it is easier for a camel to go through the eye of a needle than for a rich person to enter heaven (Mat. 19:24). While this statement doesn't apply directly to discipleship (where you are choosing between believers), the principle seems to be that highly successful people are often too distracted, and perhaps too self-reliant. They may have ego issues as well. Viewed this way, high education or professional or athletic success could actually be viewed as risk factors. Notice that none of Jesus' disciples were highly educated or notably successful. On the other hand, Paul seems to have had some well-educated disciples, such as Luke, Apollos, and Sosthenes.

As already mentioned, compliant personalities are sometimes mistakenly viewed as desirable. While a compliant personality is not a risk factor, it should not be consider as a positive feature either. Some compliant personalities make good disciples, while others do not. You should ignore this feature, and focus on the attitude features discussed earlier. For example, is she a doer? If a compliant person is a man-pleaser (i.e. always tells people what they want to hear) but not a doer, her compliance becomes a risk factor.

You should also look for initiative from compliant personalities. In other words, does the compliant person only do what others suggest? Or does she initiate creatively on her own? If a compliant person only acts on what others suggest, such action may signal man-pleasing more than genuine spirituality.

People who are physically attractive or who have winsome person-alities seem to be more influential with people in general and they also have more success attracting disciple-makers. But just as with wealthy, successful, or highly educated people, they are often disappointing. When they do develop into good disciples, this has more to do with their heart attitudes than with their appearance or personalities.

People who know a lot about the Bible or those from strong Christian backgrounds may seem like good choices, because it seems like we have a head-start with them. But this could actually be a risk factor. Unless their knowledge is accompanied by consistent action in serving and witnessing, you may be viewing a bad habit: sitting around studying all the time, but not putting it into practice. Paul warns against those with "morbid interest in controversial questions and disputes about words" (1 Tim. 6:4). Some heavy Bible students are more interested in debating doctrinal trivia than in "faith working through love" (Gal. 5:6). This feature should not necessarily be viewed as a head start.

On the negative side, people who have bad habits, such as over-eating, cigarette smoking, bad language, or even occasional drug use or heavy drinking are considered by many to be disqualified. We think this is a mistake. If such people continue to pursue the things of God, they may be worth the risk of some investment. You can always work with them on these habits during discipleship, and such sins of commission may be no worse than sins of omission that sometimes characterize more well-behaved people. Probably the most dangerous and daunting sinful habits are sexual sins (promiscuity, both hetero and homosexual or addiction to pornography), drug and alcohol addiction, and materialistic avarice. These sins are so potent in their habit-forming power, and so debilitating to one's spiritual growth that they should give you pause. You may be able to work with such people in a general pastoral way, but put off discipleship until you see convincing progress.

None of these factors should be considered decisive. Basic attitudes of the heart are far more definitive than any of these misleading factors.

Dennis: In 1997 I changed ministry venues within our church. Because my brother went to the mission field, I left adult ministry and took over his role as head of our campus ministry. In a whole new group of people, I was eager to find a disciple. A friend of mine who works as a prison chaplain brought a young man to one of our meetings who was recently released from prison. He was a street thug from Chicago, where he had belonged to the Latin Kings street gang. His history included rampant sex, violence, armed robbery, drug dealing, and even shooting people. This kid had some real rough edges! He was argumentative, boastful, distrustful, and had a bad temper. Like many in his position, he smoked cigarettes, drank too much, and used the "F-word" like punctuation after each phrase in most every sentence. He had many doubts and problems with the Bible. But in talking to him, I sensed something within that drew me. He was spiritually hungry!

I spent time with him, and before long, he agreed to do some reading with me. We formed a relationship that has lasted for eight years. During that time we have "hung out" privately every week in addition to seeing each other several times a week at meetings. During that time, I've wrestled with him in a hundred different areas of his life. Also during that time, he has led multiple people to Christ, completed college, and now leads a college and a high school home church. He's taking graduate courses in the Bible on the side, and is determined to expend his life for Christ.

The lesson? The interior may be quite different than the exterior.

THE HUNGRY HEART

In Luke 19 we read that Jesus was in a huge crowd, and he singled out one man, Zaccheus, to spend time with. Why Zaccheus? He was a criminal, a tax gatherer, and a non-believer. The reason Jesus chose him was probably because, out of the whole crowd, he was the only one so eager to hear Jesus that he climbed a tree. Imagine a grown man climbing a tree. That's hunger! And spiritual hunger should be a premium feature when it comes to picking a disciple. Jesus must have looked out over that crowd and seen a guy up in that tree. He probably thought to himself, "That's my man."

You should follow this model. Like Jesus, you should ignore apparent negatives in a person's life if they show you authentic spiritual hunger. A person who has manifested consistent hunger for the things of God is an almost irresistible opportunity to experienced disciple-makers.

STEPS TOWARD DISCIPLESHIP

If you identify someone you think might make a good disciple, how can you move into a regular discipling relationship? The answers to this question are as varied as the personalities involved. People have used scores of pathways into regular discipleship, and your creativity and sensitivity to the situation are your best guide. But some things are needed in most or all cases:

- The first step is to build a friendship. If you are already friends, your best move is to deepen your friendship. Read the next chapter for ideas on how to build and deepen friendships. You could begin discipling someone you don't know well, especially if that person asks for your help. In such cases, you'll develop a friendship while you begin discipleship.
- If you sense your friend is hungry for spiritual growth, you can move toward a regular meeting for edification. You could bring this up in a number of ways:
  - You could suggest meeting for mutual edification, as suggested earlier. This way, it doesn't seem like you are suggesting a hierarchical arrangement.
  - You could refer to a study project you did yourself in the past and

ask your friend whether she would be interested in a similar study.

- One of the best approaches is a problem or needs-based approach. This approach begins when your friend brings up a problem or need during regular conversations. For instance your friend may share concern about his marriage. You could point out that you heard a certain book was helpful to other couples struggling in the same area. Would she be interested in reading it together? Or, she mentions that she wishes she had more confidence when sharing her faith, or that her friends ask her questions she can't answer. Then you could point out that you know a book that was helpful in that very area. Instead of just suggesting she read it herself, you suggest reading it together. Or, just ask if she would be interested in going over some Bible passages that might help.

- Some people like a direct approach. In this approach, you explain to your friend what personal discipleship is. Then ask if he would be interested in embarking on such a relationship with you. This is good for established believers. It gives you a chance to explain some conditions you want to put on the relationship; level of involvement, effort you expect him to exert, etc.

• Regardless how you bring the idea up, once you study and pray together several times, your friend will probably feel gratified by the experience. Most people find God uses these study projects and times of sharing and prayer to build them up, and they naturally desire more.

• As your friendship grows, you can powerfully increase motivation by developing and sharing strong vision for your friend.

Developing Vision

When your disciple gets a vision for his future as a servant and even a leader for God, he becomes far more motivated in his service. Disciples must see where the process is headed before they are likely to give their all to growth and ministry. As a discipler, you must impart this sense of vision to your disciple. In this context, vision is a picture of what your disciple could become—how his life could be enhanced by becoming all that God has in mind for him. People operating with vision outperform those operating purely on a motive of duty.[2] Instead of doing what they feel they *should* or *must* do, they begin doing what they *want* to do— with far more energy. When people have a strong sense of vision for their future, they become heedless of the suffering and personal sacrifice needed to reach their goal. Instead of strolling toward the goal, they begin to run as fast as they can!

Jessica: Lexi became a Christian, and although she was shy, she began inviting her non-Christian friends to church right away. But when none of her friends responded to Christ, she became gun-shy and withdrew from trying to minister to others. Even though I was trying to encourage her, she seemed immobilized. As her discipler, this concerned me a great deal. I spent two weeks praying that God would give me a vision for her.

I knew Lexi wanted to be a missionary someday and had a heart for the world. The problem was, she didn't see the connection between her future aspiration and her present day ministry activities.

I tried to motivate her on a number of occasions without much success. Finally, after praying about her again, I approached her in a serious manner. I brought up her desire to become a missionary and affirmed that desire. "The only problem is that you'll never get there if you don't start doing some ministry right here." I said. "If a missions agency were to call me and ask about you, I would advise against sending you to the field. The best indicator of future behavior is past behavior."

This came as a shock to Lexi, because I almost never confronted her. We talked some more about how her passivity could be blocking her dream of being a missionary. I continued to describe what a missionary life would look like, and how she should begin now to learn the ministry skills she would need on the field. These skills would be easier to learn here, where the ministry was easier. If she was unable to succeed here, we had no reason to think she could succeed in cross-cultural ministry. "If you learn how to befriend and build people up in their faith, eventually you will most likely end up leading a group of your own, like I am doing now. When you can duplicate your Bible study, you'll be a church-planter. And a church-planter is the perfect candidate for the mission field."

In the two years since this talk, Lexi has become a different person. With quiet determination, she set about trying to build her own ministry with a new vigor. Today, she is a leader in her own home church. She is currently working with three disciples, all of whom have disciples of their own. She has succeeded in evangelism, and has become a good Bible teacher. She should soon become a church planter, and someday go to the mission field as a seasoned minister.

Imparting Vision

How do you impart a sense of vision to disciples? The first step is to get a sense of vision for them yourself. Before God, you have to go over your interactions with your disciples, asking God what they could become if all went well. God uses your imagination, combined with biblical categories to create a picture in your mind of your disciple as a successful, mature servant of God. As you linger in prayer over the strengths you see in disciples, God will give you a growing excitement about this picture. Usually, the picture is not very specific. It's usually a general picture of what victory would look like for a given person.

Achieving a sense of vision for disciples can be a lengthy struggle. Most people you will work with will confront you with many negatives that can kill vision unless you react the right way. Discouragement is a constant danger for disciple-makers because spiritual growth is so slow and so often punctuated with reversals. But it's crucial that you continue to spend time with God focusing on the potential you see, even if it hasn't been realized yet. Spend time in prayer before each get-together with your disciple, asking God to rekindle your vision for that person.

When you have a sense of vision for a potential disciple, you are only part way to the goal. Next you have to "sell" the disciple on that vision. This may take some time with certain individuals. Their own negative views of themselves often make them reluctant to believe that God could use them in a major way.

Begin by sharing your vision with other influential Christians who know your disciple. Sharing your vision helps you refine it. And it may give the other Christian leaders a new vision for your disciple. If more than one person believes in the vision and in turn shares it with your disciple, it will be more persuasive.

Then, choosing the right time, share your vision with your potential disciple. You might say, "You know, I could really see you becoming one of the top evangelists in this church!" or, "I've been watching you, and I think you have the makings of an exceptional teacher of the word!" Be ready to give details about the things you have seen that give you such hope, but don't share an unrealistic vision. Vision is too powerful to use carelessly. We know of people who have been sent on wild goose-chases based on faulty visions of their future. This is not a time for flattery. It must be a picture you really believe is possible.

When sharing your vision, your convincing tone and personal excitement carry persuasive weight. You may have to return to the subject on a number of successive meetings before your disciple begins to buy into it in a serious way. If others agree with your vision, ask them to share what they see with the person as well.

Once your friend begins to believe in the vision, barriers to attaining that vision become challenges to overcome. You can track their progress together, suggesting ways to overcome barriers along the way.

Basic Steps

Once you feel led to enter into discipleship with a friend, you need to gradually begin introducing the basic elements of discipleship:

- Friendship-building
- A regular meeting time
- Enhanced, inter-personal sharing
- Appropriate biblical and theological content to study together
- Times of prayer
- Counseling and helping your friend in areas of weakness
- Helping your friend develop a ministry
- Releasing your friend to pursue a life of service to God

These components are not sequential. Although you may see a general progression here, most of these proceed concurrently. In the next section, we will cover each of the components.

KEY COMPONENTS IN
DISCIPLEMAKING
SECTION TWO

FRIENDSHIP
BUILDING

The first step in successful discipleship is forming a good friendship. Unlike impersonal forms of education like classroom lectures, discipleship involves what Paul calls "speaking the truth in love" (Eph. 4:15a). When we speak truth to each other in the context of love relationships we will "grow up in all aspects into Him who is the head, even Christ" according to Paul. (15b). If you can make a good friend, you should be able to disciple. On the other hand, inability to form close friendships is an absolute barrier to effectiveness in disciple-making. In this chapter, we will discuss the theory and practice of developing quality friendships. As you read these ideas, think about someone with whom you could apply them.

What is Friendship?

A friendship in the biblical context is a relationship where we practice real Christian love. So the first thing you must understand is biblical love.

In scripture, love has a meaning much different than what the world today believes. Jesus said,

> *My command is this: Love each other as I have loved you. Greater love has no one than this, that he lay down his life for his friends* (John 15:12,13).

According to this key passage, simply liking someone is not enough to qualify. Jesus set a very high standard for what constitutes real Christian love. We must love one another "as I have loved you," that is, sacrificially. His following comment makes this clear. Love is all about laying down your life for your friends. According to this understanding of love, you must do anything you can—within God's will—for the good of a loved one. Just as Jesus sacrificed Himself at the cross for our good, a Christian practicing love is prepared to give up his or her own preferences, time, treasure, and convenience for the sake of building up a friend. John explains,

> *We know love by this, that he laid down His life for us; and we ought to lay down our lives for the brethren. But whoever has the world's goods, and sees his brother in need and closes his heart against him, how does the love of God abide in him? Little children, let us not love with word or with tongue, but in deed and truth* (1 John 3:16-18).

From this passage you can see that love is not just a feeling. Giving the world's goods to another in need is an *action*. Of course, such actions are compatible with feelings of affection and compassion, and may issue from such feelings. However, you can practice self-giving love even when the feelings aren't there. Sometimes your friends may be quite annoying, or you just don't feel warm for some reason. True love-givers know how to come through as servants regardless of how they feel.

These passages also demonstrate that love is not something that just happens when you "click" with someone. The moral language constantly used to describe love implies that loving others is a decision you can make at any time.

We suggest that biblical love is:

A commitment to—with God's power—give of myself in every area for the good of another.

According to this definition, if we love someone, we have a basis to do what is good for that person, but not necessarily what the person wants. This is why we have a basis for discipline in love as Christians. Your friends might want you to approve of whatever they do, but it may be more loving to confront them at times for their own good, just like God sometimes confronts us (Heb. 12:6).

How should someone without good friends develop good friendships? Let's take it from the beginning.

STEP 1 — INITIATION

In the secular world, friendships just sort of "happen." But as an effective disciple-maker, you want to develop the ability to initiate friendships at any time with people you meet. Notice that God always takes the initiative when loving us. John says, "We love because he first loved us" (1 John 4:19). He also says, "This is love: not that we loved God, but that he loved us and sent his Son as an atoning sacrifice for our sins" (4:10). This means if you are going to love others as Christ loved you, you must be ready to take the initiative. In fact, taking initiative in love-giving is an act of sacrifice in itself. The initiator is more vulnerable to rejection. The successful initiator must expend emotional energy and creativity finding successful ways to initiate. It's so much easier to respond when you sense someone likes you, isn't it?

Initiation can be costly. How does one initiate a new friendship?

Quality Conversation

First, try initiating quality conversation that goes beyond talking about the weather or sports. The easiest way to initiate conversation is to ask questions about the other person, and be a good listener.

With people you don't know, your questions must be relatively general at first—finding out who they are, where they live, what they do, and how they came to be involved in your church or small group. If your reactions are personable and friendly to these questions, you can move to deeper questions. What are their likes or dislikes? Try to get a feeling for a person's opinions and interests in areas of art, music or activities. Also, what are their key relationships? Do they have family? Who are their friends?

As you ask questions, you must be prepared to disclose as well, but your focus should remain on the other person. People sense when someone is interested in them, and they usually interpret interest as friendliness. Those who talk about themselves all the time have little success building good friendships.

Since you are focusing on forming a friendship with a Christian, you have an obvious area where you can ask questions. How did this person become a Christian? What has been his spiritual history? How does he feel about his experience so far? What groups has he been in? What were those like?

When you explore someone's spiritual background, additional questions should present themselves. You can either ask follow-up questions, or remember your questions. The next time you talk, you should build on what has already been shared. The goal is to develop an understanding of how the inner workings of the other person drives his disposition. What kind of person is this? Why does he have the attitudes he reveals?

A *careful* listener can determine not only what people are saying, but what they might *not* be saying. Careful listeners are always attentive to things that "don't add up" based on what they know thus far.

An *active* listener who is also an initiator will return later to explore these gaps in understanding. In other words, when you return to subjects you discussed in an earlier conversation with more in-depth questions, people will perceive that you are thinking about them when you are not together. This is usually interpreted as friendliness.

In your initiating conversations, the goal is to try to introduce some discussion about your lives. By helping a person talk about himself, you have the opportunity to engage in actual relational conversation. Such quality conversations, usually seen alongside the more superficial kind, lead to a feeling of friendship.

When people have interesting conversations with active, careful listeners, they feel drawn to those people as friends. While most people want to disclose and enjoy communication, some feel awkward at first. Good initiators know how to raise questions and actively listen to cut through the awkwardness.

Time

If your conversations go well, it becomes natural to initiate spending time together. Depending on the person, you might suggest joining them in one of their interests. This way, you're being sacrificial—not always asking others to join in your interests, but being willing to join into something they are interested in or passionate about. With some people, you should be able to suggest having coffee or eating lunch together. With others, you might go fishing, bowling, bird watching, running, watch a ball game on TV together, or do a hundred other activities.

Dennis: When I went to a new home church in the 80's, I was interested in finding a new friend I could disciple. A guy named Mike was new there. He was younger than me, and from a blue-collar part of our city. His background was radically different than mine, and his interest in automobile mechanics was something I knew almost nothing about. But I had an old car that was giving me trouble. So I asked him what he thought about my engine problems. He offered to look at it.

When I took my car over, he and I spent a couple of hours huddled over the aging engine while I plied him with questions about how engines worked. He explained what he was doing and why. At first, I was acting more interested than I really was. But as he unfolded his expertise in engine diagnosis, I became increasingly interested. I realized that this young man, who had never attended college and spoke with a West Virginian accent and poor grammar, was very intelligent, discerning, and friendly. He had no idea I was a senior pastor of a large church, or that I had done years of graduate study. As far as he was concerned, I was just a friendly guy who was interested in learning what he knew about cars, and he was delighted to teach me.

Mike eventually imparted a working knowledge of auto mechanics to me, even helping me buy my own quality set of tools. During the next few years, I imparted to him a knowledge of God and the Bible. He ended up winning a number of his friends to Christ, and they in turn won others. By going outside of my usual circle of interest to develop a new friend, I acquired a skill that has saved me hundreds of dollars. I also gained a disciple who eventually became a home church leader with his own disciples.

On another occasion, I met a younger guy named Jim who was a lawyer, and had recently met Christ. It turned out he also grew up on a farm, and had never lost his love of rural living. As I inquired into his interests, he mentioned that he longed for the winter days when he and his dad used to go into the woods to cut and split firewood together.

I saw my opportunity. I had just converted my old decorative fireplace into a wood-burning fireplace.

"Wow, do you think you could teach me how to find and cut wood?" I asked. It turned out he had his own chain saw, and was more than happy to have an excuse to go out hunting for good firewood.

After our first trip to a friend's farm, I was not only happy to have a nice pickup full of quality wood, I was also intrigued by his insight into quality versus "junk" trees. He could identify trees even in the winter (when trees in our part of the country lose their leaves) just by looking at their bark. I went to the library and checked out books on firewood and tree identification. I eventually learned the specific gravity of every major tree species in our region, how many BTU's per cord they yield, and can now identify any of them in summer or winter. I have my own chain saw now, and no lack of quality firewood!

Not long after a couple of trips to cut wood, I was able to interest Jim in joining me for some Bible reading and prayer. Today, he and his wife lead a home church at Xenos.

Friendships require time. You can't expect to develop intimacy on the fly. You must be prepared to invest time developing common ground with a new friend. Some of this common ground may involve sharing social situations with others. If you're going out with other friends, you could invite your new friend to join you. Or, you could look for an opportunity to join in with your friend and his or her social circle.

The best kind of time is that spent one-on-one. When you meet a friend alone, the quality of conversation is likely to be higher, and you will find you can raise questions that wouldn't be appropriate in front of others. Whenever possible, look for opportunities for spiritual conversations. Your continuing exploration into the inner workings of a friend will become easier as you spend time together.

Be ready to offer vulnerable sharing from your own life, but be sensitive. Don't overwhelm your friend or engage in long monologues.

Building a friendship requires patience and perseverance. Many people are simply not willing to invest time consistently over a six-month period in order to build a good friendship. But in disciple-making, you are contemplating investing several years into a relationship, so building a basic sense of closeness over several months is not too much to ask.

As your ability to initiate grows, you will find that you have little problem opening new friendships. But your time is limited, and this leads quickly to a situation where you may have more opportunities to spend time with new friends than you can possibly do. Now what?

If you are interested in discipling others, you must make choices at this point. You cannot expend fragments of time in a thousand directions and still expect to be effective in making true disciples. Before God, you must ask who you should invest extra time with in the hope of taking the friendship to a higher level.

By focusing on key people, you stand the best chance of building the kind of friendship that will sustain discipleship. Try to find someone who is truly willing to move in God's direction, someone with whom you feel you can make a meaningful contribution. (In fact, there may be a number of considerations that go into this kind of decision, including direct spiritual leading. Look back to the earlier discussion in Chapter 3 on some of the factors to consider when facing this kind of prioritizing decision.)

Feelings

People are emotional beings. Even those who don't express many overt feelings have emotional needs. In initiating friendship, you must be ready to initiate emotional sharing. Emotional sharing involves a wide range of expressions on many levels.

First, you need to share your feelings about third parties or external events before you go deeper. For instance, sharing your feelings about a piece of music or a movie is an act of emotional sharing with low vulnerability. People are more attracted to those who display a reasonable amount of feeling than to those who are completely unemotional. Revealing that you are really passionate about certain things (including God) is usually attractive. People feel themselves drawn to those who have passionate beliefs.

But much more important is sharing your emotions about the growing relationship with your friend. Good initiators show discretion and good judgment about how much feeling to share. In newer relationships, expressing feelings like interest, warmth, and enthusiasm is always safe. Think of a person you talked with recently who seemed interested in what you had to say. Isn't that more enjoyable than talking to someone who seems uninterested or blank?

Similarly, warmth means that you are able to show people that you are happy to see them, and that you feel positive about your interactions. A lot of warmth is signaled with body language. A smile, appropriate eye contact, a good handshake, or a pat on the shoulder suggests you feel warmth toward another. The enthusiasm with which you react to things your friend says also suggests warmth. People who don't display warmth are sometimes described as "cold fish." You will make agonizingly slow progress in friendship-building if you come off as a cold fish, or no progress at all!

Why do some people seem like cold fish? Isn't it because they are self-protective? Some people don't want to take the risk of showing they care. (Men especially fear being judged as "un-cool" if they show too much interest and warmth.) Often, unexpressive people actually do care, and may be feeling warm under the surface, but one could never tell.

It's not enough to *feel* warmth. You must *express* it in a way others can detect. And that often means you need to push yourself a bit to be more overt than you're used to being. (Of course, some people are overly emotional. People who are perceived as hysterical or who gush in an unnatural way too early in a relationship may seem threatening or artificial. Many will shy away from such a person.)

How can you know how much feeling to reveal in a new friendship you are initiating? One key is to assess yourself. If you aren't sure, ask your existing friends or family what they think. Are you a highly emotional and expressive person? If so, there's no reason to push for more. In fact you may need to control yourself! Or are you generally unemotional? If so, you must consciously push yourself out of your comfort zone to be more expressive. Seek to gradually curb your self-protectiveness and express your feelings more openly. You may need to watch people who you know are emotionally expressive and study how they express their feelings.

Dennis: When I was nineteen, I was a cold fish. I knew I was a deeply passionate person, and I felt able to express feelings with close friends. But with newer people, I tended to be extremely inhibited and shy. I was constantly worrying about the awkward silences in my conversations with new people. Sometimes it bothered me so much I would just break off conversations and even leave events early.

My roommate was the opposite. He was the most outgoing person I knew. At one point, he took me aside for reproof. He pointed out that my inability to talk to people and my disappearing act after Bible studies was being interpreted by many as an unfriendly attitude—maybe even contempt. I opened up about how difficult it was for me to express myself when I didn't know people well, and asked for suggestions. He immediately urged me to stay by his side for the whole evening the next time we went to the Bible study where most people were strangers to me. He said I should watch him relate to the new people and try to imitate him.

The suggestion sounded strange at the time, but after more dialog about the idea, I agreed. I followed him from conversation to conversation, and tried to interact. Some conversations with students at a restaurant after the meeting would last a long time and get fairly deep. I couldn't believe how well his suggestion worked! I found myself imitating the way he would lean toward people or nudge them while laughing. I noticed scores of minor actions and mannerisms, many of which I felt comfortable imitating in my own way. I saw him employing his simple formula for establishing communication with strangers: "If he says 'Moo,' you say 'Moo Moo!'"

During that year, my ability to express feelings in new relationships expanded in amazing ways. People regularly commented on how much I had changed, and how much they loved it.

Deeper Feelings

As your friendship with a potential disciple progresses, vulnerable emotions become natural. For instance, sharing your gratitude for the relationship itself is a vulnerable, but meaningful feeling to share with a friend with whom you've spent a significant amount of time. "Paula, I really appreciate our friendship. I feel like there's a growing trust between us." By sharing a serious expression of appreciation like this, you will likely boost the quality of your friendship to a new level.

The same can be said for expressing loyalty. Loyalty means telling your friend you are there for her—and that you can be counted on. Just letting the person know that you consider her to be one of your good friends is an expression of loyalty.

If you feel reluctant to express such a feeling, it may be because the relationship hasn't developed to the point where it would be appropriate. People are timid about expressing such things because they don't want to risk rejection or judgment. They're playing it safe with the self-protection of emotional distance. They probably would be willing to express the feeling *if the other person shares first*. But this is simply because they don't want the burden of initiation. Sadly, many people are not sacrificial enough to love others like God has loved them! If you wait for others to initiate, you will make very poor progress in friendship-building.

Jessica: Cassandra has a very difficult personality with past trauma that caused her to lash out in a strangely aggressive way. Most people in her life at this time eventually withdrew from her. As I tried to build a friendship, I could see why; she was scary, insulting, and irrationally hurtful. I thought about withdrawing myself and explaining that I felt unable to help her.

As I was praying about it one day, I suddenly saw her problem with new clarity. Cassandra had no real friends. Despite the fact that she was one of the most charismatic people I had ever met, she pushed everyone away. This had to be self-protection, although I'd never seen it displayed this way. Once God showed me the heart of the issue I was able to relate and empathize with her in a much deeper way than before.

That week after Bible study, Cassandra and I had an emotional discussion. She wanted to avoid me that night, but I put my hand on her shoulder and said, "Please. Let's just go downstairs and talk for a minute." After explaining my theory that Cassandra was pushing people away to protect herself, I described how I felt about it: "I feel like I'm trying to relate to you and there is some kind of block I keep running into. But I want you to know that I am not going to stop trying. You can't get rid of me that easily."

It went against my instincts to leave myself so emotionally vulnerable. She could have laughed in my face, said she didn't care or simply stated, "No thanks." Instead, we connected emotionally.

Years later, we are still friends and still bring up that conversation as being something very significant in our relationship. Sometimes unflinching, vulnerable, emotional love is the only thing that will get through to someone. Through her experience building a friendship with me, she has learned how to befriend others as well. Now she has disciples who are close friends, and leads a home church in our fellowship.

Remember, you aren't trying to accomplish all these things in a short period of time. You should envision yourself hanging out with a friend over a period of months, gradually building the pillars of good friendship: open communication, warm feelings, common experience, understanding, and loyalty.

STEP 2 — INVESTING

If you are successful at initiating a good Christian friendship, you may decide the time is right to move to a regular time of investment. You should find it easy to suggest that the two of you meet regularly for the purpose of building each other up spiritually. We suggest getting together to do some reading. (At this point, you don't need to suggest that your friend become your disciple. You may be thinking that discipleship is a possibility, but suggesting discipleship may seem hier-archical.) Suggesting a regular meeting for mutual edification is a safer option. Since you will be built up just as much as your disciple, the suggestion is perfectly honest.

Some friends may resist this opportunity, and that should tell you something. You're looking for someone who is hungry for spiritual growth. If you can't talk a friend into a weekly meeting, that friend may be telling you that he or she isn't interested in growing spiritually (or it may be that your friend simply has no category for such a time, and it seems strange). You can work with the situation gradually, seeking to understand the reluctance to meet. But you may decide that a different friend would be better to disciple.

If you've been talking about the concept of discipleship during earlier conversations, it would not be unusual for your friend to ask if you will disciple him or her. This is ideal, but don't wait around expecting it to happen. Only a minority of friends suggest this. Later, if your reputation as a disciple-maker grows, and as your group gains a corporate vision for discipleship, it will become common.

Winning a friend over to the idea of regular meetings for disciple-ship is a major accomplishment. Once you reach this point, prayer, study, accountability, and the other things we will discuss in later chapters can begin. But friendship-building must continue as well. In most cases, you are committed to building a friendship for years. These friendships become the best in your life, and you will never regret the time and self-sacrifice of pouring your life into another.

This notion of pouring your life into another is what we call *investment*. When you invest into a relationship, you give of yourself with consistency and godly concern. You give of yourself in the hope that, like a good stock investment, what you invest will come back for the kingdom of God (not necessarily to you), and much more besides.

But this is not always the case. Some disciples decide to turn away from the path of discipleship, and you won't necessarily be able to do anything about it. Nobody knows how to make an unwilling person willing. Even God doesn't do that! This is why your investment into a disciple has to be unconditional. You can never demand that you be repaid for what you have invested. You must remain aware that you have no guarantee that your disciple-making relationship will work, even if you invest several years into the person and give it your all. No wonder many Christian leaders are unwilling to disciple! Any Christian minister who is hooked on quick, big results in ministry, will turn away from discipleship. Viewed this way, investing into discipleship is an act of faith. You must go before God and decide whether you believe Jesus when He said, "the one who loses his life for my sake is the one who will save it" (Luke 9:24).

How much common experience?

As mentioned earlier, investment into friendships that lead to fruitful discipleship extends over a period of years. Of course, you're not just giving out during this process. You also receive the enjoyment of a quality friendship—one of the greatest joys in life.

Sometimes we find Christians short-changing the need for a time and activity investment in their friendships, especially after early progress has lead to success. This is a mistake. You must continually look for opportunities to add to your "relational capital" with your friends by taking the time to build a deep foundation of common experience. Relational capital means that, like a bank account, you have to deposit money before you can write checks. If you want to develop a friendship where you exert an influence as a leader—rather than being just a man-pleaser—you have to deposit often and deeply. Your friend's heart will be won through godly investment, but your own heart will be moved as well. You will experience a growing affection and care for your friends as you pour yourself into their lives. And people can tell when you care.

When you have spent years doing things together, whether it be sports, hobbies, enjoying the same social circle, and especially sharing ministry and fellowship, your friendship reaches a depth and stability that withstands difficult times with relative ease. Consider taking trips together. Trips seem to build a sense of shared memories that are hard to match. For single people, living together is an excellent way to build common experience. Even married couples sometimes have a disciple live with them for a time as a houseguest.

Sometimes people get a feeling of immediate closeness with someone, but that doesn't mean they have developed a deep relationship. As Americans who like fast food and quick information on the Internet, some find it difficult to accept the need for long-term investment. They want closeness and trust quickly, but that is not how relationships work.

On the other hand, if you accept the need to build deeply into your key relationships, you will invest the time to build up a substantial backlog of common experience. A history of common experience makes you feel like you really know a person, having seen her in hundreds of unique situations. With a close friend, you have a sense that you share your worlds. Rich times of reminiscing about your experiences together are nurturing. If you do need to bring a difficult message at times (like criticism), your friend will usually accept it because she knows how deeply you love her. People can tell when you care.

In the following chapters, we will cover several major areas of investment. But in addition to those areas, some areas have mainly to do with friendship-building.

Step 3 — Assessing and Responding

Disciplers who relate carefully are always watching and praying about their friends, trying to discover the truth in three key areas: potential or strengths, weaknesses, and points of resistance.

Potential

You may notice your friend showing empathy and sensitivity in a relational situation with a third party. You should note this and watch for more. If you come to believe these are areas of strength, you have discovered something very valuable: an area of potential. These areas are often indications of God's design for your friend. If God designed a person a certain way, that design also says something about God's will for the person. These are the keys to look for in trying to develop a vision for your disciple. For example, you may notice that your disciple is firm but loving in a situation. That suggests other potentials. Or, you notice that when sharing at a Bible study, your friend is unusually clear or insightful. That could be a sign of a teaching gift.

Dennis: When I was 18, I had just begun my walk with God. One night I went to a Bible study at a campus house. Afterward, an older student whom I admired came over and sat beside me. After a little small talk, he said, "Dennis, the way you shared tonight was so clear and convincing, I feel sure you could become a Bible teacher."

I smiled bashfully and shrugged my shoulders. I had never in my life considered teaching or preaching for God until that moment! But later that same week, while registering for spring quarter classes, I signed up for a class on persuasive speaking. Without a doubt, the reason was because of what that brother in Christ shared with me. I did well in the class, and shortly after, accepted some speaking invitations to give my testimony and teach at a couple of student Bible studies. I enjoyed it so much I never looked back.

The older brother moved out of town not long after this incident, but I went on to devote my life to teaching, preaching, and public evangelism. Nearly thirty years later, I ran into him again in another city. I always wondered if he had any idea how much impact he had on my life through that single comment. I asked him if he remembered it, and I'm not sure he did. This just goes to show that your words may have far more impact on others than you think.

When you are building friendships, you should watch for opportunities to speak along these lines, seeking to promote the potential you see in your friend through encouragement. Don't manufacture things or flatter. Instead, watch and wait until God gives you a clear sense of real potential in the other person. Then, after prayer and reflection, watch for the best way, the best time, and the best words to promote that potential.

If you plant seeds like this, you may also notice your friend acting in a way that suggests she has taken your suggestion to heart. Or she may just tell you she is excited about developing the area you mentioned. Either way, you now have the makings of motivation. You can easily agree to work together to gather the tools needed to maximize a ministry in that area. There may be books you can read or field experiences you can seek out together that will provide practice and give you opportunities for feedback.

Many people are remarkably blind to their own strengths. Even when they do believe they have potential in an area, they may be reluctant to acknowledge it to others to avoid being seen as prideful. Gifts and abilities are from God, not from ourselves, so acknowledging them is not pride. Others are well aware of strengths they have in academic, musical, interpersonal, artistic, or business fields, but have never considered how these might apply to the Kingdom of God. With many of these people, all they need is a little nudge from you to see how God could use their gifts and abilities and they will quickly show far more interest in spiritual things.

Weaknesses

If you are spending substantial time with your friend, you will also notice weaknesses. You may see him lose his temper with another person, or fail to listen. Relational problems are common and numerous, but you must distill what you see to the key, central issues that could block your friend's effectiveness with others.

During discussions, you may notice your friend is surprisingly ignorant in a particular area. Or, you may notice attitudes that are wrong. Good disciple-makers quietly mark these areas for attention in the future. While praying and planning what to study with your friend, God will often show you things you could say or read that might help. In a dozen ways you must look for opportunities to help your friend make progress in these weak areas.

Patience and grace are very important when dealing with a potential disciple's weaknesses. The emphasis in scripture when dealing with weaknesses is "help" and "patience." Paul says, "We urge you, brethren, admonish the unruly, encourage the fainthearted, help the weak, be patient with everyone" (1 Thess. 5:14). Notice the difference between being fainthearted or weak on one hand, and being unruly on the other. (Unruliness refers to points of resistance, and we will discuss these later in Chapter 10.) A weakness is not a willful refusal to comply with God's will, but an inability to do so, or perhaps blindness to the problem. All of us are weak at certain points. When you identify weaknesses in your potential disciple, you should find ways to help him or her improve.

How can you help? Clearly, this depends on the problem. The first thing is to begin praying. You will probably be praying long and often about the weaknesses you see in disciples. Part of the sacrificial aspect of Christian love is the extensive time and emotional investment in agonized prayer. No doubt this is part of the "daily burden for all the churches" that Paul said was as bad as the many beatings and imprisonments he had endured (2 Cor. 11:28). During lengthy times of prayer, God will give you insights about how to help struggling disciples.

A second objective is awareness. Is your friend aware that her weakness is a real problem? Is she excited about the need to see change? They may have elaborate rationalizations explaining why this kind of weakness isn't that bad. In some cases they may be completely blind to the problem. This is particularly common with relational weaknesses. People with anger problems, passivity problems, problems with inappropriateness, lack of forgiveness, bitterness, or selfishness (just to name a few) typically feel their reactions and attitudes are justified and normal. The same may be true with a multitude of habits or deficiencies caused by omission (e.g. failure to witness, pray, serve others, read the word, etc.). Good disciple-makers have to formulate strategies for making their friends aware of their weaknesses and the harm they may be causing. But you need to do so without seeming like an accuser or one who nags. Sensitivity and creativity are important because a friend could feel insulted when you point out a weakness.

We suggest an indirect approach. If you have reached a point where you and your friend read together, you may suggest reading a book that deals with the weakness in question. During such a reading, you can usually ask questions in a way that helps your friend through a process of self-discovery. When God directly convicts people about their problems, they usually gain a better understanding of why they need to change. You are now in a position of helper, rather than accuser. At other times, you will need to point out the problem yourself. We will discuss ideas for how to do this in the most redemptive way in the chapter on counseling.

Points of Resistance

Every growing Christian eventually develops points of resistance to God. These may involve one of their weaknesses, but the difference is that they don't want to change. In a resistant person, you are seeing an issue with his or her will—an attitude problem. Attempts to help won't do any good, because your friend hasn't agreed with the need for help in the first place.

Discovering a point of resistance is always a difficult crossroad in a developing friendship. Naturally, you earnestly want to see a change of heart. But such changes may take time, and always call for a careful approach. If you try to force a change, it may backfire. However, doing nothing shows no love.

Action here depends on a prayerful calculation of what will be best for your friend. You should not feel legalistically bound to take any particular course of action. The principle of biblical love is always doing what is best for the other person, not any need to follow legal principles. You should weight your history in the relationship along with your friend's level of accountability. Many other factors need to be measured as well. Because working with such areas is so important and sensitive, we have devoted an entire chapter to it (Chapter 10, Encountering a Lack of Progress).

If you hope to confront your friend with his needs and help him with his weaknesses, you must be willing to let him do the same for you. Endeavor to be transparent about your own struggles. You should be willing to receive insight from your friends with gratitude, even if they are less mature. Proverbs 9:8 says, "Do not reprove a scoffer, or he will hate you, reprove a wise man and he will love you." Receiving reproof with gratitude is an important lesson in humility and teachability. The best way to teach your friend this virtue is to demonstrate it in your own life. A good friendship should become a mutual commitment to develop each other's character.

This sketch of how to build friendships has been necessarily brief. We hope it sparks ideas you can combine with your own experience to build successful and deep friendships. Peter says, "Since you have in obedience to the truth purified your souls for a sincere love of the brethren, fervently love one another from the heart" (1 Pet. 1:22). If you learn how to love people fervently from your heart, you will probably do well as a disciple-maker.

5

MODELING

A well-known saying among disciple-makers is, "Disciples tend to do what you do, not what you say." Another is, "You can't give away what you don't have." Both statements point to the same thing: the power of modeling.

Books and lectures are excellent learning tools. But some things are better learned through imitation. Attitudes and values are mostly transmitted through modeling. When you see someone you respect become angry because of a selfish decision made by another, you learn in a memorable way what matters to such people. The same is true when you see the intensity of joy respected believers show when someone comes to Christ. You may see those you respect so intense about attaining a goal that they refuse to quit. How do people learn how to suffer in faith, instead of feeling sorry for themselves? How do people learn how to move deeply into intercessory prayer? How do young believers ever learn how to come forward and admit fault instead of justifying themselves? These qualities and many others are more *caught* than *taught*.

As a disciple-maker, your hope should be to transmit many spiritual and character qualities that are more subjective than objective. You can tell someone they should be loyal to God over other values in life. But what does that mean? Only when your friend sees you live it out will he truly understand it, let alone feel drawn to do the same. This is why the author of Hebrews tells his readers, "Remember your leaders, who spoke the word of God to you. Consider the outcome of their way of life and imitate their faith" (Heb. 13:7). When you notice that the lives of spiritually mature people are more healthy than others, this "outcome of their way of life" makes you want to be the same way.

Jesus was the ultimate example of a model. He said, "My command is this: Love each other as I have loved you" (John 15:12). And his life was the purest example of love anyone could imagine. What a startling contrast we see on the night of the last supper: His disciples were arguing about which of them was the greatest, and he responded by washing their feet (Luke 22:24). Afterward he said, "I have set you an example that you should do as I have done for you" (John 13:15). How do people learn humility? You could suggest they should be humble, but if you are like most believers, you know humility is something learned by being around humble Christians.

Paul knew imitation was a premier avenue of learning. That's why he said, "Be imitators of me, just as I also am of Christ" (1 Cor. 11:1). he reminded the Thessalonians how they "became imitators of us and of the Lord." And as a result, they "became a model to all the believers in Macedonia and Achaia" (1 Thess. 1:6, 7). He later pointed out that he practiced self-denial and servitude in supporting himself and his friends "in order to offer ourselves as a model for you, so that you would follow our example" (2 Thess. 3:9). He told the Philippians,

"Whatever you have learned or received or heard from me, or seen in me—put it into practice. And the God of peace will be with you" (Phil. 4:9).

He also coached his disciples to consciously present themselves as models to their people. He told Timothy, "Don't let anyone look down on you because you are young, but set an example for the believers in speech, in life, in love, in faith and in purity" (1 Tim. 4:12). To Titus his advice was, "In everything set them an example by doing what is good. In your teaching show integrity, seriousness and soundness of speech that cannot be condemned . . ." (Titus 2:7,8).

THE MAIN KEY TO SUCCESSFUL MODELING

Not all models are followed. Many people hope to lead through modeling, but people ignore them. Others are eagerly imitated, even though they aren't good models. Why is this? Jesus gives us a clue in Luke 14. First, He gave exacting requirements for being his disciple:

If you want to be my follower you must love me more than your own father and mother, wife and children, brothers and sisters— yes, more than your own life. Otherwise, you cannot be my disciple. And you cannot be my disciple if you do not carry your own cross and follow me. But don't begin until you count the cost. For who would begin construction of a building without first getting estimates and then checking to see if there is enough money to pay the bills? Otherwise, you might complete only the foundation before running out of funds. And then how everyone would laugh at you! (Luke 14:26-29 NLT)

Jesus is really explaining the old saying that if "Jesus isn't Lord of all, he isn't Lord at all." Anyone who wants to follow Jesus, but comes with contingencies, be they family, economic goals, or the preservation of his own life, is profoundly distrusting God in his heart. Why would I refuse to give over everything in my life, unless I feel on some deep level that I cannot trust Jesus completely with my life? Even if I attach one condition to my willingness to follow Christ it means that I'm still the one in control, not Christ.

Of course, the decision to enter into radical followership is different than actually carrying out that decision in practice. No Christian has ever completely lived out total commitment, including the leader of Jesus' disciples, Peter. But in this passage, Jesus is calling for a heart decision or an intent to follow without conditions. This is a big decision, so Jesus urges people to count the cost. Are we sure we can afford to sign over our entire lives to Jesus' leadership?

We believe this is a second decision that Christians make after they have come to know Christ, and realize the stakes when it comes to choosing between Christian mediocrity and vibrant, all-out Christian living. We also find that God will test our decision in a number of areas during the years that follow. We will have repeated opportunities to reaffirm our intention to go all the way with God.

But the punch line in Jesus' discourse is yet to come. He concluded the talk with these words:

> *"Salt is good, but if it loses its saltiness, how can it be made salty again? It is fit neither for the soil nor for the manure pile; it is thrown out. He who has ears to hear, let him hear"* (Luke 14:34,35)

We should read this in light of his earlier statement to his followers that they are the salt of the earth. (Mat. 5:13). Here he is warning that salt can lose its saltiness, and he implies this is the fate of those who refuse to go all-out for him. Un-salty salt is like pop with no fizz. Nobody wants to drink it. Christians who hold back in a tentative form of following (that is really not following) lose their fizz. They cannot inspire others to sell out for Christ. They cannot model radical trust, because at some level in their own hearts, they distrust God. Disciple-makers who hold back from God in one area produce disciples who hold back in ten areas.

Disciples rarely rise higher than their mentors. Even Jesus said, "A student is not above his teacher, nor a servant above his master. It is enough for the student to be like his teacher . . ." (Mat. 10:24, 25). If you haven't settled the question of radical followership, you will not be able to model real faith for your disciples.

During years of watching people try to serve God, over and over we see that some people seem to have incredible influence for Christ, while others never seem to gain much traction with people. The difference isn't their level of intelligence or gifting. Neither do circumstances have much impact. The common thread with these highly influential servants of Christ is their high level of commitment. Those with areas of compromise never develop much impact for Christ in spite of sometimes amazing levels of gifting.

Before going out to become a model, you should have a deep transaction with God. Carefully think through Jesus' proposition. Are you ready to go all the way with Christ? If not, Why? Be honest enough to admit your unbelief, and spend time thinking about what your unbelief implies about your view of God.

On the other hand, if you feel ready to make this unqualified commitment to Christ, he will use you to change people's lives, perhaps far beyond what you expect. If you long to see yourself count for God in this life, realize this is the gateway to effectiveness. Full commitment to Christ cannot be sidestepped or diminished if you want to be effective models.

Lessons from Psychology

Social learning psychologists have studied the process of learning through models extensively. Albert Bandura did research on how children choose and follow models. Included in his findings were the following:[1]

> *Children must attend to the pertinent clues. The child may misdirect her attention at the time the model is observed, and therefore fail to perform the behavior properly later. A teacher can help by directing the child's attention to those parts of the model's performance that are most important.*

According to this finding, modeling has a weakness: People may misperceive or misinterpret models. They may attribute a model's success to one thing, when the real reason was something different. Or they may not be watching or paying attention during key parts of the behavior. For instance, my disciple may watch me teach, but didn't get to see how long I studied beforehand. So, as those consciously modeling, you may need to point out the correct interpretation or features: "Did you notice what I said to that guy? Why do you think I took that approach?" By discussing recent incidents like this, you can ascertain that your disciples are correctly perceiving and interpreting what you do. You see Jesus doing this when he asked his disciples, "Do you still not understand? Don't you remember the five loaves for the five thousand, and how many basketfuls you gathered? Or the seven loaves for the four thousand, and how many basketfuls you gathered?" (Mat. 16:9,10). This also explains why Paul so often recalls and explains his own actions, like when he reminds the Corinthians, "When I came to you, brothers, I did not come with eloquence or superior wisdom as I proclaimed to you the testimony about God . . ." (1 Cor. 2:1. See also his extensive explanations of his own actions in 2 Corinthians).

Children must be able to retain in their memory what they observe, so it will be available when needed. Memories do fade or disappear with time, so memory-aiding techniques such as rehearsal, review, or practice help to maintain the image in the other person's memory.

This finding suggests that repetition is important. Disciples are sometimes surprisingly slow to pick up new skills and attitudes in a lasting way. Any disciple-maker who thinks it will be sufficient to tell or show a disciple how to do something one time is quite naïve. Only after multiple repetitions can you expect disciples to begin to pick up on your model in meaningful ways. For instance, a disciple may need to watch you in multiple conflict situations before he will begin to see the consistent pattern of Christian conflict management. A disciple learning how to teach the Bible may need to alternate attempts to teach himself with observations of your teaching during multiple cycles before he successfully acquires the skill.

Bandura also studied which people kids tend to pick as role models.[2] He found that:

Children are more likely to model their own behavior after the actions of people they look upon as important, than after people whom they do not look upon as important.

This points again to the importance of relational investment in discipleship. Close friends are considered important. If you are a part of a leadership team, you have the opportunity to "talk up" your fellow leaders to others, which will probably result in people being more willing to follow their example. Hopefully, your other team members will return the favor.

Children are more likely to adopt behavior patterns from models of their own sex than from models of the opposite sex.

This is another argument for discipling same-sexed people.[3]

Models who receive rewards such as fame, high society status, or money are more influential with children than those who do not have these kinds of rewards.

Of course neither Jesus nor Paul received these kinds of rewards, but they did receive spiritual rewards. A model's spiritual health, good relationships, and personal sense of fulfillment are attractive to disciples (Heb. 13:7).

Models who are punished for their behavior are usually not followed.

This is an important point, but remember, punishment is often a matter of interpretation. Although Paul was beaten, imprisoned, and even stoned, he viewed such things as "momentary light affliction" (2 Cor. 4:17). Even after four years in prison, and awaiting possible execution, Paul had nothing to share but the joy of the Lord and a sense that God was blessing him more than ever when he wrote Philippians. In other words, suffering and punishment are not always the same. This finding by Bandura suggests why leaders who whine, complain, and often feel sorry for themselves have trouble leading. People don't want to follow an example that leads to nothing but heartache and despair. On the other hand, leaders who undergo trials with thanksgiving and a sense of victory and faith amaze and tantalize their disciples. Disciples want the ability to rise above their circumstances like these remarkable models.

Children are more likely to follow models who are more similar to themselves in age or social status than those who appear to the child to be quite different from himself or herself.

Most parents already know this principle. A child's peers have tremendous influence, eventually rivaling or surpassing that of parents in the teen years. The main point here is that disciples need to identify with the models they follow. When disciples can see themselves becoming something similar to the role model, they will imitate. A relational investment, as well as honesty and transparency, enhances identification. Your disciples have to see you as a real person. Having common interests and common experience lead to identification. Similar age and social situations may help, although in the context of discipleship, we have not seen much disadvantage in being older. Students today seem to have less problem with older role models than those twenty years ago. Perhaps the breakdown of families in America has left more students longing for an older role model they can trust. On the other hand, age becomes a major barrier any time a younger person tries to disciple a significantly older person.

Dennis: I saw this when I was asked to disciple some older men when I was about 22. These 35 to 45 year old men gratefully accepted the Bible teaching I shared with them. And, although they admired me on some levels, they didn't seem to feel it was realistic to follow my example in their lifestyles because of the differences in our life situations and age. It was a classic case of discipleship without modeling. They learned their Bibles, and went on with the Lord, but I was unable to deliver any of them as leaders because they didn't want to imitate me.

Considering Bandura's findings while praying about our effectiveness as models should lead to some insights that will help us change for the better. Although social learning psychology is a secular discipline, we see no reason to doubt their findings in general. Ask God whether any of these points apply to you.

LOSING CREDIBILITY AS A MODEL

We have already pointed out that models who lack faith when suffering, and respond by whining and feeling sorry for themselves lose credibility as models. Also models who are not completely committed to Christ do not inspire a following. But other things can cost you credibility as well.

Dishonesty can be devastating for any would-be model. Any time a disciple catches you in a lie or any form of dishonesty, trust is broken. And trust is central to people's willingness to follow your example. If you tell a lie, the only thing you can do is quickly admit it, and apologize. "I wasn't honest with you in that situation, and that really bothers me, because I want us to be honest with each other all the time." Of course, honesty doesn't mean you have to be exhaustive in what you say. You can always tell a friend, "I'm not free to share what I know about that." They may not like being told this, but it won't result in distrust. To the contrary, the fact that you guard confidences creates more trust. The key is whether they think you are being secretive for self-protective reasons, or out of concern for others.

Self-serving is also bad for a model's credibility. When disciples sense you are serving self, rather than God and others, they may well become suspicious about everything you do. You must demonstrate that you will consistently try to do the right thing, including when it costs you the advantage. This is particularly important when dealing with people and ministry situations. Some things can appear self-serving even when they aren't, and you may have to explain why what you are doing is right under the circumstances. For instance, imagine a group of leaders taking turns teaching in a Bible study group that isn't doing well. We know of cases where the senior leader made the decision to take on a larger proportion of the teaching. That could seem self-serving to the other teachers. But if the leader explains that, given the problems in the group, he feels the need to get the most experienced teacher up more often, people will generally accept it.

You must be particularly careful when dealing with opponents. Refuting or reproving an opponent may seem self-serving, both to the opponent and to others watching. This is why Paul cautions Timothy, "The Lord's bond-servant must not be quarrelsome, but be kind to all, able to teach, patient when wronged, with gentleness correcting those who are in opposition, if perhaps God may grant them repentance leading to the knowledge of the truth . . ." (2 Tim. 2:24, 25). On the other hand, if your disciples see you handle opponents and critics graciously and fairly, their desire to imitate your example will grow, especially if they hear you pray for your opponents.

Extreme hypocrisy usually permanently ruins your chances of being imitated. You can't avoid all hypocrisy, because no Christian is completely consistent. But when hypocrisy becomes extreme, your influence with others is lost. Common hypocrisy might include situations where you don't completely do something you have taught others to do. Most disciple-makers experience a disciple pointing out one of these areas of failure. This is usually not a problem if you are willing to admit the fault and good-natured shrug, "You've got me there!" Having a gracious attitude about your own failings as well as toward others teaches your disciple a valuable lesson.

Most forms of extreme hypocrisy involve some form of implied dishonesty. A leader who continues to teach God's word, while engaging in secret, immoral sexual episodes is guilty of extreme hypocrisy. A believer who tries to seem more righteous than he really is also commits extreme hypocrisy. Consider the case of Ananias and

Sapphira (Acts 5). They gave money to the church in a way that made them seem more generous than they actually were. Their act was an implied lie, designed to impress other Christians with how spiritually advanced they were. God's extreme discipline for this act (death) demonstrates how seriously he views "the leaven of the Pharisees, which is hypocrisy" (Luke 12:1). This kind of hypocrisy will create cynicism in your disciples. They will discount what you say and do because of your hypocrisy, and at the same time, may feel more free to be hypocritical themselves. Real honesty, however, doesn't create cynicism, but trust. Even if you have to admit some fairly serious failures, your disciples will respect your honesty.

TYPICAL AREAS WHERE MODELING IS SUPREME

We already suggested that attitudes and values are best transmitted to disciples through modeling. But objective training can usually be combined with modeling to get the best effect.

Attitudes
Consider the area of your attitude toward money. If your lifestyle is one of moderation and relatively simple living instead of being centered around loving money and possessions, you may well see your disciples gradually trend toward a similar lifestyle. The importance you attach to faithful financial giving will also likely begin to appear in your disciples' lives. But by teaching principles of stewardship, you can accelerate the transmission of such values. Studying quality texts together like Gene Getz's book, *Real Prosperity: Biblical Principles of Material Possessions,*[4] can give your disciples a good biblical and theoretical understanding of the issues surrounding stewardship. Reading key Bible passages, like the parable of the unrighteous steward (Luke 16:1-15) or Jesus' teaching in

the sermon on the mount (Mat. 6:19-34) provides the opportunity for the Spirit to work through the word of God on a disciple's heart. When truth is combined with example, God uses them as a powerful force for change in a disciple's life.

Sacrificial Love

Perhaps the most crucial area you must model for your disciples is real Christian love. Nothing helps people learn how to love like having a close friend who knows how to love others in a Christ-like way. So many aspects of real sacrificial love are subjective:

- How to empathize with others – Developing sensitivity and discernment when relating to others is a key skill for servants of God. Not only caring, but being able to project the impression that you care matters. They need to learn to reflect feeling, so model appropriate emotional responses. For some, this is one of the most difficult relational skills to develop.
- How to listen carefully – Active listening includes careful concentration on what people are saying, and what they may be holding back. Body language, facial expressions, and feedback convey interest when listening. Disciples must learn patience when people are laboring to explain their burden. They may need to ask questions to see if they have understood.
- How to intercede in prayer – This will be discussed in chapter 7.
- How to think about others when we aren't with them – The Bible teaches that we should be, "considering how to stimulate them to love and good deeds" (Heb. 10:24). The imperative in this verse is not to stimulate others, but to "consider." It's too late when you are already with a friend, trying to think on your feet. Those who practice biblical love learn to spend the time praying and thinking about friends so they show up with great ideas about what to say or do that will serve others' needs.

- How to encourage others effectively – Encouragement is both a skill and a creative art. Encouragement is discussed more at the end of chapter 9.
- How to forgive – You must routinely disciple those who don't know how to forgive from the heart. For most people, true forgiveness is a real struggle at times, and a good model can guide people through that struggle.
- How to confront others in love, instead of anger – Disciples often damage or destroy relationships because of unrighteous displays of anger. However, others fail to serve their friends because they are unwilling to confront them at all. We will discuss confrontation later in Chapters 10 and 11. But for now, suffice it to say that nothing will help a disciple understand a loving approach in this area more than watching a mature believer in action.

Christians learn these abilities over a lifetime of following God. But trial and error are slow teachers, even when the Spirit is leading and teaching. To more quickly learn how to love deeply, disciples must see someone they respect and are close to practicing deep love in their presence. Being present when a mature, loving brother confronts a friend about something in his life can teach more than many hours of reading. In fact, reading may never convey all the nuances that go into a careful reproof by a skilled, spiritual leader. However, reading and studying the subject can enhance the disciple's ability to apprehend those skills for himself. Just as in other areas, the combination of modeling and studying is far more potent in effecting life change than is modeling by itself.

Outreaching Love

You model love through your own relationship with a disciple. But that's not enough. Jesus asked, "If you love those who love you, what reward will you get? Are not even the tax collectors doing that?" (Mat. 5:46).

These words highlight the need to practice discipleship in the context of the body of Christ. In community, your disciples get to see how you love people of different backgrounds and personality, including those who are hard to love. They also need to see your love for non-Christians. Your love for non-Christians and your zeal to see them meet Christ can nurture a similar love in your disciples. Disciple-makers who are unconcerned for the lost tend to produce disciples with the same weakness.

Inner Life with God

Your personal walk with God is a key area of modeling. Your love, trust, and appreciation of God are subjective attitudes that are not easily taught through book study. These are mostly learned through years of experiencing the faithfulness of God, but also through imitation. First, you learn to appreciate God through your own experience with him over a number of years. Then, your disciple can actually learn through your experience—a process called *vicarious learning*. In vicarious learning, people acquire for themselves what another has learned, by accepting the other's experience as valid and credible. This is modeling.

Most young Christians have a lot to learn about gratitude. They usually are dissatisfied with what they have been given, and only focus on what they have yet to receive. Study can help them learn a consistent habit of thanksgiving, but nothing helps more than watching a mature believer pray and worship God. Likewise, young believers don't really understand what it means to trust God with their lives. Studying scripture tends to build trust. But knowing an older believer who has learned how to trust God at the deepest level shows them things they may never understand any other way.

Victorious Suffering

A key area of trust you must impart to disciples through modeling is a willingness to suffer in faith and even gratitude. When disciples see you suffering without becoming bitter or defeated, they feel challenged. How can someone continue to trust God, even giving thanks, when they are in pain? Sometimes, only watching a close friend living out this attitude will convince people that it's realistic.

Ministry Skills

Not only does modeling excel at transmitting values and attitudes, it is also powerful for training disciples in complex ministry skills. The best way to learn how to share one's faith is to watch an accomplished evangelist witness. So much of good evangelism involves reading the heart attitudes of non-Christians during discussion. This kind of sensitivity is dynamic, because we have to practice it on the fly. When to put the question of conversion? When to back off until later? When to engage in argument and when to change the subject? These are judgments based on experience and spiritual discernment. After a witnessing experience we can discuss what happened, pointing out key parts in the discussion. When disciples see us witness, they will not only learn how to do the same themselves, they will gain motivation and desire to witness.

Teaching and preaching are best transmitted through modeling as well. Although good books on preaching can help, your disciples will excel far more if you can show them yourself how to proclaim the word in a living way. If a discipler doesn't have much gifting for preaching, all is not lost. Many Christians have developed their own gifting through trial and error, and we can always join them in listening to other effective teachers, and noting why the talk had impact.

How to Motivate Others

Leaders make it their business to be motivators. You must learn to motivate people to love, serve God, and others. You also want your disciples to learn this almost mystical power of motivation. A group may be gripped by apathy or preoccupied with other pursuits when a quality leader enters. Soon, people gain excitement for serving God. They may have already been doing things related to God, but without much excitement. Motivational leaders bring a sense of urgency, excitement, and passion to activities that may have seemed humdrum before. Under the influence of a skilled leader, people begin to gain vision and excitement. Some people have gifting as motivators, but much of this ability is learned. Anyone can increase their motivational ability, especially when they have first-hand experience with a good motivator. Ask questions to insure your disciples notice the right things: "Did you hear how I recounted recent victories during the prayer meeting?" Then ensure they connect the dots by asking, "Why do you think I did that?"

Ministry Judgment

Another key skill set you must transmit through modeling is mature judgment in ministry situations. Human behavior involves so many variables that it becomes impossible to prescribe decision making in ministry. Instead of teaching disciples *what* to think, you must teach them *how* to think. They may have to decide whether to take a hard line or to go easy in a particular situation. Or, whether to look the other way or to confront someone in sin. They will have a thousand judgement calls to make! All of these vary from situation to situation, and are informed by scripture, wisdom, experience, and the direct leading of the Holy Spirit. Learning good ministry judgment through trial and error can take decades. But nothing will accelerate the process more than being near a good model who already has good judgment.

Relations with the Opposite Sex

Married disciple-makers have the opportunity to teach their disciples how to relate to a spouse and perhaps how to be good parents. Bringing disciples into your home where they can see for themselves how you relate to your family is important. Single disciple-makers have the chance to show their friends how to relate maturely to the opposite sex. Single disciple-makers must realize they cannot do anything in dating that they would not be happy to see their disciples doing. Your disciples are watching you at all times, and they will either learn mature Christian living from you or something else.

ARE YOU QUALIFIED TO MODEL?

When you consider the multitude of attitudes, values, and skills best transmitted through modeling, you could easily feel intimidated. "Am I mature enough to be viewed as a model? Do I want to risk having a disciple imitate, not only the good things in my life, but the bad?" You may even feel it would be arrogant to put yourself forward as a model to be imitated. Take a deep breath and relax.

Remember, your value as a model is relative. No model is perfect. Even Paul said "imitate me as I imitate Christ." This could be understood as, "only imitate the part that matches Christ." The question is not "Am I as good as Jesus?" but "Am I further along than my disciple?" If your attitudes and lifestyle have progressed further than those of your disciple, he can learn plenty from your modeling. You have to remember how little newer Christians understand about God and the Christian walk. Most of the things discussed in this chapter take a lifetime to develop, and even then you may feel woefully inadequate at times. Satan tries to use accusation to persuade Christians that we are worthless as models, and we should give up.

But even a deeply flawed model is usually better than going without.

When you feel the heartbreak of personal moral failure, intensified by the knowledge that you are being an inadequate model, what should you do? Usually, you must be realistic about the power of the flesh and continue to move ahead, while honestly admitting where you've fallen short. You cannot afford perfectionism. Disciple-making is too real for that. Perfectionism will only lead to phoniness or quitting. Instead, you must learn to cling to grace.

The worst thing you can do during times of spiritual defeat is abandon your disciples. How often we have seen disciple-makers fall into a fit of self-accusation and leave their disciples, usually with terrible results. We are all damaged, and God uses an army of crippled people hobbling forward on crutches and missing legs to build his kingdom! We not only attain to salvation through grace—we also have to learn to minister through grace. Most successful disciple-makers are constantly amazed that their disciples do so well, considering how flawed their discipler was!

Becoming a better model for others is a powerful motivation to develop your own walk with God. Disciple-makers soon realize that real spirituality cannot be faked in a relationship as intimate as discipleship. Discipleship will unveil truth about your weaknesses in the same way your true self comes out in your marriage. But disciples will still benefit if you continue to "press on toward the goal for the prize of the upward call of God in Christ Jesus" (Phil. 3:14).

You might fail so badly that you have to temporarily forfeit your role as a disciple-maker. But this is a serious decision that should be made with other ministry colleagues, and not in the emotional turmoil and remorse of immediate failure. If you feel you have failed so seriously or consistently that you need to withdraw from your role as disciple-maker, you should go to your ministry leaders and colleagues first and get their opinion. After hearing all the facts, they can affirm your withdrawal or encourage you to continue. We suggest this approach because we have seen too many cases where disciple-makers have felt obligated to quit, not because they really needed to, but because Satan put them under accusation for relatively minor problems. If your failure is serious enough to require your withdrawal during restoration, that should be clear to your leaders and colleagues as well.

In a hundred different areas, modeling shapes the outlook and behavior of disciples. As they imitate you, they gradually become models in their own right.

6

THE

BIBLE

Jessica: For me, the Bible has become a pivotal necessity in the art of discipleship. When I first became zealous for the things of God, I tried to begin discipling some of my friends. It did not go well. They all left, exchanging a walk with God for worldly pleasures. In frustration, I went to an older Christian woman I respected to get to the root of the problem.

"What am I doing wrong?" I begged.

She gave the safe answer: "Maybe it's not about you. Sometimes even when we do everything right people will choose against God."

"I know, I know." I said, rolling my eyes. "But I want you to tell me how I can do a better job of discipling others."

She smiled and told me that she had something that might help. She handed me a list of elements that help Christians grow spiritually, suggesting I look at the list and see if I had helped my friends in all of those areas.

As I sat alone with the list, I contemplated my disciple-making experience. Did I talk with my friends about the importance of fellowship with other Believers? Yes. Did I pray with them? Yes. Did I encourage their strengths and possible gifts? Yes. Then I saw something on that list that I wasn't doing—sharing the Bible with them. I had never opened up a Bible in our multiple meeting times together. When I met with my friends, we usually spent most of our time catching up. I followed this by trying to give good advice, and praying about what we'd discussed.

Then an opportunity arose to disciple someone new. This time I was going to change my approach. Janet and I sat down for coffee and I described a couple of study ideas. "Maybe we could read through Colossians together, and discuss the principles we observe. Or we could do an overview of the Old Testament. What would you prefer?" We decided to do both studies, and by agreeing to this we also committed ourselves to a lengthy regular meeting time.

The result of these studies was a pleasant surprise. I noticed that Janet was becoming a powerful spiritual woman, someone with deep personal convictions and a successful personal ministry. She often talked to me about how thankful she was that I helped her "fall in love with the Bible."

Since then, I have become completely convinced that Bible study is key. I have seen that any committed Christian who is willing to become a student of the scriptures can become a powerful force for God in this world. I have seen one Janet turn into twenty Janets as the multiplication process goes on. The fruit is so much greater since I began prioritizing the Bible as part of my time with disciples that its value is unmeasurable.

Is Studying the Bible Essential?

In our experience, many disciple-makers put too little emphasis on Bible study with their disciples. Too often, we learn (usually from the disciples) that the time they spend with their disciple-makers is mostly social. They may talk about recent events and even spiritual struggles and pray together. They may even talk about biblical principles. But they often admit that little time is spent actually studying the Bible or related books. Such disciples usually don't do as well as others who have regular Bible study as a mainstay of their time with disciple-makers. Consider several reasons why knowing the Bible will radically transform the lives of young Christians.

Nourishment

The Bible is spiritual nourishment which helps us grow. Peter says "Like newborn babes, crave the pure spiritual milk of the word, so that by it you may grow up in your salvation" (1 Peter 2:2 NASB). According to Peter, scripture should be as important to us as milk is to a newborn. Paul reminds the Thessalonians that God's word performs the work of God inside believers: ". . . when you received the word of God which you heard from us, you accepted it not as the word of men, but for what it really is, the word of God, which also performs its work in you who believe" (1 Thess. 2:13).

Mental transformation

In the New Testament, we often read of the need for mental transformation. Romans 12:2 calls on us to, "not conform any longer to the pattern of this world, but be transformed by the renewing of your mind . . . ." And in Eph. 4: 23, Paul pleads, "that you be renewed in the spirit of your mind" (NASB). God wants to change the way your disciples think, not just what they do. Your actions flow out of your thinking, so mental transformation is foundational to a changed life. As a disciple-maker, you need to see that leaving disciples with a poorly developed worldview isn't good enough. Particularly in today's culture, where new converts come to Christ as passive, narcissistic, and mentally apathetic, learning scripture is urgent.[1] Those who grapple with their thought lives are the ones who have something spiritual and persuasive to offer their peers.

Victory over sin

Gaining depth in the word helps people gain victory over sin. Knowing the word is no guarantee of freedom from sin, but if combined with basic willingness and other factors, scripture is one of the key elements God uses to release us from slavery to sin. Jesus said, ". . . If you continue in My word, then you are truly disciples of Mine; and you will know the truth, and the truth will make you free" (John 8:31, 32 NASB). And in this context, he was referring to freedom from sin.[2] God uses his word to bring a heightened sense of motivation for change in all areas of life.

Motivation

As a disciple-maker, you must impart strong motivation to your disciples. But how do people become motivated? In the world, social pressure and manipulation are adequate ways to motivate people. When a TV add shows a scantily-clad woman with a certain brand of beer, guys buy more of that beer—they know not why. But the advertisers don't care what the person's motivation is. They just want to sell beer.

As a Christian motivator, this isn't good enough. You want people to do the right thing, but you want them to do so for the right reasons.

So what should a motivated Christian look like? We suggest that:

People are motivated when they are convinced of the correctness and the urgency of Christian goals to the extent that they are eager to act, and keep acting, to reach those goals regardless of what others do or think.

Notice the first objective is that the disciple becomes *convinced of the correctness* of Christian goals. The case for why these goals are correct and worthy comes from the Bible. Nothing will convince people that God's way is right more than studying scripture. When people see the truth so clearly they cannot deny it, even when tempted to leave the path of growth, they will find it very difficult because they know too much.

The second objective is to *impart the urgency* of these goals. This part has to do with modeling and other leadership issues we discuss later. As suggested earlier, seeing Christian goals as urgent is an issue of our values system. And values are best transmitted through modeling.

When you move from a "monkey see, monkey do" motivational base to one based on deeply held biblical conviction, you will see disciples go on even without your help.

Discernment and Wisdom

We all need an ability to discern between good and evil in order to flourish spiritually. Indeed, having this kind of discernment is one of the clear signs that we have grown spiritually according to Heb. 5:13,14: "For everyone who partakes only of milk is not accustomed to the word of righteousness, for he is an infant. But solid food is for the mature, who because of practice have their senses trained to discern good and evil" (NASB). According to this passage, anyone who cannot cope with the meat truths of scripture is, by definition, a spiritual infant.[3] Without a deep knowledge of scripture, your disciples will have little success understanding and battling their sinful nature, Satan, false teaching, or the worldly arguments constantly challenging their faith.

Ministry

Knowing the Bible also gives you credibility with other people. Without an intimate knowledge of the Bible, you will eventually hit a wall in your ability to influence others. 2 Tim. 2:15 says, "Do your best to present yourself as one approved, a workman who does not need to be ashamed, but who correctly handles the word of truth." This makes sense. As Christians, we want to know what God says about our situation, not just another person's opinion. When people sense someone can show them God's mind in a deep way that relates to their present needs, they gravitate to that person for counsel and advice. 2 Tim. 3:16-17 states that "The word of God is profitable for teaching, encouragement, rebuke, and training in righteousness so that the man of God may be thoroughly equipped for every good work" (NASB). The Bible is profitable in every area of a successful disciple-makers' ministry. How can we argue that we have "equipped the saints for ministry" if we have not grounded them in God's word?

Appreciating Grace

The Bible helps us see the gravity of our sin, and in turn the importance of God's grace toward us. You may understand that without God's grace, salvation would be impossible for you to accomplish, but do you realize the same is true for your spiritual life after salvation? Viewing your growth under grace implies that you see that all your progress must come as a gift from God. "Or do you think lightly of the riches of his kindness and tolerance and patience, not

knowing that the kindness of God leads you to repentance?"
(Rom. 2:4). God's kindness causes change within the heart at a deep
level.[4]

Understanding Self

The Bible is the best portal through which to see the important truths
surrounding this concept. The Bible is described as a mirror, or a
tutor. It can show us our true selves, and in the process lead us to a
new dependence on Christ. Self-analyzing can be a frustrating and
fruitless puzzle. But the more we look into the mirror of the Bible, the
more emotionally healthy we become. Most of us focus on ourselves
way too much for our own good. By turning our focus to scripture,
we get God's perspective on our lives and become closer to God in the
process.

Enjoyment and pleasure

Finally, the Bible is rewarding and enjoyable once you learn how to
partake in it. Proverbs says, "Doing wickedness is like sport to a fool,
And so is wisdom to a man of understanding" (Prov. 10:23 NASB). In
other words, gaining wisdom should become as fun as the greatest
sport. It may not be an enjoyable experience the first couple of times
you try to read the Bible, but it becomes enjoyable to anyone who
perseveres. If you can bring your disciples to the point where they
begin to really enjoy spending time in the Bible, you will have
imparted a value that they will use throughout their lives.

INCORPORATING SCRIPTURE STUDY INTO YOUR MEETING TIME

We often begin spending time with disciples on a social basis, perhaps with occasional prayer. But before long, we hope to begin incorporating times of Bible study or reading. We find that many students from generation X and Y are unwilling (or even unable!) to read books on their own, so we often actually read together, taking turns reading a page aloud, and discussing it as we go.

Some people are frustrated about learning the word, and this can be a gateway for initiating Bible study. A girl we know named Samantha recently complained that she didn't know anything about the Old Testament. Later, in private, Julie approached her and asked if she would like to do a seven-week overview study of the Old Testament. Samantha enthusiastically agreed and now these two have developed a regular discipling relationship. People don't always ask for help, but often they do have some frustration or aimlessness, and you can help them.

When you became a Christian, you received a heavenly citizenship. Imagine that your U.S. citizenship was suddenly and irrevocably changed. You are no longer an American. Now you are a citizen of Thailand and transported to that country instantly. Imagine how hard it would be if no one helped you learn the language or showed you around. You would feel intimidated and overwhelmed! You could easily become reclusive, and perhaps even give up, hopping on the first plane back to America.

These are the same emotions new believers feel if they are not guided towards spiritual nourishment. But instead of getting on a plane to go back to America, they have their old homeland—the world system—at their fingertips whenever they want to return to it.

Now imagine that you were in the same position and a Thai citizen befriended you, helped you to learn the language, showed you a place you could work, introduced you to friends, and helped you learn more about the culture. What a relief this would be! Of course, you could make your new life in Thailand work without help, but it would be nice to receive the help you need. Understanding disciple-making in this way will help you keep a deep burden for this type of work.

Deciding What to Study

This question is difficult because your approach to disciple-making may be different every time. Instead of prescribing a curriculum, we suggest some of the key areas where you may need to devote time:
- The reliability of the Bible
- Motivation to study
- The story of the Bible
- Main theological themes in the Bible
- Bible interpretation
- Helpful Bible study tools.
- How to teach others from the Bible

The Reliability of the Bible

First, you must explain what the Bible is: the inspired word of God. Your goal is that your disciples gain a basic confidence in the reliability and authority of scripture. They also need to be ready to defend biblical authority to others who may ask. Unless they view the Bible as inspired and authoritative, they will see little point in studying or following its teachings. We consistently find that disciples who lack a high view of scripture never go far in their faith. (Several good books are available for such a study,[5] and we have included a worksheet in Appendix 2.)

MOTIVATION TO STUDY

A key need for most disciples is motivation: getting to the point where they regularly feel the need to study the word for themselves.

What motivated you to begin studying scripture? Sharing your own experiences and convictions about scripture often helps to inspire your disciples. Offering direction or forming a plan also motivates people. They may feel overwhelmed by the size of the Bible. Sometimes a simple suggestion such as, "Maybe you could start by reading the book of John and writing down any insights or questions you have for each chapter" is good enough to get someone excited about reading. Any approach that allows them to check off goals as they are accomplished will be more motivating than simply looking at the Bible as a vast, unattainable goal.

Positive reinforcement is a powerful motivational tool. Show them how the Bible can be rewarding for them. Show them how scripture will strengthen spiritual gifts they possess. Be as specific as possible. Show them how knowing Bible verses could bring a lot of power to conversations they have with their friends. If they see the future incentive that comes with disciplined study, they will be more likely to persevere.

Finally, if your disciple seems too lazy to study, you can motivate through challenge. If someone has made a commitment to God, yet fails to progress in his devotional life, you can assume that he needs to be warned. For example, the author of Hebrews says, "by this time you ought to be teachers . . ." in 5:12a. Here he paints a negative vision. "You could be in one place, instead you are here." Warning can be motivating if it succeeds in causing your disciple to feel convicted and repent. However, such a style of motivation should be used sparingly. Excessive reproof can lead young disciples to withdraw from their mentors. You need to pick your battles, and pray that you are working with God and the plans he has for a given person's life. Reproof should be reserved for cases where other motivational tools have failed.

THE STORY OF THE BIBLE

Once people are motivated, they may still need help understanding the big picture in the Bible. You may find it helpful to do a short Bible overview. Numerous Bible overviews are available, including one found on our website.[6] Understanding the big picture helps give a context to each small section of scripture. How does the story of Joseph fit in with God's big plan? Why are the Israelites suffering so much in Lamentations? Why does Hebrews speak so much about priesthood? Your disciples can more easily discern the answers to these questions and many more like them when they know the basic story and themes of the Bible.

MAIN THEOLOGICAL THEMES IN THE BIBLE

You should teach your disciples a basic doctrinal framework that will help them understand the Bible. Recent scholarship has questioned the wisdom doing this because it could lead to a biased reading. We disagree.

Everyone has an interpretive grid when they read the Bible. This grid is an associational framework that ties the particulars in the narrative together in a comprehensible form. Such a grid could pose a threat to good Bible interpretation, because one's understanding of the big picture could lead him to squeeze passages into that grid in a way never intended by the author. For example, Jehovah's Witnesses have an elaborate theological framework that becomes a bias in one passage after another. So, when Jesus uses the expression that Lazarus is asleep, they think this proves that souls sleep from the time of death until the judgment day. Passages that don't fit the grid are actually re-translated to make them fit. So we see that unless we are careful, our framework could become the real authority, and the Bible becomes a collection of proof texts we plug in to the appropriate hole. This tendency is called *paradigmatic thinking*—once we see things one way, it becomes harder to see them any other way.

On the other hand, without categories, the immense number of details in the Bible become an incomprehensible jumble, especially to new readers. Newer readers tend to become discouraged unless they see the parts fitting into some whole while reading.

We don't advocate going into a detailed systematic theology with younger disciples. But we do think they benefit from a basic doctrinal framework. A simple book like Paul Little's book, *Know What You Believe,* or various outlines like those we use in our church should be adequate.[7] We think inductive Bible study should go forward along with some systematic, topical learning. It should be easy enough to teach your disciples to question any system you share as they do their own study of the text. You can also challenge them to compare different systems (such as covenantal and dispensational schools, or Calvinist and Arminian schools) as a way to avoid paradigmatic thinking.

INTERPRETATION

You also need to help your disciples with proper Bible interpretation. Even though disciples are reading the Bible regularly, some only look at it superficially. They may ignore difficult sections, they may only regurgitate things previously taught to them, or they may pick verses out that sound nice without understanding the context. You should teach them to look deeper, to find the buried treasure in scripture. While you will never be able to teach them every principle in scripture, you can give them a sort of treasure map by showing them how to interpret the Bible for themselves. Even young Christians need an overview of historical grammatical hermeneutics. One of the best ways to learn good interpretation is through inductive Bible study.[8] Basic rules of sound interpretation give a theoretical framework for reading.[9]

When teaching your disciples how to use commentaries, you should exercise caution. A commentary is one person's opinion. But unlearned disciples often seize on interpretations as soon as they read them, and their own critical faculties are not developed. Teach your disciples to use commentaries in tandem, comparing several credible commentaries to each other. This way, disciples have to use their own judgment to decide which argument is most persuasive. Disciples gain another value in comparing commentaries when they see for themselves that the commentators don't agree with each other. This helps guard them from naively accepting a commentators' explanation at first glance.

Today, Bible software is cheaper than paper books, and works faster. Lookups in several sources can be done in a flash. Drawbacks to Bible software include their tendency to include old commentaries like Matthew Henry or Darby that have no copyright protection. However, these older commentaries lack some of the scholarship available in newer commentaries.

Your church's library may be a good place to find multiple commentaries without having to spend hundreds of dollars.

SHARING KNOWLEDGE

Disciples also need to learn to teach others. Just because disciples are reading and interpreting the Bible doesn't mean they will be able to share what they know. If you are developing leaders in the church, they must be able to convey their knowledge to others, either publicly or at least one-on-one. Teaching others helps a disciple take ownership of a concept. Without the exercise of sharing insight with others, people tend to grow stale in their knowledge of the Bible. On the other hand, nothing is more potent for learning and retaining biblical insight than teaching it to others. You should urge disciples to look for situations where they can share what they learn. Whether in general conversations, discipling a younger believer, or teaching a group, once believers share Bible knowledge they seem to retain it forever. "Use it, or lose it" is the rule of biblical learning.

MOVING TO INDEPENDENT BIBLE STUDY

All Christians have the capacity to learn the word on their own. God says he has given us a new mind to understand spiritual things (1 Cor. 2:14-16). This means that any Christian should be able to develop the ability to be a self-feeder in the word.

Once people have the tools to do personal Bible study, they generally take more away from a personal study than from a cooperative study. When people take the initiative to study a topic or passage on their own they usually remember and apply results from the study long afterward. With prayer and patience, you may succeed in bringing disciples to a point where they develop a lifelong love for the word of God.

PRAYER, PART I:
GETTING STARTED

Dennis: As a young Christian, I was not strong when it came to prayer. My times of prayer usually alternated between whining sessions, where I bemoaned all my problems before God, and quick, almost despairing pleas for help. A quick "Thanks, God!" seemed adequate when things went well.

I was living on a college campus in a rooming house with some Christian friends at the time, and some older brothers asked if they could come down and cook us breakfast on Saturdays. It seemed a bit strange, but we agreed. These four men were middle-aged, mature Christians. I guess they felt burdened to help us grow.

I didn't get up at 10:00 a.m. on Saturday mornings, and they often had to drag me and others out of bed. They fed us eggs and bacon with lots of coffee. Then came the Bible reading and prayer. Listening to these men pray was life changing for me. Some of them had walked with God for more than thirty years. The zeal and heart they put into their extensive times of thanksgiving and praise of God were new to me. To an impatient young guy like me, it seemed like a waste of time at first. It took a while, but I let them lead my thought and spirit upward, away from myself and toward God. I sensed myself being filled with a vision of God in all his greatness and love. Later, when we moved to interceding for ministry and people, I noticed a different perspective—I could see who I was talking to. My usual cynicism and self-pity were banished. I felt the power of faith-based prayer.

I've read books on prayer since then, and even taken classes on it. I doubt I could have learned as much so quickly any other way than sitting with older believers who knew how to pray.

TEACH US TO PRAY

Jesus was really into prayer. According to Luke's account, "Jesus Himself would often slip away to the wilderness and pray" (5:16 see also 6:12; 9:28). Then on yet another occasion, "It happened that while Jesus was praying in a certain place, after he had finished, one of his disciples said to Him, "Lord, teach us to pray . . ." (11:1). After seeing Jesus pray so much, they apparently reached the point where they sensed their own need for instruction.

Paul's frequent references to his own prayer life show he was quite conscious of modeling prayer for his readers. He stresses that he was regularly interceding for the churches. (Phil. 1:4,9; Col. 1:3,9; 2 Thess. 1:11). He often stresses being devoted to prayer: "Devote yourselves to prayer, keeping alert in it with an attitude of thanksgiving" (Col. 4:2; also Rom. 12:12; Eph. 6:18 and 1 Thess. 5:17).

The constant emphasis that Paul and Jesus placed on prayer clearly suggests that you should make prayer a central emphasis in your discipleship ministry. Your disciples won't go far spiritually unless they become men and women of prayer. You have multiple areas to teach and model if you hope to foster a healthy prayer life in any disciple.

GETTING STARTED

Your first step is to get your disciples to pray with you. Most new Christians have never prayed with another person, and they may feel very uncomfortable doing so at first. You can always just ask, "Do you mind if I pray about this?" Then offer a short, simple prayer and go on. Remember not to make your prayers complicated, theological, or long. Any of these will intimidate new believers, who sense they wouldn't be able to do the same. They should hear you speaking simply, honestly, and personally, as though to a friend. Such prayer says to disciples, "You could do this." The more you pray in the presence of your disciple, the less strange it will seem. It soon becomes natural to ask, "Why don't we pray?" Once a disciple prays with you (no matter what was said) be sure to comment that you enjoyed being able to share coming before God together.

Any ongoing reluctance to pray will generally decline as you pray in your friends' presence. Teaching about prayer will help the process along. The more people learn about prayer, the more motivated and fearless they become.

Try introducing short prayers in the middle of conversations. For example, if your disciple is sharing about something that is really bothering her, why not say, "Why don't we pray about this right now?" If there's no objection, quickly speak to God: "Lord, I sense this really bothers her, and we'd just like to ask for your help . . . "

Frequent *shorter* prayers are better than infrequent, long prayers. Like any personal relationship, you don't save up everything you have to say and dump it in a long monologue once a day! It's more natural to speak to God as you go. Disciples should feel that entering into prayer doesn't always involve setting aside an hour.

TAKING INITIATIVE

You should watch for your disciples to cross a significant frontier: the time when they suggest prayer. Your longer-range goal must be to see your disciples become "prayer initiators" in their own right. This might happen with you or with others, but a key part of spiritual leadership is guiding others into prayer. If this doesn't happen spontaneously, you can simply ask, "Have you ever asked one of your roommates to pray with you?" Over a period of months, a new disciple should become comfortable initiating prayer with others.

At the same time, you should suggest a habit of a daily appointment with God. Most leaders agree: there is no substitute for this daily time reading God's word and praying. Morning is best because one's rapport with God tends to carry through the day. This is a time when young Christians build their personal relationship with God. You should teach them to approach this time with expectation that God may speak to them, either while they read the word, or during prayer.

A disciples' walk improves noticeably soon after they develop this habit. Once you've made the case for a personal time with God, merely asking a disciple from time to time how his personal time with God is going will usually suffice to motivate him to develop this habit.

Many Christians have never fully come to grips with the solemn verdict of James 4:2: "You do not have because you do not ask." Let us never drift into fatalistic theology, believing that "whatever will happen, will happen." James makes it clear that when we pray we have the potential to change the course of eternal history. But failure to pray can change the course of history also. Sadly, this verse could be engraved on the spiritual grave stones of many Christians: "He did not have because he did not ask." This verse teaches that, for our own good, God sometimes deliberately withholds blessings until we pray. Otherwise we may come to believe we are performing God's work through our own efforts.

Do you remember times in your own life when God answered prayer in a powerful or unexpected way? Tell these stories to your disciples. Your spiritual experience with God is one of the most powerful tools you have in impressing young believers with the truth. Such stories are far more powerful than you might expect!

GROUP PRAYER

Some people naturally pray in groups, but for others this is a major hurdle. If your disciples spontaneously pray in a Bible study or prayer group, don't miss the opportunity to share how edifying you thought their prayer was. Praying in public is a risky venture for anyone who hasn't grown up around church meetings where people pray. New Christians are afraid of sounding stupid. They need immediate affirmation that their efforts to pray are appreciated and welcome.

But what if your disciple doesn't choose to pray in public? Usually, the best place to start is with some teaching on why they should pray with fellow Christians. You may want to point out that Jesus taught us to pray, "Our father" not "*my* father" (Mat. 6:9). Jesus' ideal prayer is corporate, not individual. He even seemed to put special emphasis on corporate prayer in Matthew 18 when he says, "if two of you on earth agree about anything you ask for, it will be done for you by my Father in heaven" (vs. 19).

You should teach your disciples the difference between corporate and private prayer. Paul says when we assemble, "Let all things be done for edification" (1 Cor. 14:26). This means prayers for a sick aunt would usually be more appropriate in private, or with one or two friends. In a Bible study setting, most of the participants won't know who she is. In group prayer, we should be asking God to give us a prayer that would edify the group. A praying group of Spirit-led Christians corporately try to sense the mind of the Spirit. They try to offer praise and thanksgiving for things that would make the group feel grateful. Such corporate thanksgiving is a way to guide the group into insight and appreciation of the great things of God.

Good corporate prayers are those that come before God in a way that is sensitive to any non-Christians present. Inside jargon and "Christianese" terminology should be avoided in these situations. This is the thought behind Paul's reproof of the insensitive speaking of tongues in Corinth. He points out, "You may be giving thanks well enough, but the other man is not edified" (1 Cor. 14:17). Although their problem involved praying in tongues without interpretation, the same principle would apply to any form of prayer that is un-edifying, including prayers that alienate non-Christians (vs. 23).

We find that as young Christians understand the importance of corporate prayer, they usually feel inwardly motivated to join in—but not always. You may need to challenge a disciple directly by saying, "I enjoy praying with you so much, I just wish the rest of the group had access to what you bring." Or, a questioning posture could be taken by asking, "Have you ever thought about praying at the home group? What's holding you back?"

Young Christians who pray in public expose their spirit to the body of Christ and publicly declare their faith. In a healthy group, that's sure to be a nurturing experience that makes the young believer feel more a part of the group. God will directly bless any effort they make to pray with an inward sense that they have done the right thing, and have given out, instead of just taking in. As you encourage more of the same, you are laying the groundwork for a future ministry mind-set that will extend into many other areas.

THANKSGIVING

Teaching your disciples to be thankful is a long-term project. Most of us are working on this simultaneously, fighting our own innate ingratitude. But you have to make the case for thankfulness with disciples if you want them to develop a healthy spiritual walk.

In Jesus' life we find a striking story that puts a sharp point on the need for thanksgiving. He told ten lepers to go wash. On the way, they were miraculously healed. One of the ten returned and thanked Jesus. A real note of astonishment is heard in Jesus' reply: "Were there not ten cleansed? But the nine—where are they? Was no one found who returned to give glory to God, except this foreigner?" (Luke 17:17,18). Even the son of God seems to have been amazed (which didn't happen often) at the incredible omission of nine out of ten lepers to give thanks for such a remarkable healing! The more one thinks about it, the more strange it becomes. Can you imagine yourself walking along, and your dreadful, incurable disease suddenly is gone? You look down and say, "Hey, that worked out well!" and go on about your business.

What's wrong with this picture?
The story of the ten lepers illustrates why God makes a major point out of thanksgiving. You need to teach your disciples that God doesn't call on us to give thanks for his benefit. He needs nothing from us. The point is entirely for our own benefit. We reveal our inner sickness when we receive even the most remarkable blessings from God and think so little of it that we "forget" to give thanks. These nine ungrateful lepers are a picture of us! God knows that humans have

many problems, but few are as serious as our lack of gratitude. We are so self-centered that we can receive almost any amount of blessing and take it for granted. We tend to think far more about possible blessings we have not received than the multitude we already have received.

God's concern here is not because his feelings are hurt. Rather, he is concerned that such lack of gratitude signals a dark and deadly core of moral filth in the center of our beings. When we aren't thankful, we imply that all we have received is only fitting, and really deserved.

Discontent signals that we are angry we haven't received even more. Anxiety signals our suspicion that God can't be trusted—we must meet our own needs. Selfishness of this kind will overthrow every aspect of spiritual growth unless we confront it powerfully. God wants to transform us from self-centered people who think everything should revolve around us to other-centered people who live in self-giving love. That will never happen if we accept the legitimacy of our inner selfishness. And ingratitude is a clear signal that selfishness is ruling in our lives.

Rebellion against God is bad, too. And lack of gratitude is a major indicator of inner rebellion. Ungrateful people have never accepted the life and situation God has allotted to them. We are so resentful about our makeup and situation that it blots out everything good God has done for us. At times we see this clearly: how could anyone who has been rescued from hell at the incredible cost Jesus paid at the cross feel ungrateful? But how fleeting these moments are! All too quickly our eyes are glued again on our frustrations and the things we lack.

Quite often, we've met with a disciple and find him morose and struggling. When this happens to you, you must be willing to enter into the pain he is feeling, and explore the reasons. Shallow and simple answers serve only to alienate people. Counseling will be discussed in a later chapter. If your disciples are discouraged and in defeat, you owe it to them to address ingratitude.

We have wonderful news in the midst of this dark picture of human falleness. When God calls us to give thanks and praise, he does so not just because that's what we *should* be doing. Thanksgiving is also the medicine that has the power to heal that dark inner core of selfishness.

Yes, that's right: Thanksgiving is not just the *result* of a change of heart; it can actually be a key *cause* of heart change. Young disciples tend to think the opposite. They feel that when they finally have inner peace and happiness, they will be thankful. But the linkage between these two is spelled out very clearly in Philippians 4:6,7. After saying, "Be anxious for nothing, but in everything by prayer and supplication with thanksgiving let your requests be made known to God," Paul continues the thought: "And the peace of God, which surpasses all comprehension, shall guard your hearts and your minds in Christ Jesus." When you analyze the linkage between verse six and seven, you will see the peace and happiness promised in verse seven are the direct result (and are conditional upon) the activities in verse six. Prayer is one of those activities. You should teach your disciples that it's not enough to pray. The verse is clear that both prayer and thanksgiving are needed. Praying without thanksgiving may leave them just as carnally minded, anxious, unbelieving, and discontent as ever.

Facing God and thanking him from the heart for who he is and what he has done has a profound effect on our spirits. Thanking God is an act of faith. To thank God, you have to acknowledge how good he is, and all that he has done for you. When you do this, you will actually feel a change come over you as you move deeply into thanksgiving. The problems that seemed so hopeless just minutes ago will seem to shrink before your eyes. As the lens of your mind pulls back from the rough and tumble of daily living to embrace the whole picture of an awesome God and his personal love and care, an inner relaxation will spread over your soul.[1]

Guiding your disciple into a time of thanksgiving won't solve all his problems. But it will put those problems in perspective. Again and again, we have experienced disciples wallowing in defeat, only to leave feeling full of the Holy Spirit because we helped them move into a good session of thanksgiving to God. You may have to explain God's promises related to the current situation and suggest you give thanks for those. Or, you could just begin thanking God while praying together, and hope your disciple will pick up on your example.

After thanking God, suggest that your disciple move on to plead for answers to his requests. Then, his requests of God will probably be different. Because his perspective was aligned with the Truth first, he'll approach his requests from a perspective of faith.

8

PRAYER, PART TWO: MINISTRY AND PRAYER

OTHER-CENTERED PRAYER

Jesus included another part in his ideal prayer *before* praying for daily bread: "Your kingdom come, your will be done on earth as it is in heaven." The believer's prayer to see God's kingdom built and expanded on earth is a prayer for victory in Christian ministry. This pattern of praying for others' spiritual needs before asking for ones' own needs matches the rest of the New Testament. Paul's prayers are usually for others. Even when he asks for prayer for himself, it's usually that he will be empowered to minister to others effectively (Eph. 6:19; Col. 4:3,4; 1 Thess. 5:25; 2 Thess. 3:1).

You should teach your disciple to match their priorities in prayer with his priorities in life. First is God. Focusing on him through thanksgiving and praise is the best way to begin a time of prayer. Next, offer prayer for others. After reflecting on the faithfulness, power, and goodness of God, your disciple will know his problems are going to work out eventually. When viewing himself in Christ, his concerns for self should diminish and his concern for others will take center stage.

Over time, you must convince your disciples that praying to God for people is even more important than talking to people about God. A growing disciple hopes to see many things accomplished in ministry: people's hearts coming under conviction, their eyes being opened, lives being changed, the lost people being rescued, invisible evil spirits being dispossessed. None of these things can be accomplished through human ingenuity or will power! Nothing less than the supernatural power of the Holy Spirit will really change people's lives or build the church.

When you pray for others with your disciples, you teach them through modeling that God's power is the only hope in witnessing, preaching, counseling, and motivating others. You should make this point explicitly when you pray together: "Lord, we know nothing we can do or say has any hope of success unless you empower it." Every time you teach the word, you should pray (with your disciples if possible), "God, we ask that you take this utterance and turn it into more than words. We are relying on your Spirit to fill these words with Your supernatural power to pierce people's hearts."

Special prayer groups for the purpose of intercession are a great way to expose your disciples in this area. If your church or home group has one, try to attend it regularly along with whomever you are discipling. You may well notice your disciple feeling pleasure in joining together with fellow-servants of God for an extended time of intercession. Prayer groups are unexcelled for staying in touch with the needs and struggles in a fellow-Christians' ministry. Beyond prayer group participation, you and your disciple should commit to continue praying during the week for key needs in the group.

Don't forget to pray for each other! James calls us to "confess your sins to one another, and pray for one another so that you may be healed" (James 5:16). By praying for your disciple while with her, you effectively model other-centered prayer. She will soon pick up on the example and pray for you, especially if you are being transparent about your needs and struggles.

If you are successful in teaching your disciples other-centered prayer, it can impact many other areas of their lives. The other-centered perspective is one of the central themes of real spiritual growth, and much of this kind of thinking begins with prayer.

EXPLORATORY PRAYER

Prayers are not always declarations of thanks or declarations of need. Prayers can often be questions.

Jessica: When I first became a Christian leader, an older leader advised me: "Make sure you reserve a time each week to ask God questions about the people you will be leading." It was such a simple yet powerful piece of advice. God reveals his wisdom about people so that we can serve them in a way that cooperates with what God is doing.

We can apply this same technique to ourselves, asking God to reveal which things about ourselves he is hoping to challenge. Ask along with David, "Search me, O God, and know my heart; test me and know my anxious thoughts. See if there is any offensive way in me, and lead me in the way everlasting" (Ps. 139:23-24).

We should come to God hoping to receive wisdom about our plans or direction. We hope each day to see where God is moving and work with him. When we approach God with an attitude of submission and discovery, he will give us a more spiritual perspective. Instead of coming to God saying, "here are my plans, please bless them", we should be asking, "what are your plans and how can I be involved?" This is also the time when God will reveal how we can bless, motivate, or encourage other believers. As we pray through a list of people in our group, God will often cause thoughts to enter our minds about what we could say the next time we see a friend.

Exploratory prayer is very subjective. As we are quiet before the Lord, we may receive answers to our questions. These answers are subtle leadings in our thought patterns that gradually lead to a new conviction on a certain topic. However, we may not always receive an answer to a question during the prayer time itself. We should view any revelation we receive, both during prayer time and later, as answered prayer.

PRAYING IN THE NAME OF JESUS

Your disciples won't be equipped to pray as they should unless you teach them the difference between general requests in prayer and those prayers that qualify as "asking in my name." In John 14:13,14 Jesus made a remarkable promise: "I will do whatever you ask in my name, so that the Son may bring glory to the Father. You may ask me for anything in my name, and I will do it." This apparent blank check from Christ is often misunderstood by young Christians. Why not just pray that everyone on earth receives Christ this year? Believers often fail to notice the two qualifications on the promise.

First, the prayer must be "in my name." This expression means the one praying should ask as Jesus' agent, or as one *authorized* by Jesus. Like an employee going to the paint store to order products for his boss on the company account, he is not supposed to order products for his own use at home. He is only to order what his boss wants. To pray in the name of Jesus doesn't mean simply saying the words, "in

Jesus name" at the end of a prayer. It means asking as Jesus would ask. This qualification is another way of saying the same thing as 1 John 5:14: "This is the confidence we have in approaching God: that if we ask anything according to his will, he hears us."

Jesus also mentions another condition for this blanket promise to answer any prayer. The prayer must be such "that the Son may bring glory to the Father." The implication is that prayers that wouldn't glorify the Father won't be answered.[1]

These qualifications are important because misinterpreting this verse as a promise to answer all prayers without qualification can lead to serious trouble. The infinite, personal God of the Bible can never be controlled by anyone. Any effort to do so is supremely irreverent and misguided. You need to warn your disciples against this dangerous misinterpretation.

In other cases, young believers are unable to reconcile Jesus' promise (that God will grant all prayers) with their observations that God clearly does not grant all prayers. The resulting confusion can undermine their confidence in scripture, or in prayer itself. A wise discipler will anticipate such problems and move to give answers.

Understanding the conditions on Jesus' sweeping promise to answer prayer in no way nullifies his promise. No, God won't grant requests that are against his will. But we have extensive knowledge of the will of God. For instance, Paul says, "For this is the will of God, your sanctification ..." (1 Thess. 4:3). Talk about a sweeping statement! This passage teaches that whenever we pray for help with an area of sin, we know God's will. Likewise, we know God's will when we pray that a friend gain victory over sin. That means Jesus' promise applies. We don't need to ask in uncertainty, *hoping* God will answer. We should pray for deliverance from sin in the name of Jesus, knowing in faith that he *will* answer. These are the cases where James' teaching applies: "But he must ask in faith without any doubting, for the one who doubts is like the surf of the sea, driven and tossed by the wind. For that man ought not to expect that he will receive anything from the Lord, being a double-minded man, unstable in all his ways" (James 1:6-8).

You should teach your disciples what they can pray for in the name of Jesus, and what they can pray for anyway, but without the same certainty that God will answer. By teaching your disciples what God promises, you can also teach them to pray based on biblical authority, and claim the promises of God in faith. The result will be a more confident and powerful prayer life. For example, a believer preparing to teach a Bible study may pray that God will empower his speech for the good of the group, but may doubt whether God will answer the prayer. But based on the command that we should "Preach the Word" (2 Tim. 4:2) and that his word is effective for changing lives (2 Tim. 3:15-17; Is. 55:11), this believer should be praying in Jesus' name and in full assurance of faith.

Disciples who learn to wield the power of prayer in ministry are well on their way to a lifetime of fruitful spiritual service.

SPIRITUAL WARFARE

Paul warns that "Our struggle is not against flesh and blood, but against . . . the spiritual forces of evil in the heavenly realms" (Eph 6:12). Learning to confront and overcome Satan and evil spiritual powers is essential to the growth of any disciple. Prayer is only one of the weapons prescribed for this conflict, but it plays a central role.

Satan has important advantages over Christians. He is more intelligent and experienced than any of us. His forces are numerous and generally more disciplined than Christians. Unlike humans, they don't get tired or distracted. They are relentless, whereas we tend to give up or slack off.

We do have advantages. First and foremost, God is on our side—an advantage that should be decisive. "Greater is he who is in you than he who is in the world," declares John (1 John 4:4). And Paul adds the thought that "the weapons of our warfare are not of the flesh, but divinely powerful for the destruction of fortresses" (2 Cor. 10:4). We also hold an advantage because Satan tends to work in *relatively predictable* ways. Paul says Satan won't take advantage of us because, "we are not ignorant of his schemes" (2 Cor. 2:11). By knowing how Satan works, we are in a position to anticipate his moves and meet them with the power of God through prayer based in truth.

These "schemes" of Satan; what are they? From ancient times Satan has used deception, temptation, and accusation as his main avenues for attacking Christians and non-Christians alike. If your disciples know how these tactics work, they will learn to recognize the voice of Satan in their own lives and in the lives of those they hope to serve.

As you teach your disciples how Satan works, you will also need to undo some of their thinking about Satan. God's true enemy is not the one portrayed in popular movies and books. Are we likely to see Satan appear as a flaming monster's head? Are we likely to see people flung across the room or through a window by a demon? These are the secular visions of Satan grounded in Hollywood. You have to persuade your disciples that the power and weakness of Satan have more to do with truth. In the spiritual world, truth and lies carry far more weight than anything else.

When Paul describes our "divinely powerful weapons" that can demolish fortresses in 2 Cor. 10, he goes on to explain that "We are destroying speculations and every lofty thing raised up against the knowledge of God, and we are taking every thought captive to the obedience of Christ" (2 Cor. 10:5). Speculations, knowledge, and thoughts: these are the language of thought and belief. He seems to be saying that this battle is an ideological struggle and that our minds are the battleground. When Jesus confronted Satan in the wilderness his consistent reply to each temptation was, "It is written . . ." (Luke 4:1-13). The power of truth withstands and overthrows all Satan's lies. This indicates how you should teach your disciples to withstand Satan in prayer.

Young Christians often believe what Satan tells them. His suggestions come as inner thoughts. They have incredible plausibility because he knows how to develop maximum persuasion based on his observations of individual tendencies and life circumstances. Satan continually tries to guide believers into interpreting their world in a way that undermines faith and puts self at the center. Just as God wants to foster thanksgiving, Satan tries to foster discontent with what God provides and anxiety about whether he will provide in the future. He tries to convince believers that their ministry plans or intentions to witness will never work. He wants them to believe that God would never honor the efforts of such unworthy and unfaithful people anyway. According to Satan, God looks down in continual disappointment and disapproval. If your disciples believe any part of these lies they could be headed for outright defeat in spiritual warfare.

When Satan lies to Christians the stakes are very high. These lies are intended to manipulate believers' minds. Once we believe one lie it becomes much easier to believe the next lie. And the lies come in bunches. Satan actually weaves a web of lies as the implications of one lead to another. Temptations, accusations, and deceptions pile on top of one another; creating so much confusion and doubt that Satan may be able to virtually take over a believer's mind. The unsuspecting believer is totally unaware that he is thinking thoughts from Satan. It all just seems so obvious and undeniable!

This kind of takeover of the believer's thought life by Satan is not demon possession. He is not being *over-powered* by Satan (which could never happen to a Christian according to 1 John 4:4). Instead, he is being *persuaded*. He simply chooses to believe the super-plausible ideas presented by a being far more brilliant than himself. Unless the downward spiral is interrupted, believers could end up in "the trap of the devil, who has taken them captive to do his will" (2 Tim.2:26). Peter asked Ananias in amazement, "How is it that Satan has so filled your heart that you have lied to the Holy Spirit . . . ?" (Acts 5:3). When a believer's heart is 'filled with Satan' he isn't possessed. He simply has believed so many lies that he completely loses his way spiritually. Yet at any time, he can return to believing what God says and overthrow the whole house of cards.

Here we see the importance of praying the truth. As your disciples learn to pray using the words of faith based on God's truth, Satan's lies lose their effectiveness. A shame-filled young Christian coming before the Lord could point out, "I feel so unworthy and distant from you God, but your word declares that you see me as 'the righteousness of Christ'" (2 Cor. 5:21). A young Christian worker who has lost all confidence to witness because of an overwhelming sense of unworthiness could pray using Paul's words, "Not that we are adequate in ourselves to consider anything as coming from ourselves, but our adequacy is from God, who also made us adequate as servants of a new covenant . . ." (2 Cor. 3:5,6). Likewise, a young believer might be under temptation. A single woman could pray, "God, I know Satan wants me to believe that your provision for love in my life is inadequate. He wants me to surrender to sexual temptation so I won't be rejected. But I believe you when you say in your word, "And my God will supply all your needs according to His riches in glory in Christ Jesus" (Phil. 4:19). Here is the perfect retort to Satan's accusations. Just as Jesus uttered the words, "It is written" to refute

Satan's suggestions, you can teach your disciples how to match up God's promises against Satan's lying suggestions when they pray. With persistence, his lies lose their power.

And herein lies the challenge. You need to teach your disciples that they will experience seasons of struggle to fully believe God's promises. This explains references in the New Testament like Romans 15:30, "Now I urge you, brethren, by our Lord Jesus Christ and by the love of the Spirit, to strive together with me in your prayers to God for me" (Also Col. 4:12). If your disciples understand prayer, they should know that they have no need to strive with God—he's on their side. No amount of pressure will change his will. To the contrary, they may struggle in prayer with Satan and their own fleshly nature. When using their choice to believe God rather than Satan, your disciples will struggle with ongoing inner skepticism about what God says. If they win through, this is the shield of faith that will extinguish the fiery darts Satan is firing at them.[2]

Most young Christians don't pray this way. Normal "instinctive" prayer is based on one's feelings. They reflect their feelings to God, and plead for change. But they are often missing the key to victorious prayer—the truth. Praying the truth, backed by biblical authority, and battling to believe that truth, is a new skill for most disciples.

Ephesians 6:18 shows not only a practice that you need to teach your disciples (intercession), but an attitude. The notions of alertness and perseverance are both important when it comes to spiritual warfare. Alertness is important because of the stealthy nature of Satan. He often does his work without anyone realizing what he is doing. A Christian's superior power often never comes into play because the Christian is too dopey and muddled to realize Satan was quietly at work.

Perseverance is important because Satan is relentless. He follows one attack with another, constantly probing for weakness. If we could offer a prayer that would end spiritual warfare, we all would have prayed it long ago. In a game of basketball, you can call time-out when you get tired or hurt. But in a war, there's no time-out. Imagine yourself on the field in the movie, *Braveheart*. The screaming masses attack and you stand out from your army and hold your hands out, crying, "Time-out!"

You can take a time-out if you like, but your enemy isn't going to stop. The fact that you're tired or injured is probably a good reason for the enemy to press the attack harder than ever.

Persistence, alertness, intercession, praying the truth, and battling to believe the truth—these are the weapons of our warfare. If you teach and model their use with your disciples, you will help them avoid heartbreaking defeat in their own lives and in any groups they may later lead.

When you successfully disciple your friends in the area of prayer, they will come to love praying with thanksgiving, praying in Jesus' name, praying for others, and praying in a personal way.

9

COUNSELING

Those with experience in disciple-making know that character and personal problems block disciples' progress more than anything else. Teaching people about the Bible, how to pray, and why the things of God matter are all important. But without real character transformation, they are all for naught. You never reach your central goal: providing the Body of Christ with leaders and role models who can facilitate multiplication. That's why, as a disciple-maker, you must be ready to move into any and every area of a disciple's life with godly help. Your disciples will need advice and help in a thousand areas: relational, functional, emotional, and even physical.

To help in these areas, the discipler acts in the role of counselor. Paul says, "And concerning you, my brethren, I myself also am convinced that you yourselves are full of goodness, filled with all knowledge and able also to admonish [counsel] one another" (Rom. 15:14). In the early church, there were no professional counselors. People in the body of Christ helped each other as they were able. We believe this should still happen, especially with the ninety-plus percent of people's problems that are not clinical.

WHAT ABOUT PROFESSIONAL COUNSELING?

In the modern world, people who need counseling go to a professional and pay an hourly fee for help. We believe this is often a good idea. As a Christian lay counselor, you should work along with professional Christian counselors, not against them. Good disciple-makers have learned how to recognize when they are in over their heads with clinical cases. If your disciple needs professional care, and you try to handle it instead of referring them to a professional, you may do serious damage.

So when should you refer a friend to professional counseling? If you find yourself dealing with any of the following, you may need to seek immediate help:
- Suicidal thoughts
- Schizophrenia or other psychoses
- Clinical depression
- Extreme and unexplained mood swings
- Situations involving violence, including child abuse
- Some anxiety disorders
- Personality disorders

In Appendix 8, we've include an article from a psychiatrist on some of the things to look for when trying to determine whether to refer your friend to professional counseling. If you are in doubt, you may want to play it safe by referring your disciple to a trusted Christian professional for assessment. Many churches have professional counselors either on staff, or with whom they have developed a good relationship.

But even if your disciple goes into counseling, you should remain engaged with the situation. As someone who is actually in regular daily contact and who lives in community with this person, you are in a position to significantly add to what the counselor brings. People who work with both clinical counselors and competent disciple-makers consistently do better than those with clinical counseling alone. Professional counselor, Larry Crabb complains,

We have produced a generation of therapists, an army of counselors trained to do battle with problems they poorly understand because they have spent more time in classrooms becoming experts than in God's presence becoming elders. We have lost interest in developing mentors, wise men and women who know how to get to the real core of things and who have the power to bring supernatural resources to bear on what's wrong.[1]

Good disciple-makers should be able to counsel their people in many situations often gaining results that go well beyond expectations.

Dennis: A young man came to me with serious mental problems. He had made a serious attempt at suicide a month earlier, and almost succeeded. He was even diagnosed as schizophrenic, but later the diagnosis was modified to "clinically depressed with psychotic features." He was sullen, withdrawn, self-absorbed, and anti-social. His doctors prescribed a range of drugs which seemed to help. Because of his hungry heart and his urgent pleas, he and I began meeting weekly for disciple-ship. He also became a part of my home church and men's cell group. Later still, he moved into a ministry house related to our home church. My assessment was that his problems were multi-factorial: not all physical or chemical. Many of his emotional problems were really theo-logical and identity related. His drug use, philandering with women, and inability to develop healthy relationships seriously aggravated his other problems. His doctors agreed with this assessment.

Today, he has gradually been taken off nearly all his medicine, and seems like a friendly, relatively well-adjusted young man. He still struggles with depression and destructive habits, but he is engaged with the other men in our community, and is developing a ministry, including discipling a younger guy. Nobody would ever guess today that this guy was near death and institutionalization just over a year ago!

I'm not suggesting my work has caused this striking recovery. I'm sure I made a certain contribution. So did his doctor. Also, the young man himself is highly motivated and willing to take strong measures in his life. Finally, the body of Christ in a healthy home church has made important contributions. This is the way it should be. No discipler should see himself as the only source of help for a disciple, but should draw on any and all avenues through which God may work.

Wise Christian counselors welcome the help of lay people who will follow up with their clients. Most people need regular help, not just an hour-long session once a week and pills.

Lay Counseling

Most people's problems are not clinical, but may still be serious enough to block their growth and development as healthy people. In these areas, you, as a competent disciple-maker, need to be ready to deliver wise counsel.

In the Bible, a number of different words are related to counseling. All of them are applied to regular Christians, and anticipate that Christians will be able to counsel each other.[2] Most people counsel friends without thinking about it. It seems natural to suggest solutions when friends bring up problems. When the advice is informed by biblical principles and spiritual maturity, that advice may be very helpful.

This is not a book on counseling. But we will suggest several typical areas that may need attention, and some general directions to move in counseling a disciple. We hope these thoughts will spark some ideas, and your own creativity and life-experience can build from there. For more detailed coverage visit the organic disciple-making web site at: http://www.xenos.org/disciple.

Typical Areas to Counsel

Interpersonal Conflict

People are continually fighting with each other, and your disciples will certainly have this problem as well. In fact, studies show that the closer a group of people are, and the more urgently they feel about their shared goals, the more likely conflict becomes—and the more violent it becomes. This means that a close, well-motivated local church could become a hotbed of conflict.

Conflict provides one of the best areas to learn and display the character of Christ. But too often, conflict derails a Christian's spiritual growth and even results in permanent alienation and defection from the body of Christ. Every pastor and Christian leader knows that they lose more people to conflict than almost any other cause. Marriages and families are also often damaged by immature approaches to conflict.

Conflict is not necessarily bad. Groups devoid of conflict are most likely dysfunctional. Groups can only avoid conflict in one of two ways: they either avoid talking about controversial issues in a form of groupthink, or they stay so disengaged that no one cares enough about what happens in the group to argue.

Conflict is often the occasion for creative thought. Opposition from others might make a person re-think his position and come up with new solutions that are often better than what he had in mind in the first place.[3] Mature Christians develop a marvelous ability to engage in conflict with edifying and peaceful results. They know how to argue their case without alienating others. When alienation does occur, whether between themselves and others, or between third parties, they know how to reconcile.

As a disciple-maker, you must counsel and train your disciples in mature conflict management early and often. We routinely study Ken Sande's excellent book, *The Peacemaker* with our disciples.[4] This book is loaded with biblical principles, and has a great history of helping believers avoid the pitfalls of unrighteous conflict. Consider the following points (most of which are expanded in Sande's book) when counseling conflict problems:

- The first step in any conflict is for your disciple to adopt the right perspective on the conflict. Instead of seeing the conflict as an occasion to get their own way, or as a nuisance to be avoided, mature believers see each conflict as a stewardship from God. In a conflict, Christians have the opportunity to display the power, love, and wisdom of God. When your disciple stops seeing the conflict as mainly a horizontal engagement with his opponent, seeing it as something God has allowed in his life, his eyes move to Him. He will begin to show your disciple the things he needs to see in order to resolve the conflict God's way. Paul teaches, "So whether you eat or drink or whatever you do, do it all for the glory of God" (1 Cor. 10:31) and this includes conflict. Sande says, "In conflict, we show that we either have a big God, or we have a big ego and big problems."[5]

- After taking conflict to God, and offering himself as God's servant, ready to do as he directs, the next step is to "take the plank out of our own eye." Jesus said, "You hypocrite, first take the plank out of your own eye, and then you will see clearly to remove the speck from your brother's eye" (Mat 7:5). Human nature dictates that our opponent needs to see what is wrong with his position. But if we aren't willing to see where we are in the wrong, we are hypocrites, as Jesus suggests. Before God, you must help your disciple think through where he may be in the wrong in terms of projecting hostility, showing insensitivity, failure to listen patiently, using punishing behavior, impatience, or a host of other possible sins. As a disciple-maker, you must patiently guide your disciples into facing their own fault *before* moving on to deal with the fault of an adversary.

- Next you should counsel your disciples to purpose in their hearts to go and repent to their opponents, asking forgiveness for their own moral failures in the conflict. In most conflicts, a negative rhythm is in place: "I'm in the right!" "No, you're in the wrong!" "No, *you're* in the wrong!" and so forth. When a mature believer comes back to an opponent and says, "Guess what. *I'm* in the wrong," he disrupts this negative rhythm and replaces it with something new: humility. Now the door usually opens to progress and godly resolution. Remind your disciples that their repentance should be honest (not apologizing for things they never did or portraying the sin as a "mistake," denying intent or responsibility). Their repentance should also be unqualified (not saying "I'm sorry if you were offended by what I said" or "I shouldn't have shouted, but I was really tired" or "I was wrong, but so were you."). These qualifications or "if" statements spoil the good effects of the repentance, and are really a manifestation of pride and self-protectiveness. Finally, any repentance should be unconditional (not confessing wrongdoing in the hope of pressuring his opponent to do likewise).

- Once your disciple injects humility and repentance into the conflict he is in a position to deal, if necessary, with removing the speck in their opponents' eyes. Conflict and bitterness are often fueled by self-righteousness indignation. After coming to grips with his own fault, it will be far easier to forgive from the heart. You should cover biblical principles of forgiveness like Ephesians 4:32: "And be kind to one another, tender-hearted, forgiving each other, just as God in Christ also has forgiven you." Unless your disciples are prepared to forgive from the heart, they have little chance of resolving serious conflicts.

- Next comes the decision about how to handle the substance of opponents' wrong positions, or sinful actions. First, help your disciple consider the option mentioned in Proverbs19:11: "A man's wisdom gives him patience; it is to his glory to overlook an offense." Particularly when an offense isn't serious, the best response is often to unilaterally drop it. Then he can go on to deal with other issues. Such a response is not phony or cowardly, but gracious. Unless your disciple is able to overlook minor offenses, he will contribute to a critical, hard-line atmosphere that poisons close fellowship and cooperation. You must teach your disciples to avoid becoming hard-liners who terrorize those around them, or they will never become effective servants of God. Study Proverbs like this with your disciples: "A fool shows his annoyance at once, but a prudent man overlooks an insult" (Prov. 12:16 NASB. Also see Prov. 15:18; Prov. 20:3; Prov. 17:14).

- Alternatively, you may conclude with your disciple that some issues are so important they need to be addressed by reproof, admonition, or negotiation. (We have a chapter on reproof and admonition Chapter 10, Encountering A Lack of Progress, so we will not deal with those here.) Reproof and admonition are for moral problems and require repentance for the sake of our opponents' well-being. And here we see the importance of dealing with our own wrongdoing first. If we find it necessary to confront wrongdoing by our opponents, our humility and empathy make it far more likely that we will be heard.

• Negotiation is for issues where two may disagree, but which do not involve moral sin.[6]

A disciple who is equipped and trained in godly conflict management stands heads and shoulders above most Christians in ability to work effectively with people. You will never regret the hours you spend teaching and persuading your disciples to follow God's pattern for conflict resolution.

You can see from this section that, as a disciple-maker, you are in a position to offer terrific help when counseling common areas of need in your disciple's life. In the following areas, we will avoid going into the same level of detail, but more is available at our website for those interested in further reading.

Self-absorption

You may find that you have a disciple who virtually never stops thinking about himself. Depression and defeat usually result. Even when with other people, a self-absorbed person either cannot stop talking about himself, or sits withdrawn, wondering what others think of him.

How can you help such a person? Typical steps include:

1. *Awareness and understanding* — Self-centeredness is wrong. Challenge your disciple to set a goal to overcome self-absorption based on biblical teaching and God's power. He must learn what others-centeredness means and why a life of loving servanthood leads to fulfillment (Luke 9:23,24).

2. *Practical ideas* — Suggest specific actions, or field assignments that might help your disciple make progress in learning how to center his attention on others. These could be actions taken in conversa-

tion with others along the lines suggested in the chapter on friendship building. You could also suggest guided reflection on others while alone.

3. *Support and encouragement* — Check back to see how the field experience went, discussing problems or successes. If your disciple is confused or unable to perform, you may have to go along and model the behavior yourself. Then suggest a next step for further progress.

Working with self-absorbed people is slow, patient work. Only regular checkups on how the issue is progressing, along with a stream of suggested counter-measures will likely result in lasting change.

Eventually, you should notice the person "taking off" in the sense that he realizes how to continue developing others-centeredness on his own, without detailed coaching. You are left in a position where we can use generous amounts of encouragement to press on.

Anyone who is extremely self-absorbed will likely struggle with that tendency the rest of his life. But we have seen some remarkable and permanent turn-arounds. What a fantastic victory it is to see someone tied up within himself become one who can creatively move into other people's lives in a loving way! This is such a powerful gift to bestow that you will feel gratified years afterward knowing you had a part in it.

High expectation-relating

Personal relationships are at the heart of Christian living and ministry. When you are discipling in community, you should be in a position to watch your disciples relating to their friends. (You will also gain insight into their relational tendencies from your own relationship with them.) As you gain information over a period of months, you may notice patterns of strength or deficiency that point to opportunities for encouragement or for needed change.

For instance, you may find that your disciple exhibits a pattern of high expectations on others. These become apparent when your disciple is continually offended or disappointed by others' actions or omissions. Such people are "hard to please" or "high maintenance" in their relationships. They seem to feel like they deserve a certain standard of treatment from others. Properly understood, these expectations are really love demands that make a person a love-taker rather than a love-giver.

High expectations are signaled by regular complaining about friends. Or, you may hear your disciple describing how her feelings were hurt in situations that sound suspicious—the incident doesn't seem like it would have been that hurtful. Of course, you may not be able to judge whether the complaints are legitimate just by listening to your disciple . . . high-expectation people are skilled at "demonizing" those they complain against in a way that sounds awful.

Here is where living in biblical community together makes all the difference. Your knowledge of the other people involved may contradict what you hear in the complaints. Or, you might even have been present during an interaction that is later characterized in a way you know is exaggerated or wrong.

Even when she has been wronged, you may sense a larger problem with her inability to forgive. High-expectations seem to go along with an exacting perspective that can't overlook offenses, even when they are minor. This perspective tends to be judgmental—even reading into people's motives in a negative way.

When people like this believe their relational expectations are legitimate, those expectations ruin one relationship after another. These expectations are a system of rules that no one but the love-demander knows or accepts. Consequently, love-demanders are never satisfied for long with their relationships. They punish others for breaking their list of rules, creating more hard feelings. Their refusal to forgive leads them to build ongoing cases against people. They manifest bitterness and suspicion. How can you help such people?

1. *Awareness and understanding* — Helping high-expectation people overcome their weakness can be a real wrestling match. They are convinced their expectations are only reasonable. They can't understand why anyone would question their right to feel offended or hurt. It all just seems so unavoidable! But we know this approach to relationships is morally wrong (Eph. 4:32). As difficult as it is for such a person to accept, their way of life falls far short of God's call to Christian love. Through a process of teaching and admonition you must gradually convince this disciple that God calls us to a better way, such as that described in 1 Cor. 13.

2. *Practical ideas* — When working with a problem this serious and pervasive, remember that you probably can't completely fix the problem. You are just looking for progress. Once a disciple gains insight, the next step is trying to live out the biblical perspective. Working with personal forgiveness and projecting the grace of God in relationships takes creativity from your disciple and from you. We usually find that once high-expectation people accept God's view of their love demands, progress is noticeable from that point on, especially if we've suggested ways to respond to hard feelings and situations. Struggling in prayer to adopt a gracious, Christ-like perspective on personal hurts is central.

3. *Support and encouragement* — Maturing Christians develop a growing appreciation for forgiving and accepting others because the Holy Spirit guides them in this direction. But as a disciple-maker, you can move this process forward by helping your disciple see God's viewpoint in relational situations and by encouraging her when she responds in a more godly way. This includes calling her attention to how much better things are going when she drops her expectations for others.

Although relational habits like having high expectations, judging others, and inability to forgive are hardly unusual, they are potentially devastating, and change is very slow indeed. In the most striking cases, we have seen significant change in as little as a year. But in most cases, helping someone with this kind of problem is a multi-year project, and even then, change will be only partial. Your goal is clear: help the disciple reach a point where he or she can build and maintain deep relationships. Unless a disciple reaches this point, he or she is too immature to lead in the church.

When it comes to the field of pastoral counseling it's easy to see why so many Christian workers choose to focus on outward actions and sins of the flesh while ignoring inward problems like this. Tangling with an entrenched relational pattern like high-expectation relating is just too difficult and messy for anyone who demands quick results. Therefore, you should continually seek out God for a positive vision for the disciple who struggles in these areas. God has a vision for him or her, and you must adopt his vision as your own.

Sexuality

In a fallen world, people's sexuality is usually damaged to one extent or another. Western culture with its loose sexual practices makes it more likely that the damage will be severe. Those discipling singles today are constantly challenged by profound sexual problems in their disciples.

Compounding the difficulty is the fact that people's sexuality is one of the most shame-producing areas of life. People bearing a burden of shame become less willing to admit their problems, even to a close friend. You may find yourself relating to someone for a long period of time with no idea that a serious sexual issue and heart-wrenching shame lie under the surface.

The scope of possible trouble in this area is immense. You could be dealing with someone who is promiscuous and has developed a profoundly sub-biblical view of the opposite sex, as well as loss of self-control. Or, you may be dealing with someone who is aversive to sex because of past experiences ranging from rape to molestation to personal failure occurred in previous sexual relationships. You may also work with disciples who have obsessive sexual fixations. Homosexuality or homosexual urges are also common.

Sexual sin or dysfunction is a messy area. But this area is so important it could derail all your efforts to train up mature disciples. Paul puts sexual sin in a special category in 1 Cor. 6:18 "Flee from sexual immorality. All other sins a man commits are outside his body, but he who sins sexually sins against his own body." He argues in this passage that nothing is more damaging to one's self than sexual immorality. People struggling with problems in this area often have difficulty drawing close to God and others because of their feelings of shame. They may have difficulty building successful marriages and families as well. Because the area of sexual dysfunction and sin is so immense, we can't hope to cover it here. But several things are clear:

First, Jesus Christ changes lives, and this includes entrenched sexual problems. While change in the sexual area can be painstakingly slow, we have no reason to be fatalistic. Unlike people in the world who believe that "you are what you are" and it can't be helped, we know better. Xenos' ministry in disciple-making has resulted in hundreds of examples of restored lives in this area. In fairness, there have been many failures as well. But God has the power, and is willing to exert it for change in the life of anyone who follows him fully.

Second, deliverance is almost never complete. At the very least, people with negative sexual habits will continue to feel temptation in those areas, probably for the rest of their lives. But let's face it; we all feel sexual temptation in some area. You should anticipate deliverance to the degree that your disciples will be able to form successful marriages.

Third, with serious, pathological sexual problems, you may need to seek help from a professional. Pedophilia, severe molestation, rape, fetishism, and homosexuality are examples where the person's problems may be too severe to handle without professional help. Just make sure the professional you enlist to help won't tell your disciple in areas of sexual sin that there is nothing wrong with him and he just needs to learn to accept himself. You would be better to work alone than to bring in a voice that speaks in harmony with Satan.

Fourth, you may want to study the particular problem your disciple has, especially if it is exotic or unusual. Guesswork in these cases is dangerous. By gaining a basic understanding of the causes of unusual sexual problems you will be better able to devise a strategy for change. Disciples with sexual compulsions, fetishism, wrongful orientations, or strange aversions, including frigidity, can be helped. However, you will have to do some research.

And last—in this area, more than any other—you will face difficulty persuading your disciple to disclose his problem. Yet, disclosure is one of the most healing things a disciple can do. The power of sexual sin is magnified greatly by secrecy. The first step in appropriating the power of God for change is bringing the problem into the light. Satan binds people in failure by convincing them their problem is unique and hopeless. He keeps the person from admitting the problem with dreadful threats that everyone will reject them and all their friends will think they're a freak. In this way, Satan seals them away from others' help and adds to their sense of shame because they are also deceivers and hypocrites. Whenever a disciple discloses a serious sexual problem, you have a unique opportunity to display the grace of God through your understanding and empathetic response. You can quickly move to counter their fatalistic sense that they will never change. Given these caveats, you can move into a typical pastoral counseling approach with the following:

1. *Awareness and understanding* — You should begin with a thorough study of God's ideals for sexuality. People who gain victory over sexual sin or pathology do so because they are intent on acquiring something better. Further tirades on how sinful their problem is are not very helpful unless the person hasn't accepted that the problem involves sin in the first place. Learning right from wrong in the sexual area is necessary. But even more helpful is a vision for what the believer can have if he follows God's pattern for sexual love. Reading good books on the subject can help impart a sense of vision for a more positive sexual future.[7]

2. *Practical ideas* — Once your disciple adopts a biblical view of sexuality, you must discuss a practical plan for restoration. Depending on the problem, such a plan could vary greatly. For instance, someone who is promiscuous may need to strictly limit time alone with dates. A man addicted to pornography may need to agree to have his computer filtered with software, giving the password to you or someone reliable. Your plan may include learning to develop successful non-sexual personal relationships with the opposite or same sex. We have learned that healthy, serving human relationships are the perfect replacement for sexual obsession. The things we learn about ourselves through deep relationships are the very lessons that will heal us more than anything else. Be sure to get advice from experienced pastoral counselors or Christian leaders who have experience working with the same problem.

3. *Support and encouragement* — Once you and your disciple create a plan, you can help him further by regularly asking how things are going with the plan. By developing a level of accountability, you can strengthen your disciple's will power. Often, if you can see a period of success, accompanied by positive developments in other areas of life, your disciple is on the way to lasting change. So many disciples suffering from sexual problems find that gaining a sense of vision for

being used by God, and building successful other-centered relationships is the occasion for major changes. But be ready for relapses.
Relapses are extremely common with sexual problems, because the
sexual urge is powerful and never ceases. Each failure must be
admitted and the grace of God claimed . . . and he must really repent.

Helping a disciple struggle through a sexual problem is another
example of why making real disciples is thorny, frustrating, and costly.
But for those willing to pay the price, the reward is spiritual reality.

Marriage

You will probably work with married disciples on the biggest area of
their lives; their family. Again, marriage and family counseling are
such vast areas of need that we can only mention some of the most
common areas and refer you to excellent books on the subject.

Some marriages are "unequally yoked" (2 Cor. 6:14). In an
unequally yoked marriage, one spouse is far more interested in
pursuing the things of God than the other. Sometimes one spouse
may be a non-Christian or an ambiguous Christian, in the sense that
their testimony is unclear and you see no evidence of the Holy Spirit
in the life of the uninterested spouse.

Sexual dysfunction is also common in marriages, and may come
up in discipleship. Here, some good reading in the field of marriage
counseling can help.[8]

In the field of parenting, you will commonly see two areas that
may need attention: failure to invest, and avoiding extremes in the
permissive-controlling continuum. If you share insight with your
disciples in a way that helps them win their kids over to a life centered
in God and his values, you will have helped both your disciple and
their children in a profound way. See the organic disciple-making web
site for more ideas in these areas (http://www.xenos.org/disciple).

Avarice (Greed)

In our opinion, materialistic greed is the greatest enemy of spirituality in the American church. The Bible teaches strongly against greed. Paul says, "But among you there must not be even a hint of sexual immorality, or of any kind of impurity, or of greed, because these are improper for God's holy people" (Eph. 5:3). The word for greed is *pleonexia,* which means a continual thirst for more. Here we see greed in the same list with sexual immorality, which should give us an idea of the seriousness God attaches to this danger. Jesus warned, "You cannot serve both God and Money" (Mat. 6:24). Paul goes so far as to say, "Therefore consider the members of your earthly body as dead to immorality, impurity, passion, evil desire, and greed, which amounts to idolatry" (Col. 3:5). Greed is really idolatry, according to Paul because money becomes the thing around which our lives revolve. People caught up in materialistic avarice never seem to have time for the things of God. They are so preoccupied by their careers and enjoying their money and possessions they can't develop quality ministries. With their frequent absenteeism and divided loyalties, they are unable to build quality relationships or engender true love of God in others. One of the saddest side-effects of greed is the way it chills our love for God and for others. Just as Jesus warned, "Where your treasure is, there your heart will be also" (Mat. 6:21). Many American Christians simply cannot match the enthusiasm and thrill they feel for God with what they feel for their new home, SUV, home theater system, or fishing boat. With this area, like others, a simple pastoral counseling approach can bear fruit.

1. *Awareness and understanding* — As with other areas, blindness is our first obstacle. You will rarely meet a person who affirms that they are a materialist. Most people look to those richer and more obsessed than themselves as materialists. They view their own level

of greed as only normal. As Americans, we live in an ocean of wealth, unprecedented in the history of the world. We have come to view affluence as so normal and necessary, how would we know if we had a problem with materialistic avarice? With this in mind, you must begin with a careful study of God's word. (You can begin with the outlines on the organic disciple-making web site). As Christians, we know that happiness in life comes from the spiritual and relational side of life, not from possessions, power, prestige, or money. If you can convince your disciples of this truth, you will be sparing them a life of emptiness, and freeing them to enter into the "true riches" (Luke 16:11).

2. *Practical Ideas* — How do people get out of the mindset of avarice? Think through with your disciples what practical steps (like regular giving, reassessing purchases, changing goals, etc.) might help effect change in this area. A short-term mission trip is often helpful.

3. *Support and encouragement* — Watch for shifts in attitude and action that may follow. Never miss the opportunity to encourage such shifts when you see positive changes.

Bad habits

People generally are creatures of habit. Habits can work for us or against us. As a disciple-maker, you should build healthy habits into the lives of your disciples. However, most disciples will come to you with some habits already in place that may be very enslaving.

Jesus warns, "I tell you the truth, everyone who sins is a slave to sin" (John 8:34). The Bible constantly warns about the enslaving power of sin. But Paul reminds us that in our new identity, "You have been set free from sin and have become slaves to righteousness"(Rom. 6:18). However, those who work with people know that appropriating freedom from sin is no easy matter. Sin habits can be incredibly tenacious.

When working with any disciple who is afflicted with a significant sin habit you have several things to consider.

First, you will probably never reach a point where your disciple has no sin habits. You are forced to work for *relative freedom*, not perfection (1 John 2:10). That means you have to weigh how strong to push for change, based in part on the damaging nature of the habit. Extreme habits such as fornication, homosexuality, alcoholism, or drug addiction are dead ends when it comes to spiritual growth. You are really wasting your time if you attempt to develop spiritual growth in a disciple while failing to deal with such habits.

But other habits may be almost as bad. Congenital lying effectively blocks relationship building, and disqualifies the person from spiritual leadership of any kind. Materialistic avarice is really a habit, and we have found that few things strip a person of zeal for God more than avarice. Rage-aholics constantly destroy their own relationships, and are also disqualified from leadership. (1 Tim. 3:3). Habitual thieves or those with an extreme habit of laziness are in serious trouble when one considers that both of these are mentioned in connection with church discipline (1 Cor. 5:11 "swindler," 2 Thess. 3:3:14). So are those who are habitual slanderers (1 Cor. 5:11).

Lesser habits also do a lot of damage. Over-eating and eating disorders are highly destructive of a person's social and sexual life and physical well-being. Cigarette smoking is also destructive to the body. Pornography is a spiritually devastating habit to millions. The list goes on and on.

No matter how severe or mild a sin habit is, as Christians we don't want to be enslaved to anything (1 Cor. 6:12). But we think it should be self-evident that we should begin at the top of the list and work down.

With this in mind, timing is your first consideration. Going after a disciple's sin habit is dangerous work. None of these habits are easy to resolve, and you will face the danger of losing a disciple anytime you grapple with such emotionally charged areas of a person's life. You may find yourself waiting, and hoping God directly rescues them from some lesser habits as they grow spiritually. But in the case of the most severe habits, you have no choice but to go for change early on.

Honesty is key. The disciple-maker walks a very difficult tightrope between being overly permissive, which leads to no change, and being so hard-line that the lines of communication close. When your disciple goes underground with his sin, you will have no way to counsel them. And our experience with people coming from evangelical churches suggests that most habitual sinners in these churches do so in secret. Admitting sin is never easy. But admitting sin to a severe and unsympathetic discipler soon becomes too hard for most disciples. This is really bad, because as we argued earlier, bringing sin into the light is the surest way to see progress.

Counseling people with bad habits follows a now familiar pattern:

1. *Awareness and understanding*— Begin by guiding your disciple into a godly perspective on his habits. You need to help him learn how the dynamics of sin and habit work in the larger scope of spiritual growth. Christians are forgiven, so God is not going to withdraw even from someone caught in serious sin. But the damage done by habits goes far beyond the direct damage caused by sin. Christians also fear the damage caused by the guilt and shame the habitual sinner feels. These can be so severe that they become a wedge driving the believer away from his only source of deliverance—God and the body of Christ. Remember that when you work with people who have sin habits, you must be patient and gracious. The first key to deliverance from sin is laying a foundation of grace. Your disciple must know that Jesus says, "Never will I leave you; never will I forsake you" (Heb. 13:5). This is the ground of security from which people can face their sin and begin dealing with it.[9] You must bring your disciple to the point where he

admits personal responsibility. A person caught in a habit can feel so enslaved that they have no *experience* of their free will. They often strongly believe they are helpless, and perhaps fated to always be that way. Through the nurture of scripture and your own and others' experience, you must persuade him that God's power is greater than his habit. You may have to work in stages, initially looking for small changes, and working toward bigger ones.

2. *Practical ideas* — Next, you need a strategy for change that matches the habit. This is often a matter of common sense, combined with biblical wisdom. This strategy may often involve external constraints. For instance, an alcoholic may need to agree not to go to bars or parties where people are drinking. A sex-aholic may need to abstain from dating for a time. You may want to involve a professional counselor in some extreme habits as well. At the very least, we suggest you consult the wisest Christian leader you know on how people can win change in the area at hand. We also suggest finding someone who has been delivered from the same habit in question, and ask them what was helpful. The possible strategies are far too numerous to list here. Books have been written on most of these sin patterns, and you should do relevant reading for more ideas.

3. *Support and encouragement* — As your disciple struggles, don't overlook the principle of *replacement*. People with bad habits usually can't just eliminate a habit. They have to replace it. What have you built with your disciple that could potentially give him the same or greater emotional gratification as his old, sinful habit? Usually, personal relationships rank high, as well as the joy of being used by God in others' lives, and warm personal times with God. When Christians see how gratifying these can be, they often finally decide to take strong measures with their sin habits.

FAILURE IN COUNSELING

Any disciple-maker who tangles with a disciple's serious personal problems looking for real change—as opposed to lip service—will meet with failure some of the time. Looking for authentic change in people's lives isn't easy. What happens when your efforts don't seem to be working?

First, you have to make a sensitive determination: Are you dealing with on-going weakness? Or are you facing a point of resistance where your disciple is basically refusing to take further steps? This judgment isn't always easy to make.

For one thing, you need to be aware of micro-movement. Even the slightest movement forward is very significant when dealing with any of the problems discussed in this chapter. The tiny step forward might be disappointing, but you have to adjust your expectations to reality. With humans, change is usually incredibly slow. Thank God for those cases of immediate deliverance from sin. But don't wait for it. Cases of rapid recovery from serious emotional or sin problems are few and far between. Even when people claim to experience instant healing for their problem, the problem usually re-surfaces later: The healing wasn't as complete as they thought. We suggest you focus on slow growth in your disciples. Instead of comparing your disciple's progress to where he was just a month ago, think about where he was a year ago. Is there a difference?

Also, you should watch for signs of effort. Even if you can't see any improvement in outward behavior, a believer who is putting forth effort will probably eventually see results. But what about cases where you aren't sure you see either effort or results? A discussion of resistant cases follows in the next chapter.

ENCOURAGEMENT: YOUR MOST POWERFUL TOOL

When you see either micro-movement or effort, you have the opportunity to use your most powerful tool; encouragement. Scientists who study how people learn have proven that positive reinforcement is far more powerful than punishment for effecting lasting change in people.[10]

The Bible urges us to encourage one another whenever we get the chance: "Encourage one another daily, as long as it is called Today, so that none of you may be hardened by sin's deceitfulness" (Heb. 3:13).[11]

Positively reinforcing godly attitudes and behavior through encouragement is important for several reasons. In the first place, by noticing when a disciple is doing the right thing and stressing how happy you are about it, you indicate the importance God places on these behaviors. At the same time, encouragement often gives your disciples the emotional strength to continue while effectively contradicting Satan's debilitating accusations.

Encouragement has one limitation: it is highly effective in *sustaining* action, but far less so at *initiating* action. In other words, you have to catch your disciple "doing something right" before you can use encouragement effectively. If you encourage even though they haven't acted, you are practicing flattery, which works against motivation. Flattery works against motivation because it cheapens encouragement. If encouragement is always there, whether deserved or not, your disciple will begin to discount it. "Oh, there he goes again," might be the inner response of a disciple who is being encouraged when he knows he shouldn't be. The encourager actually loses credibility if he flatters. Therefore, you need to plead, prod, and persuade in the hope of stimulating action, and *then* encourage.

Even when your disciples take positive action, you shouldn't always encourage them. The most important time to encourage is in the beginning. When someone first tries to move out in some way for God, you must not miss the chance to encourage. But as he becomes more regular in his movement, you will actually get more response if you only encourage them periodically. Scientists have demonstrated that intermittent reinforcement actually leads to higher levels of motivation in the long run.[12] Based on these findings, you should do what God often does: encourage people repeatedly during the earliest phase of learning a new pattern of living. Then, make the encouragement more intermittent as your disciple continues.

Try to devise different ways to encourage. For instance, instead of always encouraging people yourself, try organizing indirect encouragement by calling on others who noticed something good to encourage your disciple. Perhaps someone shares with you that your disciple's comment at home group was helpful. You could relay that yourself, or you could urge the person who made the comment to tell your disciple in person. Encouragement that comes from multiple sources has more impact.

Public encouragement is good if done tastefully. Expressing admiration for your disciple's progress in the presence of others sometimes has far more effect than doing so privately. At a men's group, I might say, "Ted, why don't you tell the guys about that awesome conversation you had with the guy at work?" Then follow up the question by mentioning how cool it is that Ted is speaking up for his faith.

Your encouragement will have more power if you mention specific details that were impressive in what your disciple did. Being detailed helps convey that you aren't just being perfunctory, but you were really paying close attention. This usually leaves a strong impression.

Try to show your disciple the benefits he gained in any situation where he made progress. If he sees for himself how the change is enhancing his life or helping others, he will be able to move toward self-reinforcement. Self-reinforcement is key to a disciple being able to maintain progress without ongoing help from others.

By reserving encouragement for actual progress—rather than for routine accomplishment—you can keep encouragement special. Overuse of any reinforcer tends to weaken its reinforcing power.

Consider offering encouragement in writing. Sending a card of appreciation, detailing what you have seen and why you think it is good seems to have special impact for most people. In your note, let your disciple know how his progress made you *feel.* This is powerful.

If you know gifted encouragers in your church, study how they work. You can learn a lot from skilled encouragers. Watch their nuances, inflection, and body language and emulate them.

If you become an effective encourager, you will likely see solid progress in your disciple. When combined with deep friendship, encouragement has incredible power to motivate people. Your disciple knows that you aren't just someone who has jumped to a superficial conclusion; you are too familiar with his or her weaknesses to be fooled, so your encouragement is more meaningful.

Diving into people's real problems and helping them progress is far more difficult than merely teaching them some Bible verses. Patient and loving disciple-makers who know how to apply God's wisdom and who are strong in encouragement will see God work in amazing ways in the lives of their disciples.

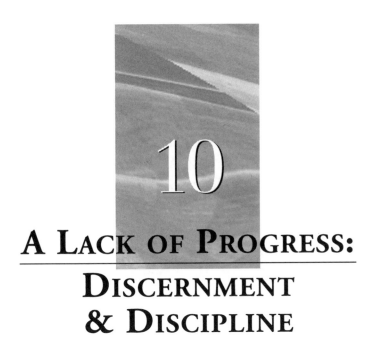

A Lack of Progress:

Discernment & Discipline

No disciple is completely willing from the beginning and continues to go all-out for God. Most disciples will encounter some kind of breakdown in their progress sooner or later. If you sense your disciple isn't moving forward, what's your move?

Make the Call

First, consider whether you have actually called your disciple to action. In many sections of this book, we have suggested that instruction will have a positive effect as a disciple develops his own inner convictions based on scripture. Sharing your vision with a disciple is also motivating, much like modeling. But sometimes these are not enough. You also have to be willing to challenge your disciple in a *direct, straightforward manner.*

Notice that both Jesus and Paul challenged people directly when necessary. Jesus' calls to those who would be his disciples are surprisingly strong (Luke 14:25-35). We see a great example of Paul calling people in his discussion in 2 Corinthians on giving (Ch. 8, 9). He persuaded, urged, and pointedly insisted that they follow through on their earlier commitment.

Much of the time, good leaders find it unnecessary to call on their people for action. People seem to sense what they should do on their own, as the Holy Spirit moves their hearts and they observe other models. Oswald Sanders argues that the ability to secure compliance without a show of authority is a mark of a good leader.[1] But such indirect leadership approaches don't always work. Not everyone picks up on subtle cues offered by others. God places leaders in the body of Christ because he wants to use them to motivate people. Good leaders aren't afraid at times to face someone and directly call on them to do something. Such a call need not be rude or bossy. It may be a case of simply saying, "Bob, you need to do this. How about it?"

The direct call is not a pitch you throw very often. Most of the time, if things are going well, disciples either sense what they need to do, or ask what they should do. When this is the case, you can take a consultative approach that helps your disciples learn how to think. But sometimes you need to throw the direct pitch without apology.

Dennis: Bob was a smart young college student who loved people more than study. Although he had good aptitude for academics, his grades were up and down depending on whether or not he wanted to study that quarter. After dropping classes repeatedly, he was offered a job that paid as well as any job he would get as a graduate, and it focused on his skills with people. He shared that he was seriously considering dropping out of college and pursuing a career with this company.

I didn't say much at the time, just nodding and smiling, but it concerned me. I knew Bob wanted to be a Bible teacher and leader as well, and I saw great potential for him there. I prayed about it for a couple of days before I saw him again during our regular "hang out" time. While there, I felt led to tell him directly that I thought the move to take the job and drop out of college was a bad idea. I suggested instead that he should get more serious about college and finish during the next year and a half. I argued strongly that, with his gifting, he would regret not having a degree later in life. At the same time, opportunities like the one in question were commonplace and he could take one any time he wanted. More than anything, I hated to see him taking the path of least resistance, and give in to his irresponsible tendencies.

My challenge wasn't what Bob wanted to hear, and he was argumentative. We actually argued for a time in heated tones as I tried to convict him about his laziness and poor stewardship. When he left, he was sullen. But I left him to mull it over. I didn't soften my words by reminding him that it was his decision, or that I would back him whichever way he chose, although I felt these were implied when we prayed together. I really wanted him to hear clearly that I had a strong opinion on the matter.

Days later, he stopped by and told me he had decided I was right. I was glad to hear it, but as his commentary continued, I realized there was much more. He went on to describe how he had been under conviction from God about his laziness in school and elsewhere, and he knew in his heart that taking the big dollar job was the easy way out. In the days after our talk, God wouldn't let him rest, and he had come to a complete breakdown before God. His whole life came into review, including a pattern of irresponsibility and self-indulgence. He repented before God and committed to go back to school and to attend to his other duties in life with a new perspective. He was amazingly thankful to me for bringing the whole thing to a head.

In the two years since that difficult time in our relationship and his life, he has gone on to finish college with good grades and is now in graduate school. God has moved him ahead in his ministry, giving him several promising disciples and two different groups to lead. He is headed toward a very promising future as a spokesman for God, and has never stopped feeling thankful for my intervention and call to stick it out in college.

DECIDING WHEN TO CALL

Based on my experience coaching other disciple-makers, I believe that many would not have made the call I did to challenge Bob. Or, if they did make it, they would not have been willing to argue or leave the situation in a state of tension while the Lord worked on their disciples' hearts. Too many disciple-makers are squeamish about pulling the trigger when it comes to making an unambiguous, direct call for action. If they do call, they qualify it so much it loses impact.

Of course, I had three years of relational capital built with Bob, and I knew he would listen. This was especially true because I rarely called on him to do things differently or make changes. Most of the time, subtle hints, story telling, and humorous jabs were enough to let him sense what I thought. He knew if I was taking a strong stand on something it must be important.

It was important. And that's one of the keys to knowing when a direct call is necessary. If you regularly call people to account for small things, you will be seen as bossy or nagging. Then, when you need to make the *big* call, your disciple writes it off as one more case of you not minding your own business.

Another key to this kind of decision is the recent history of your relationship. If I had recently made a major call on Bob, I would have been more reluctant to do so again. Part of the artistry of discipleship is knowing when you can make a call with a good likelihood it will be heeded. If you sense your call will be discounted, you're usually (but not always) better off holding your counsel back. In poker, you don't call a big bet unless you know the cards in your hand are good. You can't push people faster than the Holy Spirit is moving them.

STARTING A CAMPFIRE

When you make a direct call, you must be sensitive enough to read how the person is responding. Based on the response, you may either withdraw for the time being or advance.

Consider building a proper camp fire. When you try to start a fire in the woods, you have to do things in the right order: gathering the right kind of kindling, medium sticks, and larger wood first. Then, arrange the pieces the right way. Only when everything is set do you strike the match. Hopefully, you produce a little flame that can be nourished. Fire builders learn that a tiny, sputtering fire doesn't need more fuel piled on—maybe a little huffing and puffing, but not more wood. Only when you sense the fire is advancing should you add more and larger sticks, then logs.

Likewise, leaders learn to move *toward* responsiveness with more ideas for how to progress. They learn to retreat from unresponsiveness, waiting for a more opportune time. Giving a strong call to an unresponsive disciple is usually not just a waste of time. It endangers the relationship. Yet, we will argue later that in some rare cases, you must make a strong call even though you anticipate it will be discounted.

Some leaders simply will not make a strong call on people. Leaders who are afraid to make a direct call that creates tension become "soft disciple-makers." And soft disciple-makers consistently see very poor results in discipleship. You aren't doing your disciples any favors by failing to raise the tension in your relationship at key points that involve a change in life direction. And sometimes these calls have to be made with some force and fiber. We are so thankful for the older believers who called us to a higher level at numerous points in our Christian lives! Aren't you?

Soft discipling is a good approach when things are going well. By leaving decisions up to your disciples, or at most collaborating with them on decisions, you foster independent thinking. But good leaders know their style of leadership has to be dynamic. Sometimes the collaborative style won't work, so you must become directive.

When considering whether to be directive or collaborative, the importance of the decision in question is one factor. Another is the disciple's competence. With low-competence disciples, more direction is needed. You should assess the competence of your disciple at all times, not expecting him to know what he doesn't know, or patronizing him with things he already knows.

These decisions are complicated, so don't hesitate to consult with competent and experienced ministry colleagues. This is one reason we favor team leadership at Xenos. Each leader has fellow leaders they can consult on difficult ministry judgment calls.

POINTS OF RESISTANCE

Previously, we argued that disciples manifest strengths, weaknesses, and points of resistance. Maximizing strengths will be discussed more in the next chapter. Working with weaknesses will be discussed in the chapter on counseling. But you may also notice points of resistance in your disciple.

Points of resistance are different than weaknesses when it comes to a person's will. A disciple with a weakness wants to change, but may have trouble doing so. Such disciples exert effort to change, and are distressed when they fail. As we have argued earlier, you should be extremely patient with weaknesses. A resistant disciple is different. When a disciple becomes resistant, you will see signs that she is not on board with God's agenda for her life. Resistance is not just a matter of behavior, but of attitude.

Discerning resistance

Sometimes resistance is easy to see. The person may openly declare resistance to what you are teaching or may openly refuse to take steps you suggest. But not always.

Much of the time, resistance is not easy to discern. Most Christians want to be seen as willing to follow God, and they will speak and act in ways that suggest willingness even when they really aren't. You may sense resistance to God even though the disciple claims she wants to follow God's way. Even more confusing are those who don't realize they are resistant. God says, "The heart is more deceitful than all else and is desperately sick; who can understand it?" (Jer. 17:9). Rebellion and resistance often feel only natural to one in their grip. Then too, we are all resistant to some degree. No one is completely obedient, so how do you know when to make an issue of it with a disciple?

Determining the difference between weakness and resistance is very important, because the treatment for each is different. For most weaknesses, the greatest needs are for instruction, support, and encouragement, whereas resistance may call for confrontation and discipline. What then, are some signs of possible resistance?

1. The same questions keep coming up, and even good answers fail to satisfy. When disciples develop a resistance to God, they use

questions more as foils to deflect conviction than as ways to discover truth. That's why they begin to seem less interested in answers as opposed to more questions.

2. Resistant disciples manifest sins of omission. When Christians aren't being refreshed by their relationship with God, spiritual activities become burdensome. Prayer, reading the word, and sharing one's faith are all too much work for resistant disciples. Such a lack of spiritual energy could be caused by other things, but it's a warning sign. Always look past what a person says to what he does. Actions speak louder than words.

3. Dishonesty is not always a sign that disciples are hardening their attitude to God, but whenever they do harden their hearts, dishonesty follows. The most common type of dishonesty is when disciples avoid admitting guilt. You should always be worried when you find your disciples covering something up, especially if it becomes a pattern.

4. Responsive disciples are generally interested in spiritual things, but when they develop a point of resistance, they become relatively disinterested. You will notice a general decrease in eagerness to discuss the things of God, pray, or study the word.

5. Fruitless discussions (rabbit trails) about unimportant issues are a sign of resistance. Especially when you get into the area where the disciple is resistant, they suddenly want to go down rabbit trails instead of remain on the subject at hand. Watch for this.

6. Sometimes, you might hear comments a disciple made to others that clearly show an attitude problem. While you always must be careful with second-hand reports, these are sometimes used by God to tip you off to a problem. These second-hand reports are often where you will discover dishonesty. You should always take a questioning posture when checking with your disciple about what you heard. Don't assume facts that aren't confirmed.

7. Watch for defensiveness. While anyone might be defensive when caught in sin, it quickly becomes a regular pattern for those who are resistant. Defensiveness about sin is usually either *rationalization* (where they explain that what they did wasn't wrong), *minimization* (where they explain that it might have been wrong, but it wasn't that bad), or *blame shifting* (where what they did may have been wrong, but it wasn't their fault).

8. Resistant disciples usually demonstrate a shift in priorities. Things of the world seem to become more important, and they have trouble finding time for the things of God.

None of these signs is definitive by itself, and even seeing most of them isn't always definitive. It's normal for young believers to go through cycles where they are warmer and cooler to God. Also, emotional problems, such as depression, could result in most of these symptoms rather than a hardened heart. As a disciple-maker, you need spiritual sensitivity in addition to objective criteria when making this discernment. God will often call your attention to actions or words that signal resistance, so ask him for a greater awareness in this area.

Discernment is so difficult and so important you should not hesitate to consult with other mature believers. If you know reliable believers who are mutual friends with your disciple, you should ask what they think. When seeking this second opinion, try to avoid leading the other person with your questions. How you ask for help can bias the answer you receive. Instead of asking, "I feel like Sarah is developing an attitude problem, what do you think?" try asking, "How do you feel Sarah is doing?"

Discerning resistance is not a sudden realization. Any negative sense you receive should be sifted carefully over a period of days or even weeks. We all have negative tendencies at times, and it would be easy to jump to the wrong conclusion. Through continual prayer and observation, including ongoing conversations with the disciple in question, God will gradually confirm or disprove your sense of what is happening.

In addition to these points, you should learn to watch for one key exception: dissonance. We believe dissonance should be distinguished from resistance, even though many of the same symptoms may appear.

Dissonance

The word dissonance comes from the word *sonic*, and so has to do with sound. In particular it refers to something sounding bad. Sometimes when Christians—especially young ones—go through a hard period in their walk, they experience dissonance. This is common for young believers who experience an initial burst of excitement when receiving Christ. When the excitement fades, dissonance may ensue.

Often, it seems that God in his grace has sustained the young believer with extra protection and encouragement, which he gradually removes in order to refine the new believer's faith.

You should treat dissonance differently than resistance. When young believers begin to struggle in their faith, you should ask questions in the hope of discovering the root problem. Why is he experiencing defeat? You must be willing to show a high degree of patience with someone going through these growing pains. A young believer is more innocent than an older, resistant believer, because they are learning about spiritual living for the first time. With a dissonant young believer, it's appropriate to persuade rather than giving them a scolding.

The best thing you can do for young Christians is warn them before they ever enter a time of dissonance. You do a great disservice to young believers if you let them believe the Christian life will be an easy ride. When they begin to suffer, they will wonder if God has abandoned them.

Preventative work is usually more helpful than reactionary work. Notice how Paul went through villages talking to believers he had reached only weeks earlier: ". . . strengthening the souls of the disciples, encouraging them to continue in the faith, and saying, 'Through many tribulations we must enter the kingdom of God' " (Acts 14:22). Is this message really encouraging?

Yes! To be forewarned is to be forearmed. Paul is managing their expectations, and this removes one of Satan's key tools: the shock effect when a new believer moves from victory and excitement to a period of disaffection and estrangement.

The positive side of dissonance is the resulting strength and stamina they will gain if they persevere. Believers who withstand a bout of dissonance emerge substantially stronger than before. You should describe this positive vision to young disciples as they struggle, or better yet, before they ever struggle. As Christians, we can exclaim with Job, "When He has tried me, I shall come forth as gold" (Job 23:10).

If a disciples' faith is never strengthened in this way, he will end up as a defeated and weak Christian. Faith is what keeps us going as Christians! Dry times of dissonance are a blessing in disguise when they make our faith stronger.

To summarize, anticipate dissonance in young Christians as a normal part of spiritual growth, and not as resistance. You should forearm them by warning that they may experience dissonance, and you should make special allowance for dissonance in young Christians. And last, you should not be too reactive to negative comments and actions they may manifest.

Responding to resistance

Even when you discern that your disciples are resistant and perhaps in danger of hardening their hearts, you still have an open question:

What do I do about it? Since you are not operating under legalism, you are not required to respond a certain way in any given situation. Under law, each crime would have to be recompensed fairly. But under the grace and love paradigm, you are only bound to do what is best for the person. This means your response might be quite different for other people in the same situation. You might even respond differently with the same person in different situations.

What are some of the factors you must weigh in determining how to respond to a disciple's growing resistance to God?

First, you have a range of responses open to you. At one extreme, you may decide to "look the other way" on the issue at hand, and continue to offer general spiritual nourishment and friendship in the hope that God will directly change his or her heart. This approach makes sense with newer relationships and young believers who may not realize fully what is wrong with their attitude. Quite often, we have seen remarkable turn-arounds in disciples we were praying for, even though we never got around to confronting them with their problem.

At the other extreme, you could strongly rebuke the person, and demand a change of heart. Such a rebuke could be accompanied even with threats of various sanctions. Paul urges Titus to "rebuke them sharply, so that they will be sound in the faith" (Titus 1:13). But the reason he calls for such strong medicine is that these are "rebellious men, empty talkers and deceivers . . . who must be silenced because they are upsetting whole families, teaching things they should not teach for the sake of sordid gain" (Titus 1:10, 11). Consider the Christians involved. First, these false teachers were knowledgeable, and therefore more accountable. Second, they were doing significant damage in the body of Christ. In some extreme cases, scripture teaches that we should be prepared to put someone out of fellowship rather than let them continue in sin (1 Cor. 5; 1 Thess. 3:12-14;

Mat. 18:15-18). Jesus was also capable of sharp rebukes. On at least one occasion whipping the people he rebuked! (Mat. 23; John 2:14-16).

Discipline is not the opposite of love. Discipline is a part of love as God presents it. God certainly loves us, and he is also committed to disciplining us as needed for our good. Hebrews 12 explains:

> *"And have you entirely forgotten the encouraging words God spoke to you, his children? He said, "My child, don't ignore it when the Lord disciplines you, and don't be discouraged when he corrects you. For the Lord disciplines those he loves, and he punishes those he accepts as his children."* . . . *If God doesn't discipline you as he does all of his children, it means that you are illegitimate and are not really his children after all"* (Heb. 12:5-8 NLT).

God doesn't need to apologize for disciplining us. Anyone who watches a loved one destroy himself and does nothing is simply not loving, according to the Bible. You have to care enough to confront. The book of Proverbs teaches that, "If you refuse to discipline your children, it proves you don't love them; if you love your children, you will be prompt to discipline them" (Prov. 13:24 NLT).

Even though many Christians accept the validity of discipline when it comes to children, they lose this perspective when it comes to peers in discipleship. One may even have a vague sense that discipline could be appropriate for adults, but in practice he isn't willing to apply it.

People usually fail to exercise needed discipline simply because they are self-protective and unloving. They just aren't sacrificial enough to risk the displeasure that might be unleashed if they dare to discipline. Or, worse, they won't risk losing popularity.

Disciple-makers who refuse to discipline become "soft" disciple-makers. We already argued that soft disciple-makers are among the worst at being able to foster life change in a disciple. We all desperately need to be reproved at certain points in our lives. And no one is in a better position to meet this need than a caring discipler who has invested into the relationship over time.

We know of cases where soft disciple-makers finally disciplined their disciples and were surprised to find that their disciples felt more loved at such times than any other. It's one thing to have a relative stranger come and tell you you're in the wrong. But how different when someone loves you, agonizes before God on your behalf, and in the end comes and reproves you. You realize they wouldn't be saying this if it wasn't important. We have often had the experience of disciples returning days later to thank us from the heart for telling them what they needed to hear. No wonder Paul reminds the Thessalonians that, "night and day for a period of three years I did not cease to admonish each one with tears" (Acts 20:31).

We have argued several times that disciple-makers must be patient. But patience is not softness. Consider the following comparison:

Patience	Softness
Accepts the fact that people change slowly	Accepts lack of any change
Continues to warn, encourage, and admonish	Encourages, but little or no warning or admonition
Withstands the pain of honest assessment	Pretends things aren't that bad no matter what happens
Makes people feel secure, but challenged and motivated	Nothing seems important because "anything goes"– People are bored and discouraged
Workers are able to go the long haul because their lives are changing	Great danger of people quitting because they see no progress or purpose
People are gratified by gradual but real progress	Spiritual depression increases temptation to sin

Considering then, that your response to resistance could range from deliberately "looking the other way" to mild reproof or strong discipline. How do you decide what to do?

Accountability

First, consider the question of accountability. Different believers are accountable to different standards. Paul urges his readers to "keep living by that same standard to which we have attained" (Phil. 3:16). New believers are hardly accountable to any standard. They don't understand Christian living, and often have a very distorted view of what is right and wrong. A home group leader, on the other hand, is highly accountable. Paul doesn't give lists of moral requirements for membership in the body of Christ. But he does give such a list of requirements for leaders (1 Tim. 3 and Titus 1). Leaders may need discipline even for sins of omission, like failing to fulfill their role in their home group. Most believers are somewhere between these extremes. The careful discipler weighs what a disciple knows and the progress made so far. Then, drawing from multiple options, he selects the most appropriate response.

History

Recent and distant history can have a major impact on your choice of responses. Is this the umpteenth time this disciple has become resistant? Or is resistance a new thing? A disciple who slanders and backbites other believers on a regular basis, especially after several people have complained about it, may need some strong discipline. On the other hand, you should go softer if you have not seen such behavior before. A repetitive pattern of resistance suggests the need for stronger discipline, whereas a softer approach would be appropriate for any first-time problem.

Another feature to consider is your own relational history with the disciple. If your relationship has been stressed recently, this would suggest a lower likelihood of success in discipline. If the issue isn't crucial, a wise discipler will possibly wait until a more opportune time for confrontation.

A person who has been consistently responsive to reproof whenever it is offered will probably respond to a milder form of admonition.

Seriousness of the sin

Sometimes resistance is not connected to a particular sin problem (although you should always consider whether a sin problem could be involved). Students of scripture know that some sins are more damaging than others. We hear Christians say, "All sins are alike before God." This statement is true, if considered from the perspective of what it takes to fall short of God's requirements for going to heaven. But all sins are not alike in terms of the damage they do to the one sinning and to others. These highly damaging sins are the ones the New Testament singles out as meriting stronger discipline.

Among these most serious sins are sexual sins. Paul says fornication is really joining the members of the body of Christ to a harlot (1 Cor. 6:15). He is also referring to sexual sin when he says, "a little yeast works through the whole batch of dough" (1 Cor. 5:6). In other words, the presence of sexual immorality powerfully defiles the church. He also points out that sexual immorality is worse than many other sins because "the immoral person sins against his own body" (1 Cor. 6:18). Anyone believer who is engaging in fornication, adultery, or homosexual immorality is involved in a sin so harmful that a serious warning cannot be delayed. Even young Christians engaged in sexual immorality must be admonished without delay. If the immoral one is your disciple, you are wasting your time trying to foster spiritual growth until such a sin is resolved. We have never seen any Christian grow spiritually to any significant degree while engaging in sexual immorality.

Other sin areas are also very serious. Drug addiction, false teaching, alcohol abuse, divisiveness in the church, extreme laziness, and even materialistic avarice are on the same lists of sins requiring formal church discipline (Titus 3:10; 1 Cor. 5:11; 2 Thess. 3:10-15; 1 Tim. 1:20). Any of these sins will block further spiritual growth, so as a discipler, you should be more inclined to lovingly confront a disciple who is entangled in such a serious problem.

Even lesser sins could become points of resistance that might contaminate one's whole spiritual life. The point is, when a believer stops struggling with sin and gives into it, resisting God in that area of his life, he is in danger of a hardening his heart. A believer who says "No!" to God is in real spiritual danger. But with sins that aren't that dangerous, defiling, or damaging, at least in the short term, you may want to consider working in ways other than strong discipline.

11

A LACK OF PROGRESS: PRACTICING DISCIPLINE IN LOVE

When things go wrong with disciples, the disciple-maker must go before God to gain discernment. In the last chapter, we discussed ways you can discern, and different options you could pursue. Now you need to consider, in depth, one of those possibilities: Loving discipline.

PREPARING FOR DISCIPLINE

Once you discern that reproof is in order, you need to prepare. Careful preparation greatly increases the likelihood that reproof will work. "Shooting from the hip" in these situations is very dangerous. Even experienced disciple-makers—who might get away with spur-of-the-moment reproof now and then—know that preparation is important for effective and loving reproof.

Your first act of preparation is prayer. By asking God to precede you and work on the person's heart before you speak, you greatly increase the likelihood that your disciple will listen. You also need to pray for guidance while you think through how you are going to confront your disciple.

You can prepare for reproof by carefully thinking and praying about each of the following:

1. Assemble the facts. How do you know this problem is real? Think back about what you have seen and why you feel sure this issue requires change now. Especially with subjective issues, such as attitude problems, you must think about how the problem is affecting the person's behavior and demeanor. People in sin are usually blind to some extent, and may need some convincing that their problem is real and serious. So you may have to build a case for why you believe he or she should change.

2. What are the main reasons why your disciple needs to have a change of heart? Think in terms of biblical arguments, damage being done to the person, and damage being done to other loved ones. What does the Bible say about this problem?

3. What measures can the disciple take to overcome the problem? This is a difficult question, especially if the problem is mainly one of attitude. But you must come to the table with practical steps your disciple can take. If he or she is responsive to your reproof and wants to change, you should be ready. Nothing is more discouraging than being reproved, but left without positive ideas for how to break free from an enslaving problem. Remember: people caught in sin are often confused and may have false beliefs you must address. People caught up in habits may need outside help as well. Some should be referred for counseling. Others may need a support group where they can learn how to win against their habit. You might recommend some reading based on similar cases. Do the research required to discover realistic suggestions. As you pray over the situation, God may speak to your imagination showing

you a particular prayer of rededication or repentance the person needs to pray. Ask yourself, "If my disciple is totally responsive, exactly what would I like to see her do?"

4. Think through the consequences that will result if your disciple fails to change. A negative vision based on the current trajectory of the person's life is required here. Part of reproof is warning, and you will be more persuasive in your warning if you have thought about similar cases and where they led. Don't exaggerate or you will lose credibility. The truth about where sin leads is bad enough without exaggeration.

5. Consider an analogous problem with which you struggled in the past. Remember how difficult it can feel to face repentance and change when you were caught up in a wrong attitude or action? It's hard to admit you are wrong! By identifying with the person in this way, you can build strong empathy. Studies show that persuasion is more powerful when it comes from an empathetic speaker. Mentioning a past problem you have faced also helps prevent the impression that you are self-righteous, which is always a potential concern when confronting someone.

6. Consider the benefits if the disciple changes. Your positive vision should reflect on all you know about the person and all you can imagine them becoming if they succeed in dealing with their problem. The juxtaposition of a negative and positive vision has more persuasive power than either of them by themselves.

7. Consider your words and demeanor. Although you can't script out what you are going to say during the whole conversation, it's wise to at least plan out how you will begin. Formulate an opening statement that affirms your relationship and sets a tone for the discussion. For instance, "Bob, you've become one of my best friends, and I'm continually thankful for our friendship. That's why I feel I need to talk to you about a problem I see . . ."

Beginning a discussion like this gives the context for the reproof. Your friend needs to see that although you are critical now, this should be viewed in light of the larger positive history of friendship. You should always be concerned that defensiveness may interfere with clear communication in these situations. Beginning with a truthful (but not flattering) statement is one of the best ways to reduce defensiveness.

Before you meet, decide how you are going to describe the problem, and what you will call it. Your choice of words is important! Wording can be either unnecessarily inflammatory or easy to accept. Telling someone he was not honest, for instance, is better than telling him he is a liar. Telling someone she is harming herself with sexual immorality is more easily accepted than telling her she is acting like a tramp. Proverbs teaches that, "A gentle answer turns away wrath, but a harsh word stirs up anger" (Prov. 15:1).

Your demeanor is also important. If you seem harsh or cold, your disciple will have difficulty listening to what you say. In your mind's eye, imagine how you want to be received and prepare accordingly.

8. At what point will you finish your description of your concerns, and put the ball in the other person's court? You shouldn't preach a sermon and walk out. Instead, you should be thinking about when you are going to ask, "So, how do you feel about what I'm saying?"

9. Form a contingency plan for different responses. If the person rejects what you are saying, what will you do? Continue to argue the case, or let it go for now? You could continue if the issue is urgent, or if you feel you can win the person over with more argument. Or, you may decide that if the other person rejects your message you will retreat temporarily: "Okay, it sounds like you don't see what I'm talking about at all. Will you agree to at least

pray about it, and ask the Lord if there's anything here?" After this you may try to conclude the discussion and wait several days before bringing it up again. You aren't giving up by taking a retiring posture. You are simply backing away long enough to give God time to work. With strong-willed people or those who are too proud to admit fault, this kind of response often gives good results. You may find that the next time you discuss the issue, your argument has already been won for you by the power of the Holy Spirit. If not, you can always return to further efforts to persuade and plead.

This approach has other benefits as well. For one thing, a major change of heart may take time. By spreading the reproof over a number of days, you will avoid giving the impression that you require a change of heart on the spot. This makes real change more likely. You certainly don't want to batter anyone. Some argumentation may be needed, but you don't want to end up with a change of heart produced by compulsion. Such changes are usually superficial and won't last.

What if the disciple explodes or the tears flow? With serious problems, some emotional response is to be expected. But be sure you aren't manipulated by emotional pyrotechnics. Plan for this and consider the proper reaction.

What if the person agrees with you? What encouraging thing can you say that will reward the person for listening? "Sarah, I'm really moved that you have the humility to admit this, and I think God will use your humility in awesome ways!" Don't forget to plan for a positive response.

HOW SERIOUS IS THE ISSUE?

There is one last area to consider before you approach your disciple to discipline them in love. You must accurately determine the seriousness of the issue relative to other factors. Disciplinary acts are not all the same. Here are three categories to help you determine the severity of the problem and how to approach your disciple:

Problems that are significant, but not serious

Problems in this category are significant enough that something should be said, but they are not spiritually life-threatening, or overly damaging. Many attitude problems may fit in this category, because they are more subjective. This might be where you see a believer who committed a fairly serious sin, but only once, so there is no pattern. It could be a highly accountable believer, like a fellow leader, who did something fairly minor, but you feel he should know better. Or, it could be a younger believer in more serious sin, but at a low level of accountability—he simply hasn't been transformed in that area yet. With situations in this first category, you may feel that something needs to be said, yet you are not prepared to press the issue to the limit. If your disciple refuses to listen, you may just leave it. He may change his mind later, and it wouldn't be worth endangering the relationship by pressing the issue further than is necessary.

Dennis: Larry was a young brother living in a house with other committed Christian young men. After reports from others and my own observations about the amount of time he spent playing video games, I sensed his habit was becoming a barrier. Watching for the right opportunity, I planned to share my concern with him. When I saw my chance, I took it.

He thought I was being legalistic, and didn't agree that it was a problem. I made a few observations about how any pursuit could become a barrier if it was out of control by sharing 1 Cor. 6:12. I also reminded him how he had recently claimed to be too busy to do his homework for a Bible class he was taking, and wondered how many hours a week were wasted at this pointless pursuit. (I had reason to believe it was more than twenty!) I urged him to take my words seriously, and at least pray about it. This conversation was not a long exchange, lasting only fifteen minutes at the most.

Although Larry laughed off most of my comments, throughout the next few weeks two different brothers commented that Larry was showing moderation in his gaming. In the time since, he has gradually lost interest in marathon gaming sessions all together.

This was a minor disciplinary episode, although it wasn't easy for me. I didn't feel like talking about it in the first place, and when we did talk, I was tempted to press my point hard when he laughed. But I'm glad I restrained myself, and I believe it helped him out considerably. Since that talk, I have overheard him making the same points to a younger believer who was gaming too much.

Problems that are serious, but not spiritually life threatening

Do you have a disciple who is demonstrating a fairly serious problem, such as dishonesty or fits of rage? It could also be someone who is being extremely lazy and won't get a job, or one who is in the grip of avarice. These are potentially very damaging, but often take time to resolve. In this second category, you should probably take a harder line, including arguing the case for a longer period of time.

Dennis: Barry was from a cultural background where financial success and owning expensive things were important. As a disciple, he showed promise, but would again and again get into trouble with expensive purchases that cost him extra time at work and left him in debt. I approached the issue as a counseling problem, or a weakness. Together, we read several books I knew were good for ministering to avarice, but they didn't seem to have much effect. He developed the ability to talk about godly values in the area of finance, but continued to practice the same impulsive, showy spending. He also made a commitment to financially support a ministry, but his spending prevented him from keeping his word.

Eventually, I realized things weren't going to progress in his spiritual maturity unless he made more progress in this area. His excitement and pride about new wasteful purchases often dwarfed his excitement for spiritual things. In dozens of ways, I saw his avarice was choking out the fruit that God wanted to bear in his life, as Jesus had warned (Mat. 13:22). My periodic, mild disapproval at his way of life seemed to have little effect. Because I'd seen Barry fall into avarice repeatedly for two years in our friendship, I felt I needed to draw a line with him on this issue.

When we finally had a lengthy time to talk, I frankly stated that I was very pessimistic about his future for God because he couldn't seem to decide whether to serve God or mammon. He was resistant, feeling that I was exaggerating, so I poured out the case I had been building. I went on at some length, and made it clear that I was upset about his lack of progress. I had stories to tell him of other disciples I had lost to the same failing. The hurt was visible on his face and in his voice, but I pressed on. I didn't actually threaten to stop meeting with him, although the thought was in the back of my mind. I made it clear that I was despairing over his lack of growth.

He admitted it was a problem, as usual, but alternated between pleading that he had improved and a fatalistic sense that he couldn't change. Again, I pressed the issue. I pointed out that he always made such excuses, and that he was refusing to believe God or submit to him in this area. I pointed out that he was making up for deficits in relational and spiritual areas by these efforts to impress people with his possessions.

At the point where he fell silent, I went on to share what a fantastic future I believed awaited him if only he would have a change of heart on this issue. In the end we prayed together, and although he said the right things in prayer, I didn't have any confidence that a major break-through had taken place. The talk lasted longer than an hour.

As I drove home that day, I resolved that this wasn't over. I knew that if he continued to fail in this area, I would return to the reproof immediately. Because I was certain this area was going to either wreck his walk or be dealt with, I was ready for a running battle. I knew he enjoyed our friendship as much as anything in his life, and I was determined to draw heavily on that relational capital to press for change. Instead of adopting the posture of passive advisor, I was ready to become the active disciplinarian and to stay that way. At the same time, I felt sorry for him. I knew it was confusing to experience such a collision between values he had pursued his whole life and those of his new Christian life.

During the next several months, I won this running battle with Barry. By God's grace, he was granted a widening revelation about the state of his own heart. As he progressively curtailed his avarice, his spiritual life soared accordingly. Within a few months, he was a different man. Everyone who knew him commented on how well he was doing, and how his attitude seemed to have changed dramatically. Barry himself reported how he felt happier and more fulfilled than before.

As Barry's discipler and friend, I paid a very heavy price for this victory. But as he went on to become a strong leader and teacher of truth . . . the result was so fantastic that I hardly remember the pain.

I have had similar struggles with most successful disciples. Few will fully develop without a major point of resistance and a corre-sponding struggle. As a sacrificial lover, you must be prepared to pay the price of bearing the cross for your disciples. And discipline is sometimes the supreme price.

Problems that are spiritually life threatening or menacing to others

Some situations are so serious and extreme that you cannot take "no" for an answer. An addict who won't seek out help is destroying himself before your eyes. You cannot say you love him if you passively watch this destruction and are not willing to go to any length to stop it.

A believer who is involved in discipleship for spiritual growth, but also is sneaking periodic fornication is a walking contradiction. If you love that believer, you cannot allow him to go on believing that these two agendas are compatible. If he refuses to repent, you must press the issue to the point where you are prepared to impose sanctions.

These sanctions could include ending your discipleship relation-ship, confronting the person before the community of believers, or even removing them from Christian fellowship. (The latter of the three will probably require the participation of your church leadership.)

You must make clear in such situations that some things won't be tolerated in the community of God. You are also hoping that even if these sanctions are imposed, the person will realize the error of his ways and change his heart. You also must consider the well-being of your church. Severe cases of division, defiling sexual sin, or violence all threaten the spiritual lives of others. By being too soft on one person, you could endanger many others.

Dennis: Sid was raised in a divided family that was extremely dys-functional. When he came to Christ in his late teens, he had many serious problems. He lacked drive or control in almost every area of his life. But during one of his positive swings, I decided to try to disciple him. I knew he was a hard case, but he seemed eager and I had the time. I was also attracted by the fact that he periodically shared the gospel with friends, and had brought people around to Bible studies.

As time passed, I realized I wasn't making progress. His fits of rage terrorized the men in his rooming house, as well as guests. His over-eating was destroying his body. Sid's periodic drinking episodes seemed to be repeated at roughly the same frequency. Worst of all was his terminal laziness and self-indulgence. He couldn't hold a job. He couldn't bring himself to study, go to school, or anything that required saying "no" to self at any point.

Even though he showed excitement for God and fellowship at times, it became clear that our discipling relationship of more than a year was going nowhere. Not only was he not progressing, but he was poisoning the atmosphere at his house, and had even frightened and alienated non-Christian guests to whom we were reaching out. After talking to other leaders, we decided something had to be done. Our periodic reproofs were being ignored.

In stages, the body of Christ gradually cornered Sid. After another particularly awful rage episode in front of guests, we told him we were seriously considering removing him from the rooming house unless he went to counseling and convinced us that things were going to change through his actions, not just his words. He agreed, but four weeks later, had still not called the counselor we suggested. His excuse was that he didn't have the money, which would have been minimal.

I let him have it with both barrels. In a deliberately angry tone, I pointed out that he always had money for huge piles of food, and expensive disc-golf discs. I said I wasn't going to meet with him until he delivered what he had promised. I followed that with the statement that we were obviously fooling ourselves by talking about discipleship while he lived a life that totally contradicted every aspect of a disciple's character. I clearly remember saying, "You can talk to me after you've been to your fourth counseling session."

Nothing happened. Later, additional episodes led the others in the house to expel him. He left Christian fellowship not long after, and moved in with a girlfriend.

Was this episode an example of failed discipline? Not necessarily. I believe Sid may be better off now in the world than in the church living in rebellion. In the world, God takes over the disciplinary process like he did with the prodigal son (Luke 15:11-32). Notice that the waiting father didn't go chasing the prodigal into the distant country. He waited. And the savagery of the world broke down the son's resistance.

In our years of ministry, we have seen hundreds like Sid come back after a lengthy journey into the terrors of the world. (Sid himself recently ran into a believer in our group and said he's thinking about coming back). The loneliness and lack of love in the world is a painful experience that becomes unbearable for true believers. When people return to the Lord after such an experience, they usually have a whole new attitude and far more resolve.

Of course, some never return. But the church is still better off, and if the discipline was necessary, the person is probably better off as well. A person who draws comfort from the community of believers while pursuing a life of sin will not grow, and their heart grows increasingly hardened. This makes repentance even more unlikely. Believers who choose to leave fellowship know they have made a decision to walk away from God. When suffering results, they are less likely to blame God, and more likely to realize they are to blame.

If you know you are dealing with an issue of ultimate seriousness with a disciple, it must change how you approach the question of how to discipline. Adjusting all these factors based on your disciple's spiritual age and accountability, special circumstances, and past history makes for a difficult assessment. The greater the seriousness of the situation, the more urgent it becomes to get plenty of consultation, including your church's leadership. Fortunately, most disciplinary situations are resolved long before this point. Only rarely will you find yourself facing the most extreme cases.

THE MEETING

Your main goal in your first meeting is to clearly express what you have planned to say. Your hope is that your disciple sees the problem in his own life, and comes to view that problem the right way—not in despair or unbelief in God's power to change lives. Whether in the first meeting or in subsequent discussions, you also hope to see your disciple agree from the heart with your message, and decide to take the measures you will suggest, or other measures that accomplish the same end. Your prayer should be that acting in discipline will not alienate your relationship, but actually deepen it.

Don't beat around the bush. Remember to begin with your opening statement, already planned out. Be tactful but direct. People sense when you are talking around a subject, and it seems "shifty."

As you make your points, watch closely for your disciple's response. A disciplinary talk is a fluid situation and you need to adjust your approach based on the response you sense. Responsive people don't usually need heavy conviction. Resistant people may need more argument or you could decide to retire, as we discussed earlier. The key is that you are aware of how the person is responding. Ask questions if you are unsure, and be willing to wait in silence for the answers. A person who falls quiet during a talk like this is hard to read. You must help them to talk about how they feel if you are to correctly read their response.

Whether you are calling or reproving someone, you should always do it with respect for the person's individuality, never pestering or browbeating. Galatians 6:1 says, "Brothers, if someone is caught in a sin, you who are spiritual should restore him gently. But watch yourself, or you also may be tempted." Accepting reproof is always difficult because our flesh is naturally resistant to instruction and correction. But when ego-punishing rhetoric is added to reproof, it becomes doubly difficult. Spend some time thinking about what it looks like to be firm but respectful. Always stress the free choice your disciple will make, clear that you are not making choices for the person.

Follow Up

Always follow up on a disciplinary talk. It would be very unnatural to have such a talk and leave silence afterward. Whether you felt your disciple was responsive or not, you should ask her soon afterward whether she has thought any more about your conversation. Often, initial responses can be misleading. Some unresponsive people reveal later that they were more responsive than you thought. Others who initially seemed responsive will later see problems with what you said. You must discover what direction their subsequent thinking has taken. Particularly disturbing is the disciple who seems not to have thought about it at all!

Most disciplinary interactions are actually a series of talks. If you are not satisfied with the response you saw, you should continue seeking ways to persuade and urge. In cases you believe are relatively important or even urgent, you must make it clear the issue won't go away. "Sand-bagging" is a tactic where people in sin neither openly resist nor fully agree. Instead they give vague responses and little or no action. Their hope is that by doing nothing, they will eventually out-wait you and be relieved of the burden of change. To be effective in discipline, you have to make it clear that you cannot be sand-bagged. Note that you usually don't need to escalate the debate. Simple persistence is usually enough to convince this kind of disciple that sand-bagging won't work.

When disciples respond negatively, and the Holy Spirit has been unable to change their minds, you must face some difficult alternatives. We already mentioned the option of dropping the issue if you feel it is relatively unimportant. But when the issue is important, you must be ready to create a significant level of tension in the relationship until you see some movement. You can create tension by regularly showing your disciple the discrepancy between where she is and where God wants her to be.[1] In addition, you should periodically make it clear that you are unhappy or worried about her lack of change.

Tension is a sense of discomfort in the relationship. Without tension, the disciple may lack motivation for change. If you have built up relational capital with your disciple, she will feel significant motivation to resolve the tension and return to a point where the relationship is enjoyable. Some disciple-makers find it difficult and unnatural to raise tension in a relationship that is loving and positive. But you owe it to your disciples to offer long-term, loving tension when the issue is serious. If you reduce the tension even though you see little or no change, you become a soft discipler. Your overall effectiveness as a discipler will be compromised if you are unwilling to engage in a lengthy wrestling match over serious sin.

At the same time you create ongoing tension, you should be alert to any change in attitude or action. You will not normally see complete resolution of serious sin or attitude problems after one disciplinary encounter. God needs time to work. More often, you will see partial movement, and you should move to encouragement. Encouragement is far more powerful than punishment when it comes to reinforcing change, as we explained earlier.

If you lean toward perfectionism, you must take care to avoid taking an overly hard line in discipline. Especially after the first disciplinary encounter on an issue, you may have to find satisfaction with minor movement in the right direction. You may still feel inwardly distressed because you know what you have seen thus far falls short of what God wants. However, growth is a slow process made up of many tiny movements strung together. If you seem too hard-line, a disciple may feel you are impossible to please or overly critical. In these cases, the tension no longer serves to stimulate positive change, but instead turns against you as her discipler. If you alienate your disciple, your chances of seeing the needed change decreases dramatically.

So which is it? Do you worry about being soft? Or do you worry about being too hard-line? Part of the answer has to do with knowing your own tendencies. Some people are hard-liners. Others are soft. If you know what kind of person you are by nature, you are in a position to make a course correction and proceed. Hard-liners must learn to err on the side of grace. Permissive (soft) disciple-makers must learn to hold the line on important issues, possibly well beyond what they instinctively feel is right. Both positions require movement that will not come naturally or easy. Ministry colleagues can often help you with this judgment if they are in your spiritual community and know the disciple. Involve them as to how to approach the person in balance and love.

FAILURE IN DISCIPLINE

Discipline in love is biblical, and it does work . . . but not every time and with every disciple. In some cases, even after a lengthy struggle over a serious issue, your disciple may remain essentially unchanged. When disciples refuse to respond to discipline, even moderately serious problems can become very serious.

Such unresponsive disciples will confront you with more difficult choices. Are you prepared to go on pursuing discipleship with a brother who won't make efforts to confront his own laziness or unwillingness to read? Would you be willing to pursue discipleship with a woman who continues to see nothing wrong with avarice? If you do continue, where do you see the relationship heading? Even moderately dangerous problems like these will effectively block your disciple from any significant leadership role. Track the trajectory of your disciple's current refusal to change and consider the character requirements for leadership roles. His or her future looks hopeless! All the same questions you asked yourself when selecting this disciple resurface in situations like this.

Sometimes your disciple will answer this question for you. Because of the ongoing tension in your relationship, the disciple may begin to move away from further involvement in your discipling relationship. Disciples who refuse to repent usually don't enjoy spending time with someone whose very presence reminds them of their problem. We have often seen disciples in this situation skipping meetings with their discipler and making lame excuses for their absence. At other times, resistance to God in one area begins to cascade into other areas. Lying, new attitude problems, and omission may all worsen when discipline is not accepted.

Hopefully, you have already counted this cost when you entered into the disciplinary phase of your relationship. Discipline often tends to "polarize" people. In other words, while some move closer to God, others are hardened in rebellion and actually get worse. This risk suggests that you shouldn't enter into discipline lightly. The dangers of polarization argue that discipline should be primarily reserved for more serious problems, and only where more positive measures have failed. Surgery on a tumor may involve significant risk, but if the tumor is dangerous, the risks are justified. Doing nothing involves risk as well.

How should you respond in the face of disciplinary failure? You may be right to unilaterally end the discipleship relationship. You can openly discuss this possibility with your disciple as a part of the disciplinary process. "Jim, I feel we're fooling ourselves by continuing to go through the motions of discipleship when it's clear you aren't willing to change." You can call on our disciple to give us a reason for continuing. You could ask, "What would you do if you had a disciple who wouldn't change his mind on an issue this serious?" As with other complicated decisions in disciple-making, multiple factors must be considered:

1. *Consider a change in the situation.* Some resistant disciples reach a point where they no longer feel like resisting God, and spontaneously change their minds. However, this possibility becomes less likely the longer resistance continues.

2. *Consider the needs of your church.* If other believers are eager to be discipled but no one is available, it becomes harder to justify continuing with a disciple who isn't willing to change. But if no other potential disciples are available, you may decide to persist even when facing a low probability of success.

3. *Consider the amount of investment you have already made in the relationship.* If you have years of investment with the person, you may be tempted to persist rather than write off all your efforts. On the other hand, you have probably heard the expression, "throwing good money after bad." You must be willing to face the truth, and a disciple persisting in serious sin is more likely to cost you additional years of wasted effort.

4. *What do your ministry colleagues think?* While the decision to end the discipleship relationship is yours to make as the disciple-maker, we recommend that colleagues should be consulted (probably multiple times) before making the decision to abandon the disciple-making relationship.

5. *How long has the refusal been going on?* If it's only a matter of days or even a few weeks, you should usually persist. The stakes are too high to make a hasty decision. The decision to terminate discipleship is usually made only after several months of struggle.

Most disciple-makers are very reluctant to end a discipleship relationship in failure. Some feel that such a move is judgmental and unloving. We don't agree.

First, you are not cutting the person off as a friend. You are merely ending the purposeful pursuit of discipleship. Discipleship is not right but a privilege. Disciples cannot demand this level of personal attention and at the same time refuse to make key decisions to follow God. By warning a disciple that you are considering ending the discipling relationship for basic friendship, you add another component to the disciplinary effort. We have seen disciples finally change their minds when confronted with this loss.

Second, you aren't removing the possibility of returning to discipleship later. Often, after losing the blessing of discipleship, a disciple realizes she would rather change. On several occasions, we have seen disciple-makers who stopped meeting with a resistant disciple later begin again because the disciple's attitude changed. Prodigal sons do come home.

While you may consider it harsh to put your disciple-making relationship on the line, what is the alternative? Can you reasonably consider it discipleship if the disciple has set preconditions that she be allowed to continue in serious sin? When the sin involved is serious enough to block future leadership or growth, the answer is obviously, "No." This would be *pseudo-discipleship*. You truly are wasting your own time and your disciple's time when you continue under these conditions.

Dennis: A disciple named Jim wouldn't stop going to drinking parties. At these parties, he regularly succumbed to heavy drinking and make-out sessions with girls. I told him firmly I would not spend time with him until he started taking his walk with God seriously. I felt bad when I saw he was hurt. But the time I was wasting with him became available for another young man who was being ignored. That brother is now proving to be a promising disciple. Meanwhile, Jim is still attending my house church, and I talk to him regularly. I may re-engage with him when I see he has a grip on his problem.

Offering discipline may hurt both you and your disciple for a time, and even separate you for a season or permanently. However, disciple-makers with integrity will put their discipling relationship on the line and be willing to lose a disciple rather than compromise with serious sin.

COACHING
SECTION THREE

Through helping disciples build faith, understanding, and good spiritual habits, you are laying a groundwork for healthy spiritual growth. But when Christians are growing spiritually, the natural response should be to turn around and use that spiritual progress to bless others. At this point, you move from being a disciple-maker to being a coach.

Although these stages have been presented sequentially, they usually overlap extensively. Spiritual growth develops best when believers are *doers* of the word. Young Christians should begin with the things discussed in this chapter early in their Christian lives while learning how to grow in other areas. Ministry to others provides a powerful incentive to spiritual growth. Those who fail to minister cannot understand why they should be zealous to strive and even suffer for the sake of growth.

12

Early Ministry
Development

Most Christians know that prayer, scripture study, and Christian fellowship are key avenues through which God feeds and nourishes spiritual growth. These "means of growth" are so essential that missing any one of them will eventually short-circuit a disciple's growth. Not all Christians are equally clear that ministry is also a means of growth. In fact ministry is no less important than any of the other avenues God has given us for spiritual health.

Ministry is the English translation for two main Greek words meaning "service." It is sometimes used in the sense of doing general good for others, but even more often for doing good aimed at accomplishing God's mission for Christians. When we render service intended to build up the body of Christ and expand the kingdom of God on earth, we are carrying out Jesus' instructions in the great commission (Mat. 28:18-20). All the passages on the body of Christ make it clear that the health of the church is the result of "the proper working of each individual part" (Eph. 4:16). Ministry is not just for church leaders. In your efforts to lead disciples into ministry, your hope should not only be to see them serving in general ways, but also to see them build defined ministry roles: roles where they have specific people and tasks for which they feel responsible.

Clearly, Christians should be zealous to accomplish the mission God has given them. Teach your disciples that more is involved than "doing my duty." Ministry is also a vital link to God and a crucial component in the healthy growth and happiness of any Christian.

In traditional western Christianity, ministry has often been restricted to the clergy. "Lay" people, or common people can do some forms of ministry, like painting the church building or singing a song. But advanced ministry roles like counseling, teaching scripture, leading groups of people, and discipleship are sometimes considered inappropriate for lay people. If your disciples come from a church tradition where ministry is not seen as essential for every Christian, you have some re-educating to do. The New Testament teaches that the Body of Christ depends not on the clergy, but on "the proper working of *each individual part*" (Eph. 4:16).

You have an immense volume of scripture you can use when conveying the importance of personal ministry. After sharing the Gospel with the Samaritan woman, Jesus expressed how doing God's will in evangelism fed his spirit: "My food is to do the will of him who sent me and to finish his work" (John 4:34). And he added, "I sent you to reap" the harvest.

Why does ministry feed our spirits? Probably the most important reason has to do with the connection between ministry and the New Testament concept of serving love. Understood properly, ministry means loving others "not with word or with tongue, but in deed and truth" (1 John 3:18 NASB; also see 1 Thess. 2:8). Giving ourselves to others is part and parcel of our ministry to them. All the passages that stress the centrality of love in the Christian life are really stressing the importance of ministry.

Happiness comes to those who learn to serve others in Christian love. After washing the disciples' feet, Jesus said, "I have set you an example that you should do as I have done for you" (John 13:15). And he went on to point out, "Now that you know these things, you will be blessed if you do them" (John 13:17). To be blessed is to be enriched, or to be happy! Many Christians today lack the blessedness God wants for them because they have not understood that they must serve others in ministry. The joy of others-centered living far exceeds any passing pleasure a believer can gain through living for self.

Learning to faithfully engage in ministry counteracts a selfish, temporal value system, replacing it with investment in eternal things like other people (See Mat. 6:19-21 and interpret in light of 1 Thess. 2:19, 20). Ministry also gives an outlet and an unselfish purpose to other means of growth. Apart from ministry, people view prayer, Bible study, and fellowship as mainly self-serving. Therefore, these avenues of grace will not result in growth beyond rudimentary levels.

In this chapter, we are going to discuss strategy and methods for helping your disciples develop their own ministries. We begin from the most basic level—with disciples who either do nothing in terms of ministry, or are brand new Christians. Then, we will think the process through all the way to completion—a disciple who has a fully developed ministry in several key areas.

DISCIPLES WHO DON'T MINISTER TODAY

Few disciple-makers would be happy with a disciple who rarely or never prayed. Why should you be happy, when such an omission would completely wreck your disciple's efforts to grow spiritually? Yet, some disciple-makers seem to see little problem when they work with disciples who never, or rarely give themselves away in ministry. Instead, you should see your disciple-making task as incomplete and indeed pointless unless it issues in "faith expressing itself through love." Paul says this is "all that counts" (Gal. 5:6).

Some disciples seem reluctant or ineffective in developing a personal ministry, believing ministry is inappropriate for lay Christians. Others aren't convinced ministry will be fulfilling, or are too selfish to be eager to serve. Some feel discouraged over past efforts to minister, or believe they are not qualified. They may resist the idea of ministry because they know they are completely untrained. You should explore your disciple's understanding and attitudes in this area to identify barriers.

But even disciples with willing hearts and a healthy sense of the adequacy of God still need training. We turn now to that task.

BUILDING CONVICTIONS

Your first goal is establishing firm convictions in your disciples that ministry is God's will for them, that it is doable, essential, and that their Christian life will be impoverished without it. Jesus taught that loving others is just like loving God (Mat. 22:36-40). John goes further still when he says, ". . . anyone who does not love his brother, whom he has seen, cannot love God, whom he has not seen" (1 John 4:20). You must convince your disciples that pursuing God apart from pursuing ministry is ultimately pointless.

It begins with working on your disciples' understanding of love. He may entertain a definition of love that centers more on feelings of affection than on sacrificial service. In the modern world, love is a feeling. It can happen at first sight. It may come and go unexpectedly, and whether we love depends on the person we love. Do your disciples understand the Bible's unique take on love? You can use hundreds of passages to show the difference between the modern conception of love as mere sentimentality, and the Bible's view of love as hard-core, committed servitude. At their root, most modern conceptions of love are self-centered—love is when another person makes us feel good. Biblical love takes the self out of love and replaces it with self-sacrifice. Jesus taught that, "Whoever wants to save his life will lose it, but whoever loses his life for me will save it" (Luke 9:24). This "losing our lives for Christ" means we turn away from the self-first approach to life, and give ourselves away to others.

As a skilled motivator, you should not downplay the enjoyment you derive from ministry. The thrill of leading a friend to Christ is too wonderful for anyone to live without, and you need to make sure your disciples see your enthusiasm. You should be sharing how fulfilling it is to have disciples, teach the word, lead groups of people, serve the needy—the whole range of Christian ministry. By pointing these things out, you are offering yourself as a model. In groups where people actively minister, they do so, not mainly because it is a duty, but because they enjoy it. In your presentation of ministry, you should stress what a privilege it is to serve God and others.

As you build these inner convictions into your disciples, they will usually make some faltering steps to minister. These may be as simple as sharing a thought at a Bible study, or helping a friend move from one apartment to another. The careful discipler is alert to each such occurrence. Watch and wait for something to encourage! Good encouragers usually are able to stimulate further efforts by suggesting specific possibilities for further ministry.

PRAYER

Earlier, we suggested teaching your disciples how to pray for others. Ministry is the natural context for many of these prayers. Begin early praying alone and with your disciple for his ministry. When you regularly plead that God will grant ministry opportunities for your disciple, you will usually see those prayers answered.

Each time you meet, you should ask how interactions have gone with non-Christians in your disciple's life. Then you should pray for each one by name. The same goes for believers your disciple has tried to build up. The things you pray for signal what you think is important. God uses these times of prayer by answering the prayers, and by causing your disciples' burden for ministry to grow.

EVANGELISM

Young disciples should be sharing their faith right from the beginning of their Christian life. Without some consistent effort at evangelism, disciple-making turns inward and will not result in authentic growth. Do not accept a version of disciple-making that merely focuses on self-improvement and ignores the mission Jesus gave us.

Each early attempt at witnessing is vitally important, and you should take every opportunity to thoughtfully encourage these attempts. Teach your disciples that even unsuccessful witnessing is a huge victory. The sower must sow the seed on all kinds of ground (Mat. 13:1-23). If possible, you should look for opportunities to meet your disciples' friends so you can help win them to Christ. If one of your disciples succeeds in winning a friend to Christ (with, or without your help) she will usually be excited about evangelism from then on. Such a new Christian could, in turn, be the gateway into your disciple's further ministry development as she helps her new Christian friend grow.

We recommend you read some good books on evangelism with your disciple. Faye's *Sharing Christ Without Fear* and Hybels and Middleburg's *Becoming A Contagious Christian* are good for motivating evangelism. (*Dennis:* Even my book, *Christianity: The Faith That Makes Sense* is good for getting ideas about what to say.)

At the same time you encourage witnessing, you can add some advice. After praising his efforts to make some points with a friend, you could also say, "That's a great start! You know, another point you could have made is . . ." Or after hearing that a disciple didn't know how to answer a hard question, "Oh, I know a good way to respond to that . . ." These suggestions often register visibly on the face of a young disciple. They may even say, "Man, I wish I'd thought of that!" To which you can reply, "Well, it's not too late. Maybe the next time you see her, just say, 'I was thinking about your question the other day, and it occurred to me that . . . .'" By doing this, you will send disciples back to people with whom they are sharing, armed with new ideas. You are actually training the disciples in ministry, but because the tidbits you suggest are linked to actual conversations, the disciples will remember them years later. This is field training—where the best kind of learning takes place.

EDIFICATION

Another area where even very young disciples can experiment with ministry is making efforts to build up (edify) other Christians. Most young Christians who are making friends in a local church will find opportunities to share or encourage others' faith. Again, you must be alert to simple acts of giving like these so you can powerfully encourage your disciples.

For instance, if you see one of your disciples talking with a friend at a home group, you could check in with that friend and ask what they were talking about. If you detect that the person enjoyed any aspect of the conversation with your disciple, you have the opportunity to stoke the fire of ministry zeal in you disciple by saying something like, "So, Jim was saying how meaningful your talk was . . ." Or, "Sherry said she felt encouraged by what you said the other night." Even if you don't have inside intelligence, you can always fish for information: "It looked like you were having a good talk with Bob. What was that about?" Usually, you can find something to encourage your disciple.

BUILDING MOTIVATION

If you succeed in getting your disciples to witness and build up other believers, you need to call their attention to the right things. Did they notice the power of God moving through them as they spoke? Do they realize how important their acts of ministry are, even in small areas? Do they feel honored to be used by God in his service? Have they realized they may have spiritual gifts in these areas?

Regular questioning is a key tool. "What do you think you could say to Julie that would help her in this situation with her roommates?" Or, "I sense that George has been discouraged lately. I wonder how we could build him up?" By putting such questions in a thousand different real-life situations, you teach your disciple how to think like a servant minister. At the same time, you are placing subtle suggestions for more ministry to others.

Suppose you discuss with your disciple how to help a mutual friend. Afterward, you may strategically take the opportunity to serve that person along the lines of your conversation. Later, you can share with your disciple that you used the ideas you discussed, and it seemed to help. Of course, what you're really hoping is that your disciple gets there first, serves the person and reports back to you. Then you can be the encourager again.

We find that disciples who are witnessing and trying to build up other believers soon come to love ministry. Watch for signs that your disciple is actively looking for opportunities to minister in small ways. These small acts of ministry begin to form a pattern. The others-centered way of life will begin to replace the self-centered way of life. You will soon find your prayer times expanding to others' needs as you pray for situations that come up in the course of ministry. Any conversation with non-Christians where your disciple didn't have the answers opens a new area for possible study. Hunger for learning grows rapidly within the ministering believer.

GIVING

This is also a good time to suggest a giving ministry. Giving is an essential part of a well-balanced personal ministry, and has a potent effect on the giver as well as the church. By beginning a habit of regular giving, disciples learn that God is the true owner of their money. Bringing their financial lives under the leadership of God ministers to potential dangers that could later derail their ministry development. Jesus said, "He who is faithful in a very little thing is faithful also in much; and he who is unrighteous in a very little thing is unrighteous also in much. Therefore if you have not been faithful in the use of unrighteous wealth, who will entrust the true riches to you?" (Luke16:10,11). According to this passage, God is not going to entrust ministry responsibility (our true riches) to one who is not faithful in the use of their money. If this passage is true, you are wasting your time helping a non-giving disciple build a ministry. God will oppose his progress until he begins to give back financially.

Jesus also said, "For where your treasure is, there your heart will be also" (Mat. 6:21). Believers who invest regularly into the things of God will see their hearts drawn to the place where they invest. Enhanced spiritual growth is a common by-product of giving.

EXPANDING MINISTRY

Evangelism

Disciples must learn ministry principles and methods. But we recommend teaching them to serve first. This way, they understand the principles at a deeper level. They can put methods into practice immediately, and this keeps methods from seeming like uprooted ideas that are hard to remember. Real life ministry situations call for good methods and principles, and when disciples are doers, they feel this need intensely. They will drink in your coaching like camels at a desert oasis. Quite often, learning ministry methods is a source of motivation in its own right. Disciples who learn excellent methods are usually eager to put them into practice, provided they already have the habit of seeking out ministry opportunities on their own.

Consider evangelism for example. Many disciples find that a major roadblock to sharing their faith with friends is the ability to bring up the subject of God and spiritual things with non-Christian friends. One way you can help is to role-play. You can do this informally by imagining scenarios with them, or recounting some of your own experiences when you discussed the Gospel with people.

For instance, you might recommend that your disciple bring up spiritual things by asking a friend, "Would you consider yourself a spiritual person?" Most people answer yes to this question. Regardless how they answer you could follow up either by asking, "Why not?" or "What does that mean to you?" Or, as Fay suggests, one could ask, "Do you have any spiritual beliefs?"

New Christians often find it easy to say, "Boy, I've been learning some interesting things about God lately." Or, "I feel like I might be having some experiences with God recently." After sharing this, they can easily go on to share what has happened in their lives. When you suggest concrete statements in this way, you will find your disciples will be far more likely to try some of your ideas.

You should make sure your disciples are able to articulate the Gospel of grace, and can share their own story effectively. Telling their story is often the best way to open positive and non-argumentative dialog. When one well-known pastor surveyed his non-witnessing church members to find out why they weren't witnessing, he discovered one leading reason: People didn't know what to say. This will happen with your disciples as well unless you equip them with ideas and content they can share in their own words. After this pastor introduced a training program for evangelism, his members witnessed to friends in great numbers.

As you coach, suggest ways to respond to various questions or comments they encounter. The discipler is a counselor/consultant in this situation. "So, have you had any more talks with so-and-so?" "What did she say?" "And what did you say to that?" "Not bad! Here's another idea if that comes up again . . ."

Equip your disciples to deal with rejection or hostility when they share their faith, and teach them to respond properly and patiently to those who are not initially responsive. New Christians are often surprised to discover the level of hostility from some people. Support them by helping them process this without becoming defeated or timid.

When you sense your disciple was stunned by rejection, bring these things to light for the person:

- "At times, people are defensive when they are under conviction. In other words, they are hostile because your sharing reminded them of the emptiness in their lives."
- "Weren't you the same way shortly before you received Christ? You can't go by a person's first reaction. There are too many examples of people who seemed hostile, but came to Christ soon afterward."
- "It takes time for family and friends to accept radical changes in one of their own. People will naturally be skeptical about any major change. Just because they made fun of it doesn't mean they won't be watching to see whether it's a passing phase or something real."

As a general rule, people fear rejection and ridicule. So, you should try some role-playing to show how a person can respond graciously and victoriously to a rejecter. For instance, a disciple might try to share with his friend, who retorts, "I'm not interested in that kind of crap!" If our disciple says, "Oh," that will be the end of the conversation, and probably the end of that witnessing opportunity. But if he answers, "Really. Why not?" the conversation will go on. If he follows with a question such as, "What experiences have you had with Christianity?" the person's misconceptions or fears may be revealed, leading to fruitful discussion. Most successful evangelists are heedless of resistance or negative comments. Many who ridicule a believer come to Christ in a powerful way later.

We also find that many Christians are too passive when sharing their faith.

Dennis: A believer recently told me how he invited his next door neighbors to come to a Bible study in his home. They shook their heads and said, "No, we'd never come to that."

His reply? He said, "Oh, that's cool."

He was way too passive. He should have said, "Why not?" and even been prepared to pursue it further: "I can't believe you're judging this before you've even seen it!"

As you coach your disciples, suggest they be bold enough to confront rejectors by saying, "I thought you believed people should be open-minded?" Often, people offer a rejection to invitations as a knee-jerk reaction. A moderate challenge to their position will often cause them to change their minds. Even if it doesn't change their minds, it leaves the conversation in a better place. The believer isn't endorsing their refusal by saying "Okay, that's fine."

As you give your disciples ideas for witnessing, they will usually try them out, especially if you are regularly praying together for opportunities to witness. You must be able to share recent experiences you had while witnessing or you will have little chance of inspiring consistent efforts to reach out for God. Remember, disciples will always see actions speaking louder than words.

As suggested earlier, the best thing you can do is go with your disciples to meet their friends. So often, you will find opportunities to witness, and your disciples will get to see with their own eyes how you do it. They will probably have far less trouble continuing the process after you are gone. Also, you will find it easier to coach them if you actually know the people involved.

When disciples become comfortable witnessing and trying to build up other Christians, they will also probably begin to see God bear fruit through their efforts. If you follow up their early efforts with ongoing suggestions, two things become increasingly likely: their witnessing results in someone meeting Christ, and their efforts to build up believers results in growing friendships with other Christians. Either of these becomes a door to expanded ministry.

Discipleship

If your disciples succeed in leading someone to Christ (particularly of the same sex) you should encourage them to see their responsibility to nurture further growth. You can suggest areas of truth they might teach their new Christian friend. New Christians urgently need training in the basics of the Christian walk. Understanding how and why to pray; why being in fellowship with believers is important; how to view suffering; and the role of the Bible are all issues your disciples should begin covering with new believers within the first days of their conversion. Biblical teaching on the nature of grace and on Satan will also protect them in the most vulnerable period of their Christian lives. If the new believer is in your Bible study or home group, you could do this training yourself. But why not have your disciple do it? By learning how to nurture a new Christian, your disciple learns crucial ministry skills that will be useful for a lifetime.

At the same time, disciples who nurture newly converted friends are building an important relationship. Such a friendship already includes sharing truth and feeling responsible for the other's spiritual well-being. This kind of relationship could easily grow into a disciple-making relationship. Your goal, as one who believes in multiplication through discipleship, must be that your disciples win disciples of their own.

Likewise, if your disciples are building up Christian friends, a door may open for disciple-making. The more someone encourages, serves, and instructs another, the more likely it becomes that the person benefiting from that help will look to the one who gave it for more help. In cases where no one is discipling the believer in question, and you sense one of your disciples commands a level of respect, you should suggest moving the relationship from simple friendship into discipleship.

Jesus said, "The harvest is plentiful, but the workers are few. Ask the Lord of the harvest, therefore, to send out workers into his harvest field" (Luke 10:2). If a young disciple is willing to disciple others, he should pray to the Lord of the harvest and let God know that he is willing to do this kind of work. Tell him to pray for opportunities, and pray together as well. Some win a disciple relatively soon after they begin to actively seek one. Others take a year or more. Either way, your disciples need to know it's important to seek out and find a disciple of their own, no matter how long it takes.

Once your disciple begins to disciple, you have crossed an important threshold. Instead of doing only informal, ad-hoc ministry, the disciple is now formally meeting with another to build maturity.

This is the point where coaching goes into high gear. You are now mentoring disciple-makers!

13

MOVING TOWARD
INDEPENDENCE

Unless you foster independence in your disciple, you may create an illusion of growth based on the disciple's desire to please you. This is manipulative and shortsighted, whether or not you realize it. Excellent coaching begins with a desire to help a disciple "fly solo." One of your main objectives in this advanced area of discipleship should be to help your disciple develop into an independent brother in Christ who has his own convictions and functions well apart from you. To such a disciple you can entrust leadership responsibility.

As a disciple-maker you may feel a type of herding instinct that you don't fully understand. It feels good to have people "with us," communicating, asking for advice, and working together in a group. If someone goes in another direction, or begins making decisions without consulting you, you may instinctively feel that you are being deserted. You may even find yourself thinking that he or she is unspiritual! If you feel this way when a young disciple begins to spread his wings, you should ask God to reveal any ego-centrism or control issues you may have. Quite often, a disciple-maker never realizes he has issues in these areas until his disciples become disciple-makers. It is a new life experience that reveals new issues to be dealt with.

Without independence, the process of multiplication quickly breaks down. Your goal for a disciple must be to reach a point where they no longer need you. A well-taught disciple will continue to serve God and others years into the future with little or no support from you! Even if everyone else quits, a committed servant of God will go on. To reach this goal, you must consciously foster independence from spiritual adolescence onward.

Once you learn and practice the art of coaching, seeing a disciple begin to spread his wings will be an exciting experience! You'll know it means he or she is close to spiritual maturity, and you will feel happy that you were there to help them. Elton Trueblood wrote, "The glory of the coach is that of being the discoverer, the developer, and the trainer of the powers of other men. But this is exactly what we mean when we use the Biblical terminology about the equipping ministry."[1]

As your disciple grows, your role changes. Instead of seeking to stimulate action, you must realize the disciple is already motivated to act. Coaching involves stepping back to take your place at the sideline. Give your disciple tips and advice on strategy, but remember . . . he is playing the game on his own.

COACHING THOSE WHO DISCIPLE

Disciple-making is a skill that takes years of practice to develop. Many have a hard time the first year they disciple. This is normal and should be expected. As a coach, you should become friends with anyone your disciple is trying to mentor. Knowing the third party will help you ask the right questions during coaching sessions.

When you do this, be careful not to take over. You should only help in ways you feel will enhance the discipling relationship so as not to accidentally discredit your disciple or rob him of the friendship forming by becoming too close to his first disciple. Most of the time, you'll want to work with this new person *through* your disciple.

Some new disciple-makers need lots of advice on what to study, how to motivate, when to move to the next level, and when to confront. When you meet with your maturing disciple, it's natural to ask how things are going with his new relationship.

When we meet with new disciple-makers, we usually subject them to a regular battery of questions about what they are seeing in their disciples and how they are assessing progress. If they don't know the answer to some questions, this shows what they need to explore. When they do have answers, we compare what they see to what we see. We are always careful not to undermine our disciple's confidence by doubting too many of his opinions. A good coach must assume God is helping a disciple discern the needs of others. We're careful not to make him feel like he is clueless. Consider this strategic, encouraging mindset when you meet with your disciple-makers.

Asking questions will play an important role in reminding your new discipler of key steps she may forget otherwise. For instance, you may know she tends to be weak in encouragement, and your questions could help her remember to encourage. Eventually, she will probably develop this habit when she sees how helpful encouragement can be. But early in the process, a coach needs to remind her.

Many of your questions should focus on prioritization. Although she may see many areas of weakness and need in her disciple, which one should she focus on next? By prioritizing, you help new disciple-makers refrain from calling for action in a hundred areas simultaneously. Too many imperatives lead to a sense of defeat, making spiritual growth a hopeless endeavor.

PLANNING

Experienced disciple-makers are able to make plans instinctively. They sense where disciples are in various areas, and know what they need most of the time. But new disciple-makers don't have this ability. They don't know how to assess and anticipate a disciples' needs, and they haven't developed the instincts needed for good planning.

As a coach, help your new disciple-makers along by discussing the principles of discipleship and the ever-changing conditions they face with their disciples. Here is where you will see the value of maintaining a friendship with the one your disciple is mentoring. You can use your own instincts, trained by experience, to sense progress and needs in the younger believer. Subtleties like shifts in attitude or a rise or fall in motivation are easier to see through personal contact.

If you aren't in a position to build a relationship with the person your disciple is mentoring, you have to gather your information through a strategic series of questions. Skilled disciple-makers know how to read between the lines and sense problems and opportunities during a questioning process. When you do this, don't jump to premature conclusions. Pray for a sensitivity to remember things said during sequential discussions, leading you to a growing certainty in your conclusions.

Try walking your disciple through discipling material like this book or others you like, stopping periodically to ask how your disciple feels she, or her disciple is doing in the areas covered. Be sure to follow up with the "why" question. Why do you feel that way? By thinking through these questions, the disciple-maker is forced to go beneath feelings and impressions to consider the actual data that does, or does not support her answers. This is the kind of thinking the disciple-maker needs to exercise in order to learn how to create helpful plans. As a coach, your hope must be to move your disciples away from "flying by the seat of their pants" and toward careful, prayerful analysis.

When you and your disciple-maker agree on a need to be addressed with her disciple, you should step her through a planning process. Help her anticipate possible reactions and create a response or direction for each possibility. Role-play is helpful here. What are some ways she could state the issue that would be sensitive? Be sure to point out the role of prayer and reflection *before* trying to effect change in a disciple. God can prepare people's hearts to hear what others need to say. Remind your disciple-maker to begin most interactions with positive comments. By sending your disciple-makers in to ministry interactions with a good plan and helping them become spiritually prepared, you their make success far more likely.

DEALING WITH SETBACKS

Making disciples always sounds like a great idea. But those who have the courage to actually engage with disciples soon realize it's a lot harder than they thought! Disciples often disappoint their disciple-maker. Progress is usually slow. And expectations often exceed what is realistic.

As a coach, you will play a major role adjusting your disciples' perspective on what they are doing. You will find many occasions where you need to calm anxieties, renew faith, and encourage success. The coach is a major source of positives in a project that could easily discourage an inexperienced discipler.

Here are a number of typical conversations you may need to have with your inexperienced disciple-maker:

Patience

First-time disciple-makers usually aren't used to the length of time required for real life-change. You might respond with . . .

"You have to realize these things take time. Think about where you were spiritually when you were just two years old in the Lord . . ."

"Your disciple was raised in a highly dysfunctional home; he doesn't understand how normal people relate. Give him some grace."

"Don't forget this guy's only about nine months old in the Lord."

Perception

Your disciple-maker may be missing key signs of micro-movement. Movement in the right direction can be quite subtle from one month to the next. You'll need to help her become sensitive to the slightest progress so she will be good at encouraging by saying . . .

"Yes, your girl fell into sin, but she's enjoyed a longer stretch of spiritual freedom from that since the last time it happened. A year ago she was doing this several times a month."

"She did that? That's impressive! I don't think she could have done something like that six months ago."

"Yes, she hasn't won anyone to Christ, but she is witnessing. That's a lot better than some believers!"

"Did you notice she asked about that Bible passage in the meeting last night? She must have been reading. That's progress."

Negativity

Satan will try to overwhelm your new disciple-maker with negative thoughts. An excellent coach's response might sound something like . . .

"Let's not forget that defeats like these are typical in ministry.

I remember having something similar with so-and-so and he ended up pretty good."

"Yes, you may have to give up for now, but this story isn't over. A lot of people in his situation change their minds after a time."

"God is powerful. I hope we're not discounting his power to change people's hearts. Maybe instead of despairing, we should pray."

General encouragement

Take opportunities as appropriate to point out how God is using your disciple-maker to bear real spiritual fruit . . .

"I don't know whether you realize how awesome it is that you have persuaded this woman to take an interest in someone other than herself."

"Boy, it would have been so easy to give up a couple of months ago when things looked so hopeless. But you just persevered and won the victory! I hope you remember this turn-around when disappointment hits again."

"A year ago, you were just focused on your own survival. Now you're focused on helping someone else. You should feel good about your spiritual progress."

These and scores of other situations call for the creative disciple-maker to engage in thoughtful dialog when coaching.

SKILLS NEEDED IN COACHING

Coaching is probably the most creative part of the disciple-making task. Good coaches must continually read complicated situations and creatively devise suitable responses. They must also try to anticipate needs and pitfalls so they can move in ahead of time with needed preparation. This new level of ministry competence calls for new ministry skills.

While Jesus was conducting his earthly ministry, he sent his disciples on short-term trips to spread God's word. One such time is recorded in Luke 10:

> *"After this the Lord appointed seventy-two others and sent them two by two ahead of him... He told them, 'The harvest is plentiful, but the workers are few. Ask the Lord of the harvest, therefore, to send out workers into his harvest field. Go! I am sending you out like lambs among wolves. Do not take a purse or bag or sandals; and do not greet anyone on the road. When you enter a house... stay in that house, eating and drinking whatever they give you, for the worker deserves his wages... Heal the sick who are there and tell them, 'The kingdom of God is near you.' But when you enter a town and are not welcomed, go into its streets and say, 'Even the dust of your town that sticks to our feet we wipe off against you...' 'He who listens to you listens to me; he who rejects you rejects me; but he who rejects me rejects him who sent me.' The seventy-two returned with joy and said, 'Lord, even the demons submit to us in your name.' He replied, 'I saw Satan fall like lightning from heaven.' "*

From this description, one can easily see Jesus used a number of key skills when coaching his disciples.

Directing

Jesus was very clear and directive when it came to describing the goals of the mission. He gave them a picture of what he wanted them to accomplish. He even set up possible scenarios and explained how to deal with them. He told them what to say, what to do, where to go, who to look for, and when to leave.

Yet even though he gave so much strategic direction, he still left room for enormous responsibility and freedom for the disciples. Jesus trusted that if they understood the big picture, along with some specific directions, they would figure out the rest.

Vision

While vision was covered in an earlier chapter, you need to see how vision is conveyed in the context of coaching. When Jesus sent out the seventy-two, he used vision in three ways.

First, Jesus explained their mission in a way that could be visualized. As he explained going from town to town, it is easy to imagine the things they had to do. They needed to meet a 'person of peace', stay at his house, accept his hospitality for as long as it was offered, and preach the kingdom of God. They were to go from town to town, and go without provisions. It's easy to picture being an empty-handed traveler looking for hospitality from strangers. Jesus wanted them to have the kind of vision that enabled them to see what they needed to accomplish.

Second, Jesus helped them to understand the potential failure they may face, adopting the kind of vision that looks beyond super-ficial circumstances. What if we encounter people who persecute us? "That's ok," Jesus says, "you can think of them as wolves and yourselves as sheep among them." What if we encounter people who reject us? "That's ok," says Jesus, "shake the dust off your feet when you leave that place. They are not rejecting you, but Me." Jesus does not send the seventy-two out wearing rose-colored glasses. He was very honest about the difficulties they may face, and he challenges them to look beyond those things. Appearances can be deceiving. What looked like failure may actually be to accomplish what they needed to accomplish.

Lastly, Jesus looked beyond the natural world into the spiritual world. As the disciples returned full of joy, Jesus encouraged their work with a peculiar statement, "I saw Satan fall like lightning from heaven." Something about their work had positive spiritual consequences that could only be seen with God's help. If God permits you to see something like this concerning the work of your disciple-maker, you should share it! If God does not give you any insight into the spiritual repercussions of your disciple-maker's actions, you must simply persevere in faith that our earthly actions are having supernatural consequences.

As you coach your disciple-makers, paint a clear picture of their mission, the spiritual truth behind difficult circumstances, and the supernatural reality beyond what they might experience with their senses.

Practice

Humans learn things the best through practice. As a coach, you should help your disciples practice ministry in two ways: role-playing and beginning true ministry.

Role-playing can be awkward and condescending, but it doesn't have to be. For instance, you can bring up a situation you have faced and ask your disciple how he would respond if in the same situation. Continue asking questions until a satisfactory resolution is reached. Or, bring up a situation he is facing and ask how he is planning to approach the situation: What is he is planning to say? What does he hope will happen? What will he do if the worst potential outcome is the reality? Hypothetical situations work well too, so explore these with your disciple-maker to practice adequate responses.

In addition to practicing conversations and teachings in your one-on-one time, disciples also need to get a taste for doing real ministry. Just as Jesus gave his disciples opportunity to minister while he was still physically with them, you also should push your disciples to begin ministering while they are in close proximity to you.

Goal-setting

God does not want his children to be aimless. Without ordering our thoughts and intentions, we will often be left in a self-centered rut, occasionally crying out to God for help. That's why successful disciple-makers create spiritual goals with their disciples. As the saying goes, "If you never set a goal, you'll make it every time." Spiritual goals are not antithetical to faith. The Bible affirms setting spiritual goals. Paul says, "Therefore I do not run like a man running aimlessly; I do not fight like a man beating the air" (1 Cor. 9:26). In other words, he set goals and pursues them.[2]

The proverbs warn that those who refuse to work according to a plan bring disgrace: "A sluggard does not plow in season; so at harvest time he looks but finds nothing" (Prov. 20:4). Unfortunately, many Christians could be described in these terms as well. By failing to do the early work in view of a later goal, they end up with no harvest.

Coaches who practice goal setting with disciple-makers usually have fun and see exciting results, especially when goals are understood under grace.[3] Make sure the goals you set together are achievable and measurable so you can celebrate success. An example of a measurable goal is, "I want to spend time with one new person each month this year." You could see whether you met this goal or not. It would be much harder to measure a goal like, "I want to be more relational this year." See the difference?

Under a grace approach to goal setting, you should rejoice even when a goal was only partially met . . . a partially met goal indicates more growth than meeting no goal at all. Aimlessness is bad, but no worse than the opposite extreme: legalism. The legalistic mentality turns goals into laws that define one's self-worth. Spiritual goals are a tool, a means to an end, not the be all and end all. Warn your disciple-makers that any goals you create may not be met. A person under grace views failure as an opportunity to set new goals and try again.

Persuasion

Paul says, "Since, then, we know what it is to fear the Lord, we try to persuade men" (2 Corinthians 5:11). The ability to persuade is of pivotal importance to every Christian worker. In Proverbs we read, "The tongue of the wise makes knowledge acceptable" (Prov. 15:2, NASB).

One of the best ways to persuade a disciple is to demonstrate that you understand him. Spend time praying about the disciple-maker you want to persuade. Then observe and attempt to appreciate the disciple more. Listen when he prays, take note of when he serves someone, and notice what kind of things bring him down. The ability to understand others is one aspect of wisdom.

Your persuasion will also increase if you demonstrate tact and sympathy. Remember this: kindness is not flattery. You can tell the truth in a compassionate way. If you become harsh with others, you will speak more from personal frustration than concern. It's easy for people to pick up on such frustration and discredit what you are trying to say. An even-tempered approach usually affects people in the most potent way. "A soft tongue breaks the bone" (Prov. 25:15b, NASB). However, we are not suggesting that you should never employ emotional heat! Jesus Himself rebuked his disciples on a number of occasions. But you must be sure your anger is righteous, and pick your battles carefully. Angry conversations should be rare.

Flattery is not persuasive. Honesty is. "He who rebukes a man will in the end gain more favor than he who has a flattering tongue" (Prov. 28:23 also Prov. 26:28b; Prov. 27:6). If you tell the truth while retaining the intimacy of friendship, your disciple-maker will trust and probably eventually appreciate any hard things you may need to bring up. Persons who habitually flatter others forfeit respect because they seem to be shallow and dishonest.

What some of us consider persuasion may be closer to begging.

Begging and "guilt-tripping" are only effective for temporary, superficial change. Persuasion is not manipulation either. Good persuasion involves effective use of scripture rather than out-of-context proof-texting. Persuaders are also able to develop good, critically sound arguments that make sense.

Coaching disciple-makers involves persuasion in a thousand situations. Your goal is to convince those you mentor that a particular approach is right. When you see a disciple taking a wrong approach to a ministry situation, don't say, "No, do it the other way." If disciples are continually told what to do, you will fail to develop independence. But if you can argue the principle involved, you equip disciples to understand similar situations in the future and react accordingly.

Not only should you hope to be persuasive with your disciple-makers, you also hope to teach them how to be persuasive with those they serve. Paul says to Titus, "These things speak and exhort and reprove with all authority. Let no one disregard you" (Titus 2:15). How could Titus prevent people from disregarding what he said? This is probably a call to use his powers of persuasion, as well as the spiritual conviction supplied from God's side. Paul had taught Titus how to persuade others. He would have used his own example, as well as regular feedback on what was, or was not persuasive in Titus' speech.

Discernment

Discernment is the ability to judge the difference between right vs. wrong, truth vs. falsehood, and wisdom vs. foolishness. Any Christian can acquire this skill. Hebrews teaches that, ". . . solid food is for the mature, who by constant use have trained themselves to distinguish good from evil" (Heb. 5:14). Mature Christians have been trained to discern through deep study of the Bible and regular practice. This passage implies that all Christians can enhance their ability to discern.

Without discernment, disciple-makers are taken by surprise in ministry. They won't notice that a disciple is slipping into an alienated state. Then when things get really bad, it seems like a slap in the face. Without discernment they may miss opportunities to give preventative advice, or buy into dishonest masquerading. Without discernment they may also write off someone with a good heart because of the person's rough edges. These examples result from only looking at the external. "So we have stopped evaluating others by what the world thinks about them" (2 Cor. 5:16a, NLT), or in NASB: "Therefore from now on we recognize no one according to the flesh."

Bible knowledge helps a disciple develop discernment by showing him God's perspective on life. The disciple must learn to look beyond first appearances. To drive this point home, find an older Christian whose discernment you respect and make it a point to go to them for advice. Ask how they came to the conclusions they share with you. Wise disciple-makers realize that discernment does not always have to come from within. Sometimes the wisest thing to do is go to someone else.

In coaching, another goal is to enhance the disciple-makers' level of discernment. Many of our coaching discussions center on comparing discernment regarding people or situations with which we are both familiar. When you see things differently than your disciple, you have the opportunity to ask how she reached her impression. These discussions often lead to investigations of people's motivations or underlying spiritual principles. Group dynamics, God's work in people's lives, the dynamics of sin, and Satan's next moves may all come up when discussing discernment.

Part of refining discernment includes teaching a disciple not to over-discern. Some people think they can tell what others are thinking or feeling in a way that becomes prejudicial. Good discernment is useful in showing what questions to ask. Any final conclusion in subjective areas like others' attitudes or secret motives must await confirmation through facts, including the person's own disclosures. In other words, if you think a person is bitter at another, you should ask questions to discover the truth. When the person admits she is bitter, you can confidently reach a final conclusion. If you jump to conclusions based on your supposed ability to discern, you will damage a relationship.

As you coach, take your disciples back to situations they misdiscerned and ask why they think they may have erred. Learning good discernment involves many trials and errors. Noticing errors in discernment helps us avoid putting too much confidence in our discernment. Applying the spiritual principles from God's word takes practice, as the author of Hebrews argued. By patiently guiding a learner through the process of refining his discernment, you can greatly increase his fruitfulness for God, and reduce frustration.

Try going over the goals for discipleship as described in Appendix 1 with your disciple-maker's person in mind. Looking at the list of traits and ask, "which of these is a real sore point for this person?" This will help awaken your discernment as you coach the mentor.

If you can coach your disciples into the disciple-making role with the insight offered here, you will equip them with all the most important ministry skills. Once believers succeed in discipling others, they are usually able to return to success again and again, creating a long legacy of fruitful believers.

14

COACHING

GROUP LEADERSHIP

If everything goes well, some of your disciples should reach a point where they are ready to lead a small group. We believe the best way to move into leadership is to first learn to lead one other person. If disciple-makers learn to lead one person successfully in discipleship, they are in good position to try their hand at leading larger numbers. In our church, we need to see disciples lead a small group successfully before leading a larger group, like a home church. This is in harmony with Jesus' principle that, "Whoever can be trusted with very little can also be trusted with much" (Luke 16:10). We also like to see a prospective leader actively witnessing. Leaders who don't regularly share Christ with the lost usually cannot lead their groups into witnessing.

At Xenos, we think that if we encourage people to teach and lead who have not witnessed or taken on private ministry like discipleship, we would present our church with models who are inadequate and will send mixed signals to our members. To build real evangelism and discipleship into the DNA of any church, the pastoral staff must use caution when placing individuals into public roles like teaching. In our opinion, having Bible knowledge and a gifting to speak aren't enough. We know that the rest of the church watches who we honor and respect as role models, and therefore effective and convincing service in non-public ministry is a prerequisite for public roles. Put differently, if someone wants to teach or lead at Xenos, the priorities are:

1. *Teach and lead yourself* – gain the character qualities typical of a serious Christian believer.
2. *Teach and lead others* – win a disciple (preferably a new convert) or two or three, and show that you can guide them into commitment and life change.
3. *Teach the public* – first in smaller groups, then in larger settings.

GETTING STARTED

How does your disciple end up leading his own group? He may initiate a neighborhood or workplace Bible study with friends. Or, a home group might be ready to plant a new group and will be starting small. In an organic approach, any disciple who is ready to lead a group will have one or more disciples, and other people who were brought in by him or his disciples. These would naturally be the first members of the new group.

Group leadership represents a new level of responsibility, with new dangers and opportunities. If you have adequately coached your disciple-maker, he should have a good chance of stepping up to this role successfully. But you will need to continue coaching for a number of months or more to guarantee success. People who succeed at leading their own group usually retain a high level of motivation indefinitely, so this is a solid move for any disciple-maker who is ready for the role.

One way to get started in coaching the role of group leadership is to co-lead the same small group with your disciple-maker for a period of time. By leading together, you get a chance to see how she thinks about situations and people you know well. That way, you can compare your own thinking with hers. If you currently lead a small group, you could have your prospective leader(s) sit in your leadership meetings for a number of months before sending them out with their own group.

At Xenos, we routinely have the prospective leadership team join the existing team for several months before a group plants. This way, we get to see the dynamics of their new team and get extra chances to comment on issues we see in their private lives or ministries. At the same time, the new leaders get to see how the older team relates. We model team dynamics for them: showing respect for each other, talking openly about issues, stressing prayer, encouragement, unity, etc.

Some churches design small groups led by teams of leaders. Others have single leaders. But even if your disciple is the only recognized leader in the group, he will need to cultivate a group of coworkers who help lead the group—which is really a team. A successful small group must maintain the unity of its leaders and top influencers. Disunited leaders are incapable of leading group growth. To maintain unity, group leaders must learn to deal with their conflicts maturely and quickly. Your task is to teach your disciple-makers how to work with their team to build unity and motivation. Your own example may be the best teacher. However, you should also go over principles like those found in Appendix 10.

If you can show your disciple how to build a unified ministry team, you have given her one of the most potent ministry tools possible. Quality leaders are consistently able to assemble teams of people who enjoy working together. Bringing people together and helping them overcome barriers to understanding, personal resentments, jealousies, and prejudice is typical work for leaders. Good leaders often engage in conflict management with peaceful results. Out of this set of opinion leaders comes a consensus that will motivate most groups to action.

LEADERSHIP THEORY

Most Christians are not fully aware of what leadership should look like. You may need to offer instruction in the areas of leadership responsibility and leadership characteristics. A vision of godly leadership can be extremely motivating.

Christian leaders have spiritual responsibilities. As Christian leaders we are accountable to God for the way we conduct ourselves. James 3:1 says, "We who teach will be judged more strictly." Before we send someone out as a leader, we need to be sure they know what roles they should be playing. Christian leaders have to function in a number of areas, and different leaders will perform better in some areas than others. Leaders should appraise their own strengths and weaknesses, not hesitating to get help in their weak areas when possible. At the same time, all leaders need to be ready in principle to perform in all of these areas on occasion.

In Appendix 11, you will find a summary of the main biblical roles leaders should fulfill. This would be a good study to go over with your disciple-makers before they go out as leaders. By teaching what leaders should and should not do, you protect your disciple-makers from being manipulated into assuming improper roles later.

Delegating and Empowering

When your disciple-maker begins leading her own group, coach her on the process of delegating leadership to members in the group who will become the next leaders. Coaches provide needed discernment during the process of empowering and training new leaders.

For one thing, you should watch for signs that your disciples are trying to do everything in their new group. New leaders often think they are responsible for all the spiritual work in their group. They may be weak in delegation skills. Any time we find new leaders reporting that they are tired or "stressed out" in their new group, we investigate whether some work could be delegated to others in the group. Quite often, we have to remind leaders that their role is not primarily fishing, but teaching others to fish. Of course, feeling stressed out or burned out can also be the result of failure to depend on God for ministry results.

Another area where a coach is powerfully used by God is the discernment as to what tasks group members are ready to take. Over-delegation can lead to discouragement if your disciple-maker puts people into positions for which they are not ready, resulting in failure. At the same time, group members need to be stretched or their growth will be stunted. So, because this area is not always easy to determine, frequent discussions between you and your new group leader will be very helpful.

Teaching

Disciples who move toward group leadership need to learn how to teach scripture if this doesn't come naturally. These involve spiritual gifts, but are also learned skills, and you can greatly enhance a disciple's ability to communicate with groups through careful coaching. Begin this training while your disciple is still in your own group, so you know for sure he can communicate effectively to smaller groups of believers.

Teaching or preaching usually involves larger groups like home churches, youth groups, children's classes, or special events. At Xenos, we usually have to show disciples how to put a Bible teaching together.

We work hard to ensure they know how to develop the key elements that should be present in every teaching: Introductions that arrest attention, conclusions that summarize the big picture in a way people will remember, and clear content in the body of the teaching.

We also like to teach our disciples how to present information in a thesis-antithesis format. In this approach, each major point is argued alongside an antithesis. The antithesis is what we argue *against*. The approach, "We want to do this, not that," or "This is true, not the other thing some believe," adds conflict and interest to a teaching. People like debates. In this approach, the teacher debates with himself.

Even when our disciples have excellent content in their public teaching, they at times lack affect, or feeling, in their presentation. Many new teachers are too inhibited when speaking to groups, so we provide them with input and observation about their presentation. We teach them to monitor their volume, facial expressions, eye contact, and body language.

If possible, especially when a disciple is beginning to learn how to speak to groups, you should encourage him to bring his teaching notes and practice it with you. This serves two purposes: it helps him get used to giving his teaching in front of an audience, and it gives you the chance to share pointers that could improve the teaching. Your effort should be to engineer success in early teaching experiences. This will prevent your disciple from developing aversive feelings about public speaking.

LEADING DISCUSSION

Even more common than public teaching is facilitating or leading a group discussion. Leading discussion doesn't require any particular spiritual gift, so most disciples should be able to learn how to lead discussion skillfully. Developing this skill will empower your disciples to effectively lead smaller groups where so much ministry occurs.

When you teach discussion skills, you need to cover the main sections in a guided discussion. Here's what we coach our disciples to do at Xenos:

Introduction

In our introduction, we touch on the skills of public speaking. The leader must stimulate and excite the group about the subject under consideration. During this first part of the meeting, the burden is completely on the leader to raise the group's consciousness of the issues. This is done by defining what the issues are, and why they are urgent. Also the leader should emotionally engage the group with both the subject and with the leader himself. If this part goes well, the leader will have achieved arousal. People sit up, furrow their brows, smile, laugh, and in other ways show that they have been impacted emotionally, whether excited, disturbed, provoked, or inspired.

Probes

Next, the leader will introduce "probes" or questions intended to prod members toward a particular line of thought. We teach our disciples how to devise effective probes that lead to good discussion. The most important thing we explain is that discussion is not *recitation*. Recitation is when the instructor calls on the group to clarify content or asks questions requiring specific knowledge of study content. For instance, "Where does Paul teach on the body of Christ?" is a recitation question because it requires prior knowledge which is recited in the group. This will not lead to discussion. Discussion questions, on the other hand, involve creativity, problem-solving, personal opinion, and personal experience. One could set up an apparent contradiction in an introduction, and then ask the group how it might be resolved. For example, we might open with an illustration like this: "Paul says 'knowledge makes arrogant, but love builds up' in one passage, and 'may your love excel in all knowledge and discernment' in another. How do we reconcile these?"

Or, we ask them how a particular truth might apply either to life in general, or to specific situations we might imagine. "How would you apply this to someone who is worried about a shortage of income?" The point of good discussion probes is to stimulate thinking and sharing that is accessible to anyone. They don't have to know the material in advance, but they do have to *engage* with the material. Overly simplistic questions and yes-no questions also make poor probes.

Responses

As group members suggest answers, the discussion leader must respond. Responding during discussion is a complex skill involving a brief summary of what the person meant, approval for their efforts to share, and a call for more from the group. But responses can't be long and drawn out. The leader shouldn't give mini-sermons after each comment from the group or discussion will collapse. Then too, the leader has to decide when to move on to another subject. These skills and the others involved in successful discussion leading take practice. We coach our disciples to respond the right way by sitting in on the discussions.

After a practice session or an actual discussion, we offer a critique on content and delivery. We are careful not to be too critical, but we know disciples won't progress unless we are willing to offer needed correction. Some times, we record a teaching or discussion and go over the tape interactively with our disciples. We point out the good points as well as those needing improvement. After one or two successful discussions, we simply review our disciple's discussion probes and plans, just to make sure they will be good for discussion.

Any disciple who learns to give edifying teachings or discussions has a valuable ministry tool that will increase her credibility and lead to additional ministry opportunities.

ASSESSING A GROUP

Hebrews 13:17 mentions another role for leaders: "They [leaders] keep watch over you." If you are coaching disciple-making small group leaders, you are a church leader. Part of your role is to keep an eye on the spiritual health of the part of the church you oversee. Just as good shepherds watch out for their sheep, you must be shepherds who follow Jesus' example. A good leader periodically asks questions like, "Are there any unhealthy trends in our church? What is the cause? What will help to turn this around? What part should I play?"

If you have a disciple leading a Bible study or fellowship group, you must show him how to think strategically about the group. Good leaders are continually asking themselves questions about the group's health. Only the most natural, instinctive leaders ask these questions without prompting. For most disciples, you should go over what questions to ask in a number of areas. The more specific these questions are, the more you can rely on your assessments. Consider going over questions like those in Appendix 9 with your disciple-makers.

ENCOURAGEMENT

Whenever new servant leaders emerge, their coach has a great opportunity to encourage them. This encouragement could be some of the most powerful encouragement ever. New leaders are not sure what they will be like as leaders, and they may come under accusation that they are inadequate. You should let them know what you think.

Honesty is important now, even if you have some hard things to say. You should show an emerging leader something about his tendencies before he is leading alone. Move through the various leadership roles (teaching, disciple-making, administrating, etc.), and leadership characteristics (patient, self-disciplined, self-giving, etc.), asking your disciples how they would rate themselves in each area. Ask, "Which are key areas of strength? and, Which are areas of weakness?" Consider your own thoughts about their strengths and weaknesses before you ask these questions. Then, you can compare your impressions with theirs and have a solid dialog.

As the rigors of group leadership wear on your disciple, only strong encouragement will sustain her. Help her understand why disappointment and setbacks are always part of a life of service. Be sure she notices and rejoices over every victory, no matter how small.

You should also check the effectiveness of your disciple's level of encouragement with her own people. How does she try to move her group forward? Issuing regular directions is far less powerful than asking questions and offering lots of encouragement. But remember, one can't encourage until there is something real that deserves encouragement! If you are not attending the group your disciple leads, only lengthy conversations will enable you to sense conditions in the group and how your disciple is leading.

RELEASING:

PREPARATION

Releasing a disciple means your task is complete. When disciples are released, you will send them off to continue their own ministry without much ongoing support. Sooner or later, if you are to continue raising up new disciples, you have to let the old ones go. This should be a natural process where both disciple-maker and disciple agree. You will no doubt continue to enjoy your friendship, but at this point, it will be at a somewhat distant level. You will probably no longer have time for weekly meetings, but you may get together occasionally.

The most natural way to release disciples is in association with group multiplication. If you lead together with your disciples for a time, and your group is growing, you naturally reach a point where you need to multiply and launch a new group.

In a model used by some churches, mature disciples go out alone to begin a new group, which may be made up of people from the larger church who want to join a home group. In other cases, disciples begin a new group from scratch, often with friends and neighbors to whom they have witnessed. In churches without home groups, a disciple may join a different ministry team, or just move into a different sphere of ministry within the same team.

Just because your disciple is leading his or her own group doesn't mean you are done! Even though the process of releasing may begin when disciples start leading their own groups, it may not be complete for months thereafter. You should continue to meet for some time, monitoring their progress with the new group and completing the coaching process. You also have to make sure key points have been covered that will help them withstand the rigors of Christian service. Only then will you be ready to fully release them.

TEACHING GOD'S PART IN MINISTRY

If disciples are to survive and flourish in leadership, they must develop a clear understanding and dependence on God's part in ministry. Be prepared to teach specifically on what you expect God to supply in your ministry to others. Many disciples have a vague idea that God should help, but may not understand what to pray for. Teach them to look for God's help in the key areas that follow.

First, God wants to *direct* the ministry of a leader. They should go to the scriptures and to the Lord in prayer, seeking to know his will for their ministry. Ministry that departs from God's direction may bear some kind of fruit, but becomes "wood hay and stubble" the further they depart from the leading of the Holy Spirit (1 Cor. 3:10-15). Interestingly, God seems willing to continue using some ministries and church leaders that are off-target, apparently because he places a higher value on reaching the lost than on complete fidelity to his leading. Paul observed this phenomenon in Rome. (Phil.

1:15-18 see also Mark 9:38-40). Even in 1 Corinthians 3, the "wood hay and stubble" may be used by God, but it will not be rewarded. In fact, the Bible abounds with examples where God continued to use leaders who went astray, sometimes very badly. What are we to conclude?

On one hand, since God wants to direct our ministries, we should seek that leading often and earnestly. Even though God may continue to use off-target ministries, we assume that we will bear more spiritual fruit the closer we are to his ideal. This is increasingly obvious as time goes on. In the short term, human-based ministry may look good, but it tends to deteriorate over time or bring disgrace upon the Lord's name. On the other hand, we should never become paralyzed by the notion that "Unless I know exactly what God wants in each situation, I can't move forward." We can move forward based on the general knowledge of what God wants, and in areas we are unsure, we can remain open to any correction in our course that God may want to show us, knowing that he will not let us come to irreversible harm (Phil. 3:15).

God's direction extends not only to major issues like whether to preach the word or to disciple others, but to more subjective areas like when someone is ready for leadership, or who we chose to disciple. Teachers have to consult God on what slant to take when teaching a particular text. Evangelists must ask when to make a more direct call on the lost. Leaders must plead for insight as to how much to expect from a particular disciple. All believers need discernment as to Satan's next move. In all, there are thousands of decisions in ministry requiring divine guidance.

Secondly, God *empowers* the ministry of a leader. Jesus' declaration that "apart from me you can do nothing" (John 15:5) is again, a figure of speech. He doesn't mean we can do nothing at all, but that we can do nothing of spiritual value apart from him. As Christian leaders, we realize that we depend absolutely on God for things like:

Evangelism

While a warm demeanor, patience, good arguments, and heartfelt pleas matter in evangelism, only the Holy Spirit can finally convict a person of their need for Christ and bring them to repentance (John 6:65).

Conviction

We can preach truth, but we must depend on God to convict people's hearts to follow the truth. Apart from spiritual conviction, people will listen to the truth with passive curiosity. This is probably the power Paul referred to in 1 Cor. 4:20: "For the kingdom of God is not a matter of talk but of power."

Development of Christian character

No amount of blustering and Bible-thumping will transform human lives, "for it is God who is at work in you, both to will and to work for His good pleasure" (Phil. 2:13).

Overthrowing Satan

How could any human hope to impact a spiritual being like Satan apart from the power of God? (2 Cor. 10:3-5; Rom. 16:20).

Filling Christian meetings with spiritual power

Paul asks his friends to pray that he be "given utterance" when preaching (Eph. 6:19). He knew that preaching must be anointed by the Holy Spirit in order to be effective.

Failure to understand or believe in God's role in ministry will always have negative results. These results include arrogance during "in season" times, as well as panic, pushiness and discouragement during "out of season" times. On the other hand, reliance on God's role in ministry will promote thankful humility during "in season" times, and stable perseverance during "out of season" times. Those who depend on God's part in ministry have confidence in God's adequacy to minister through us.

When your disciples achieve balance in their view of God's and human's part in ministry, their ministry will reflect that balance. You should watch for signs of imbalance in this area right up to the time you release your disciples.

PERSPECTIVE ON FAILURE

One key goal with outgoing disciples is to make sure they develop a biblical theology of failure. Experienced servants of God know that real ministry includes failures as well as success. This could include failure in their new group. Some new leaders become soft from experiencing too much success. Such leaders are like a child riding a bike on training wheels who thinks he has actually learned to ride. His parents warn him, "It's a little harder when you take the wheels off," but until they actually do take them off, the kid continues to enjoy a false sense of mastery. Once the wheels come off, the child may have to endure a few nasty crack-ups that could lead to tears, and even a refusal to ride any more. However, without removing the wheels, he will never learn to ride. Successfully leading a group of people for God is a complex task that takes time to learn. Like any complicated task, there is no reason to believe success will be found instantly or repeatedly without failure.

In our own training, failure has played a prominent role, and in fact a crucial role that success never could have played. We have failed at group leadership, where groups disintegrated in spite of our best efforts. We have failed at evangelism, personal discipleship, and assorted ministry projects, often with embarrassment and a feeling of public disgrace. While we still don't enjoy failure, we increasingly realize that nothing teaches us more than our failures!

Dennis: Some years ago, I was asked to teach a group of young athletes from an area high school. I took a guy I was discipling at the time, and we began meeting with this exciting group of twenty-five promising new Christians. For six months, we held meetings which seemed to be quite good. But for some reason, the group was steadily declining in attendance. Within six months, attendance had dwindled to less than ten students. And it continued to drop. Eventually only two to four guys were still coming. But we carried on.

One evening in early summer, we arrived at the house where the study was to be held that week, and nobody was home! We sat on the front lawn and waited a full half hour. Nobody came. I turned to my young friend and said, "I think our work here is done."

Not all failures are so clear-cut. But we have presided over dozens of failed groups and projects. Why does God let failure come to sincere servants? This is a wonderful question to discuss with your disciples *before* they actually experience failure to prepare them for the inevitable.

Out of failure your disciples (and disciple-makers) will learn to be effective. Biblical guidance is important in ministry, but disciples are still left to apply biblical teaching in area after area, and these are often judgment calls requiring wisdom and experience. Success in ministry can often lead to the wrong conclusions.

Suppose a disciple concludes—based on his success—that his ministry methods must be extraordinary. However, in reality his success was the result of something completely different. His attributing his success to superior methods may be wrong, but he has no way of knowing it until he fails using those same "miracle methods." The experience of failure typically throws a disciple into state of amazement and disillusionment. This confused state of mind is exactly what God needs to bring him out of his ego-driven paradigm. Only then will the disciple listen to new ideas, new ways of explaining past success, and engage in original thinking for the future.

Through failure, disciples learn the importance of dependence on God (2 Cor. 11:30-33). At the heart of a carnality in leadership is often a self-sufficient attitude. A shortchanged prayer life is a warning signal, but this easy to ignore. Failure, however, is much harder to ignore. As a disciple strikes in one direction and then another, failing at each turn, God is able to corner him into conclusions he wasn't willing to look at before. A growing sense of ineptitude at the deepest level begins to strike a note of caution in all he does. Ironically, this sense of helplessness grows at the same time he knows he is increasing his competence in the basic skills of ministry. Such an inner tension is exactly what God uses to convince a disciple that he alone can bring ultimate spiritual success. As Paul expresses it, "We have this treasure in earthen vessels, so that the surpassing greatness of the power will be of God and not from ourselves" (2 Cor. 4:7).

Through failure, disciples deepen their discernment: Is your disciple working toward the wrong goals? It is common for believers to assume that good results, like greater numbers, are the will of God, and that certain types of people are best suited to lead. These assumptions may be partly right, but they often overlook important exceptions that could lead to unfairness or corruption in the church. God often shows us through failure that we are looking at things superficially and that we need goals more in harmony with the deeper picture. We may realize that our pragmatism leads to outward results without inward spiritual reality. At other times, we may see that our super-spirituality has led us to ignore the plain facts of our situation.

Through failure disciples learn how to minister under grace. God may have to work with us for years to bring us to the place where we understand in our hearts how it can be possible that our abilities matter, and yet take no sense of egotism from it. Most young ministers insist on taking their identity from their ministry results. Usually, only profound failure will convince us that "apart from the vine we can do nothing," and yet we need to strive all the harder (1 Cor 15:10). This is the paradoxical outlook of the mature worker—an outlook only accessible through a combination of success and failure.

Through failure, disciples develop deep spiritual convictions about ministry: Most disciples become excited about doing ministry because of the thrilling experiences they have while doing it. Such profound thrills are some of the most gratifying pleasures we can experience in life. On one level, God must approve of our feeling good from ministry victory, because he says we will be more "blessed" if we serve (John 13:17). But feeling pleasure is not the foundational motive for serving God. We must learn to do it because God wills it, even if no one else does it, even if we don't succeed at it, and even if it brings us pain and frustration. 1 Cor. 4:2 says, "It is required of stewards that one be found trustworthy." The text doesn't say "successful," but "trustworthy."

Failure separates the quitters from the servants. Failure is a painful experience that puts the question squarely: Am I going to continue doing something that often brings me pain? God also uses other painful experiences to put this question, such as betrayal by friends, suspicions, lack of appreciation, and accusations from our people. But failure seems to be the supreme negative experience. God wants to know whether we are prepared to serve in failure, or only in success. In 2 Tim 4:3, Paul urges Timothy to "be ready in season and out." Isaiah's call in Is. 6:8-13 promised a ministry characterized by failure throughout. But Isaiah was willing and faithful to that calling—and he did fail. Nobody ever listened to Isaiah, and all the judgments he warned of eventually happened. And this in spite of the fact that he spent three years preaching buck-naked! (Is. 20:2, 3). Talk about hard duty! We may not be called to anything as difficult as Isaiah, but God will test each minister on this point (often though failure) to purify our motives.

Leaders broken through failure become suitable tools in the hands of the Lord. But unbroken leaders pose a threat to the health and spirituality of the church. Leaders accustomed to nothing but success become hard to lead. They are always convinced they are right, and will fight to preserve their base as though their self-worth depended on it, which it often does. In their dread of failure, they may become downright unethical and manipulative. When success becomes the be-all and end-all in ministry, God must throw down that idol. Failure may come in an area other than our main ministry, but it will surely come.

Leaders inexperienced in failure not only fear failure in themselves, but also in others. They may become unwilling to let others have the chance to fail, and this leads to poor delegation in discipleship. Young leaders are hardly ever as competent as older ones, and history shows they are more likely to fail. But this observation begs the question: Is such failure necessarily a bad thing? We argue that it need not be bad, especially when new leaders have been well trained in their view of failure. Those who dread failure tend toward a conservatism that seeks to protect the existing ministry rather than open new ministry. When the church becomes conservative and self-protective, it loses the offensive spirit needed in spiritual war. We find ourselves unable to penetrate tough sectors of the non-Christian community.

Convince your disciples that nothing will advance them more than getting some good failure under their belts! Assure them it isn't that bad once you get used to it, and the fruit over the long haul is well worth the pain.

The experience of failure is always a crisis, because Satan will move in and suggest God let them down, or that they are unworthy for such work. Therefore, you should actively prepare your disciples for failure as well as for success.

If your disciples suffer from fear of failure, tell them to ask themselves, "What is the worst thing that can happen to me if I fail?" Does failure in ministry really endanger our lives, or only our egos? The ego-centered minister dreads failure mainly because he will have to admit it to colleagues or others he hopes to impress. Just imagining himself admitting defeat can send the ego-driven leader into a panic of self-protection. But God calls us to deny self and serve in ministry, not to glorify ourselves through it. Your disciples should imagine themselves shrugging their shoulders before colleagues and saying, "Yeah, that didn't work out, but at least we tried." And they shouldn't forget to add, "I guess we'd better try again!"

Disciples who have developed deep convictions about how to handle failure are truly prepared for the rough and tumble of real-life ministry.

INTEGRITY AND STABILITY

Leaders are regularly battered by circumstances, by Satan, and by their own people. All good leaders must demonstrate that they can take it without losing composure. People are drawn to strength of character, and tend to believe what strong people say. While they may feel sympathetic toward the weak, they tend not to follow them. This doesn't mean leaders should pretend they are not suffering, but that their determination and integrity dictate that they maintain consistency even in the face of suffering.

It also means that a leader would continue to pursue the right goals and live for God even if no one else follows. A good leader is not afraid of rejection by his followers because his concern is doing right, not being followed. Jesus taught that the good shepherd "goes out before them" which means such a shepherd sets a course knowing the sheep will follow after. (John 10:4). When people sense that a leader is more concerned about being followed than about what God wants, they grow cynical about following. Most people are suspicious of leaders anyway, and will test leaders by threatening not to follow. Only when they see that a leader can't be manipulated will they realize their choice is to follow or to take their chances elsewhere.

Stress the value of stability with your disciples. Good leaders are relatively stable over a period of years. While poor leaders periodically strike off in radically different directions, good leaders commonly stick with their handful of central values and convictions. Innovation takes the form of finding new and different ways to achieve old goals that haven't changed in decades. Another common form of instability is quitting. Unstable leaders leave the work for various reasons, while good leaders are present and accounted for year in and year out.

Many who demonstrate terrific natural charismatic leadership ability end up being poor leaders because of the erratic course of their lives. Others, who manifest little natural leadership end up being respected and effective leaders because of their sheer dogged focus on basic biblical principles. In times of crisis, people tend to fall apart and panic, often proposing destructive radical solutions to the problems at hand. The good leader is the one who stands firm under crisis and cannot be moved from the foundation of truth. People are attracted to such stability and reliability, rightly discerning that such reliability is the result of clear vision for God's way.

COMPROMISE

Teach your disciples when it's right to compromise. Ironically, good leaders are also compromisers at times. While doggedness and determination are important, perfectionism works against effective leadership. We live in a fallen world where our visions will never be completely fulfilled. People never quite do what they should, and life always presents us with the unexpected. As a result, leaders realize they need to get the best they can, while not insisting on perfection or even on complete agreement.

Wise leaders realize that the closer they come to their goal, the better, and that any movement is better than no movement. They also realize that their following will be very small unless it includes those who have a different view in some areas, even though they generally agree on the most important issues. They must prioritize goals and feel good when major goals are attained even though lesser goals are not. Leaders who fail to prioritize, or who are perfectionist, run the danger of eventually breaking themselves and those around them. They are poor at team building, and cannot negotiate effectively. In the end, they nearly always forfeit their following.

As your disciples progress in leading their own disciples, and you complete the task of teaching key values like these, you'll naturally reach a point where you begin to sense you are no longer needed. If you succeed in discipleship, you work yourself out of a job.

16

RELEASING:
THE TRANSITION

In our experience, the best and most common way to release disciples is by agreement. Successful disciples naturally become busier as their following grows. Eventually they have trouble fitting an extra meeting with their mentor into their schedules. Your disciples may suggest ending your meeting, and you should agree. You will sense they have more areas in which to grow, but that sense will never dissipate completely. Disciples often develop a healthy urge for independence. If they feel the need for help, they know your number, and you can suggest periodic get-togethers.

In other cases, disciples won't suggest ending your meetings, but you will hear them complaining about being too busy. In these cases, suggest reducing your meetings from meeting weekly to meeting monthly. This suggestion is usually welcomed without much argument. Monthly meetings are sufficient to stay in touch with how things are going, and the longer intervals between meetings encourage more independent and creative thinking. Whether the monthly meetings happen, or how long they happen depends on how much you or your disciples desire them. Usually, they taper off and become irregular.

Alternatively, you can suggest moving to unscheduled meetings as needed. You will both understand that you won't be meeting as often as before, but you are still expressing availability. If you are involved in different groups, these meetings also tend to diminish in frequency. However, you will both still enjoy infrequent meetings where you catch up with each other.

In some special cases, you may continue with weekly meetings, even though the discipling component is over. If you are anything like the two of us, you may simply enjoy getting together regularly with a close friend.

Dennis: I continue to meet weekly for breakfast with my original disciple, Gary. We've been meeting now for over thirty years. Of course we long ago moved away from a discipling relationship and into a peer fellowship meeting. Jessica and I also meet weekly for dinner, as we have for many years. The point of such meetings is pure enjoyment of a good friendship. Even though we lead different groups, it's wonderful to track each other's lives and share insight and encouragement.

NURTURING ONGOING MOTIVATION

When disciples have been released, they hopefully continue to serve God, but now without the regular coaching and support they had when you were discipling them. But when disciples are no longer reinforced with your support, a crisis may result. They still have the rewards that come from a life of service, but this may be noticeably less gratifying than the encouragement you were supplying. Some disciples begin to feel a sense of isolation or lack of appreciation. They begin to face the question of why they are living this way if no one appreciates it. Viewed biblically, you must realize they are under pressure from God to shift their motivational base off sociological support and human appreciation, and directly onto God. Moving back in to a close support role would usually be a mistake. Although it may be hard to see a friend suffer, recognize that this adjustment is needed and healthy.

This crisis may be very acute if most of their motivation has been based on human emotional support from their discipler. Therefore, wean your disciples off any dependence on your encouragement well before you release them. The crisis will also be worse if they have little understanding of why they do what they do, or little personal conviction about why their goals are right and urgent. This danger also suggests you work well ahead of time on building a deep under-standing and deep convictions about ministry.

If you sense a released disciple is struggling during periodic meetings after releasing them, you must be ready to enter into a counseling process to help your disciples process their feelings. They need to see the importance of shifting away from a wrong to a right motivational base. They must learn to draw their life directly from Christ at a new level. Point these things out and offer insight about their motivations and emotional needs, but they must figure out for themselves how to integrate the insight into daily living.

This period after releasing a disciple is when you will find out how well you did as a disciple-maker. The foundation you thought was adequate is shaky when you see a decreased level of motivation or even a desire to quit. If you re-insert yourself into their schedule with periodic meetings, you can usually talk them through such an adjustment period.

You can also significantly help release your disciples by introducing them to other disciple-makers for fellowship and encouragement. We will discuss this option in the last chapter.

LEADING
DISCIPLEMAKERS

With diligence and hard work, pastors, ministry team leaders, or para-church leaders can succeed in building an ethos of discipleship in their groups. When people buy into the notion of discipleship, the result is multiplication. Over time, the group may include a growing number of disciple-makers. Successfully leading a group of disciple-makers is a key challenge for upper-level leadership.

As leaders in a church where more than a thousand people meet weekly with their disciples, we have some ideas to share on how to lead a group of disciple-makers. Visitors to Xenos constantly ask us how we cause blue and white-collar family-aged adults to exert themselves so strenuously to disciple and be discipled.

The answer is complicated and involves multiple factors. For example, our church's DNA includes high commitment and aggressive ministry efforts by all. In addition, our leaders study motivation and take deliberate steps to keep people excited about what God can do through their ministries.

DISCIPLE-MAKERS NEED OVERSIGHT

Some self-starters have such clarity of vision that they continue to work hard even without any encouragement from others. But many people lose their way unless leaders periodically call them back to their foundations. When you leave people alone, you should expect a gradual decline in their zeal and focus. The same people, if skillfully led, will grow in competence and fruitfulness.

The best time to begin gathering a group of disciple-makers together is early. If you work with two, three, or four other disciple-makers, why not get them together periodically for mutual encouragement and learning? These meetings need not be frequent. Once a month is best, but even once a quarter is usually enough to keep people on-mission. If your meetings are quarterly, you should supplement the meetings with ad-hoc discussions one-on-one with your disciple-makers during the time between meetings.

If you oversee a number of home groups, your combined leaders' meetings can serve as your chance to lead the disciple-makers who lead the groups. Disciple-making issues share time with issues like evangelism and pastoring, but we believe discipleship should remain front and center. If people pursue disciple-making effectively, other issues like evangelism and pastoral work should automatically go forward in home groups. Evangelism should go forward because each discipleship dyad is striving to succeed in evangelism. Pastoral work goes forward because no one can counsel and encourage better than a trained and motivated discipler.

When you gather your disciple-makers for a meeting, make sure the meeting is excellent. Whether you spend time yourself, or delegate leadership of the meeting to a rotation of speakers, make sure these busy leaders never feel like they are wasting their time. A periodic meeting of fellow disciple-makers can be a high point in life if done right.

We met regularly with the group leaders and disciple-makers in our church when we had about twenty. As the excitement in that meeting spread, others wanted to join in. The group grew, as home groups also multiplied. Within a few years, more than a hundred disciple-makers and home group leaders attended. Today, that group has grown to more than nine hundred. Our meetings usually include a presentation on a passage or key ministry issue, and time for group interaction and prayer. The leaders usually socialize before and after the meeting.

Leaders should view involvement in a disciple-makers' meeting as a privilege. Attendance is by invitation only, and for those who have been discipling for six months or more. People regularly report that these meetings are their favorite times in our church. One meeting each year is a weekend retreat especially for disciple-makers and group leaders. Leaders usually leave these meetings eager to return to the work.

Goals: Reminding Them of the Vision

Making real disciples is slow work, and progress can be so gradual that people bog down. Disciple-makers often have to struggle with a litany of personal problems and ministry details. When do they get to lift their heads up from the work and re-acquire the big picture?

Good upper-level leaders know how to re-cast vision when they gather their colleagues for a meeting. Don't make the mistake of thinking that because you already covered the vision, people don't need to hear it again. Repetition is necessary, but should also be varied to avoid boredom. Teach key passages on discipleship. Illustrations like the duplicating church versus the super church, like that in chapter 1 of this book are also helpful. Waylon Moore tells a great story about a discipleship chain that began with Edward Kimball and eventually included Billy Graham in his book, *Multiplying Disciples.*[1] In fact most books on discipleship have some good stories.

Testimonials from people in your group who are getting good results serve a double purpose. The stories help build a sense of vision, but they also give you a chance to recognize and encourage disciple-makers who are doing good work.

At Xenos, we continually remind our colleagues that discipleship isn't easy, and it's not a shortcut. We stress that we are doing what we believe is God's will, and that we are willing to pay a higher price to get the authenticity and quality that good discipleship brings.

REPORTING

Multiple factors tend to sap morale in disciple-makers:

- Even in a discipleship network that is vibrant and growing, people may not see much progress in their particular circle during any given month.
- Satan actively sows defeatism in the minds of any group of disciple-makers.
- Simple impatience prods people to give up the long road of discipleship in favor of faddish gimmicks that can produce quick, but shallow results.
- Reversals and disappointments are part and parcel of a disciple-making ministry.

For all these reasons, we believe it is well worthwhile to gather the facts about your discipleship network and present those facts as feedback. When people see objective feedback about their work they usually find new resolve—especially if the feedback is positive.

To accomplish this part, you'll need the cooperation of group leaders in helping you gather information. The larger the network becomes, the more difficult gathering information becomes. If you start early, leaders will be used to the minor nuisance of reporting progress, and they will realize it is important because they enjoy the feedback.

Our group leaders report monthly on their group attendance and the number of first-timers visiting their group each month. With these facts, we construct objective charts showing our progress. We like to put up a chart showing progress to date that looks like this:

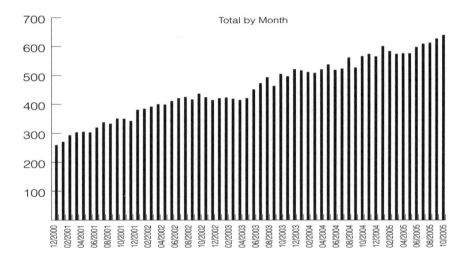

This chart shows a network of home groups that is doing very well. In just five years, the network has nearly tripled in size. Whether the group will be able to sustain this rate of growth is open to question. But if they did, you can see the group would grow to five thousand people during the next ten years! Leaders are excited to be a part of such a movement, and will exert themselves with urgency to see the dream come true.

DEVELOPING A SENSE OF TEAM

People in the world, and even many Christians simply don't understand why someone would devote so much energy and time to something like making disciples. We have found that disciple-makers love spending time with fellow workers who "get it." Committed disciple-makers enjoy a special kinship with each other.

Upper-level leaders are in good position to foster fellowship between disciple-makers. Periodic meetings or retreats are a good base. But on that base you should build mechanisms for mutual sharing. One of the easiest measures you can take is to establish an invitation-only E mail group for your disciple-makers. These forums are free, and an administrator can control who has access to the email. Anyone posting to the forum automatically sends E mail to all the members. The administrator can also publish rules for the forum. We urge our people not to flood other members with meaningless or unimportant chatter. The forum is for discussing issues of interest to disciple-makers.

Book recommendations are helpful. Sharing victories elevates the morale of the group. Sharing problems gives other practitioners the chance to give advice. We have email groups for small groups of disciple-makers (like a home church leadership team) as well as big groups (like our 900 member servant team). The forums are also a great place for upper level leaders to make announcements. Whenever a group plants a new group we announce it via email, and congratulate the leaders.

If your group of disciple-makers gets large, additional measures are necessary. Large groups of disciple-makers have to be divided into manageable groups. Groups of several dozen disciple-makers can develop good community. But if the group gets larger, they need to divide. You can still hold large meetings for the special sense of inspiration people get from being a part of a large movement.

When a group of disciple-makers grows to more than thirty or forty, your church should also consider hiring its first staff coach. We strongly recommend hiring one of your own who has an established record of good discipling work. When churches hire from outside, they run the risk of sending a negative message to their discipling leaders: none of the existing disciple-makers are considered competent enough to be a coach. Long-term disciple-makers usually have many connections with other disciple-makers and will be trusted more than an outsider. Hire from within whenever possible.

Manageable groups of leaders should gather for leaders' social nights. We like to hold these after a regular fellowship meeting, so they don't have to commit an additional time slot. We usually meet at someone's home and begin by enjoying snacks together. After half an hour, we get everyone together and the senior leader present gives a short presentation announcing any new developments, and any grounds for hope. Then we go around the room for a report from each home group, usually according to some script: "Tell us something your group has learned during the past year, and your biggest area of need, so we can pray for you." Or we might ask, "Describe your upcoming leadership team, and estimate how soon they might be ready to lead their own group. What do you see as the main barriers they face?"

Corporate prayer with a group of disciple-makers is always enjoyable and edifying, and we invest time in this as well. Whether the group breaks up into smaller groups, or pray together, they really feel each other's enthusiasm and love for the things of God.

A group of fellow disciple-makers who meet, socialize, share, and pray together gradually develop a deep-seated sense that they are a team. Being part of a team prevents disciple-makers from feeling isolated. Leaders who see themselves as part of a team tend to develop a level of consistency good enough for the long haul.

Ongoing Training

Training is motivational. People who invest their time and effort acquiring training want to use that training in the field. Your presentations at periodic team meetings can include useful equipping. Retreats are especially suitable for ongoing training. But you should also consider offering three to five week classes for disciple-makers and leaders. At Xenos, leaders take seven ten-week classes as part of their basic training (although most of these can be taken after they are already leading). We also offer continuing education once every two years. Leaders invariably enjoy the classes, and report that their ministries were invigorated as a result. Make sure any classes you offer are high quality. This is a good time investment for top leaders in the church. Equipping those who are actually doing the work of ministry is one of the most strategic things pastors and top leaders can do with their time.[2]

Our key servanthood and leadership classes require that students are meeting with at least one disciple as a prerequisite. Committed Christians in our fellowship look forward to taking these popular classes, and it becomes one more reason to seek out discipling opportunities.

One of the main benefits of ongoing training is increasing competence in our disciple-makers. Because of the complexity of the discipling task, and the confusion that can result, disciple-makers become uniquely open to training. They appreciate receiving a constant stream of ideas from upper level leadership. Some ministry principles cannot be properly learned until one is actually struggling with problems in the field. We find that leaders drink in practical training in a way they never could as younger Christians.

COACHING

Even though disciple-makers belong to a team, they still have specific questions that need individual answers. Upper level leaders need to practice a high level of availability with other disciple-makers, regularly checking on how things are going, and giving counsel and advice.

As suggested earlier, when a disciple-making group grows large, the top leadership in the church may need to seek out staff coaching help. We have had success hiring part-time coaches. Learning about groups and the people in those groups takes time, and for coaching to be effective, coaches need a good level of familiarity with the personalities, special needs, and history of the groups they coach. They also benefit from warm personal relationships with the leaders they coach. We find that coaches often do a better job overseeing only a handful of groups in their part time, rather than trying to cover dozens of groups as full-time coaches.[3]

Coaching is a multi-faceted skill. Part of this ministry involves simply letting leaders know someone is interested in what they are doing. But coaches also assist group leaders and disciple-makers in their thinking. Coaches typically ask a range of questions that cause the leader to think about her ministry in the way she needs to in order to be effective. Leaders can easily become reactive in the swirl of events and problems in a typical home group. The tyranny of the urgent crowds out thinking about less urgent, but often more important issues, like discipleship. Such leaders benefit greatly from being asked questions that require proactive thinking. Meanwhile, coaches help keep us, the top leadership, aware of developing situations in home groups.

Coaches typically set up meetings to go over conditions in the group. But they also do a lot of work by being available for unexpected calls and emails seeking advice on a wide range of ministry situations. We teach our disciple-makers and leaders to seek outside views on complex ministry judgments. While coaches usually leave actual decision-making in the hands of the person on the spot, they can suggest options and principles he may have overlooked. Even if the coach has nothing additional to offer, leaders feel comforted knowing that an experienced colleague saw things the same way.

RECOGNITION

We have argued that delivering a disciple who is "complete in [Christ]" is a monumental piece of work. The hazards are many and the short-term rewards are few. Motivating people to give their lives for disciple-making is not a simple proposition. Yet in many churches, successful disciple-making is never publicly recognized. And our church was no exception.

Years ago, we realized that at Xenos, those who sing or play music, those who prepare events, and those who preach and teach are all recognized. We also recognized evangelism when people baptize those they lead to Christ. But strangely, when someone completed the awesome work of discipleship, nothing happened! One reason was that "completing" the work of discipleship is a subjective concept. What does it mean? After all, mentoring might continue for many years.

We decided discipleship should be recognized and celebrated in the church just like we celebrate new believers when we baptize people.

First, we defined a point where we could say discipleship was successful. The point we defined is when disciples qualify for membership in our servant team. The servant team in our church is a group of highly committed Christians who have devoted themselves to living for God and serving him. These servants have typically spent several years growing, learning, and practicing Christian living. We deliberately make entrance into the servant team difficult. We would rather see people excluded who could qualify, than include people who don't belong. If we are in any doubt, we wait. Our requirements include:

- Character qualities in line with those of deacons in the New Testament (1 Tim. 3:8-12). These qualities must be witnessed and confirmed by people in their home group over a period of years.
- Regular participation in Xenos large meetings and a home group for a period of years.
- Completion of at least four quarters of our basic training classes with passing grades.
- Practicing regular personal times of prayer and Bible study.
- Practicing defined ministry, including evangelism and personal discipleship at a level considered to be effective by their home group members.
- Currently leading a home church except for special exceptions.
- Becoming a committed giver at the level of our Fiscal Support Team, (implies at least 5% giving).
- Help with shared ministry needs like children's ministry, youth ministry, music, light, sound, snack bar, etc. at least one quarter every other year.
- Nominated for the team by a current member and confirmed by other members.
- Approved by upper-level leadership.
- Willing to sign the Xenos Servant Covenant, which promises ongoing obligations such as more classes, attendance at servant team meetings, and general mature Christian living.[4]

Meeting these requirements typically takes two to five years of concentrated spiritual growth. In our judgment, any disciple-maker who helps a young believer mature to the point where he qualifies for the servant team has succeeded at making a new disciple. Most new members of the servant team continue to be discipled for some time after joining, but you have to draw a line somewhere.

With this objective definition of success, we were in a position to begin publicly recognizing success in the disciple-making process. We set up harvest celebrations where more than a thousand people attend. At these festivals we introduce each new servant team member *along with his or her primary discipler*. We explain the new member's ministry contributions. The crowd cheers furiously. We also introduce each new home church planted since the last meeting, and the new leaders in those groups tell their stories.

Our church really enjoys these celebrations. They are celebrations of success in the most important ministries going on in our church—discipleship and church planting.

Of course, being recognized before the church as a successful disciple-maker is not the reason for making disciples. But we see no harm in encouraging good work. New servant team members and leaders appreciate being congratulated, and disciple-makers enjoy their recognition. At the same time, these celebrations make a statement to the church about what matters in our fellowship. But we teach disciple-makers that the real reward is not being on the stage with their disciples, but seeing their disciples on the stage with other disciples. When we see multi-generational discipleship, we know it's working.

Anyone who manages to coalesce a group of disciple-makers has developed the most potent possible force for expanding the kingdom of God. By leading them, helping them, and recognizing them, you will fuel a ministry that can change the world!

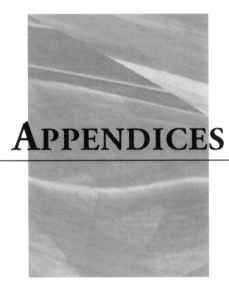

APPENDICES

To save space and cost, we have moved some appendices and our bibliography to the *organic disciple-making* web site. There you will also find a free study guide and other helpful material: http://www.xenos.org/disciple

GOALS FOR
DISCIPLESHIP

The worksheet on the following pages summarizes nine areas where we should look for improvement in disciples' lives, as mentioned in chapter two. You can think through where your disciple stands on these issues, recording your impressions in the spaces provided. A full explanation follows the chart. If you don't know where your disciple stands on a particular issue, just say "unknown" and look for an opportunity to explore that area later. For more information on any category look below to the corresponding text.

Name _____

1. Law and Grace	Comments:
Knows how to confess sin and claim grace.	
Able to set goals under grace, and able to shake off failure and carry on.	
Knows, articulates, and depends on God's part in ministry.	
Has developed reasonable ethical priorities, in the sense that the disciple knows what constitutes serious sin versus minor sin. The disciple is focused on the main issues in sanctification rather than "straining out the gnat and swallowing the camel."	
Understands the true role of the law.	
Understands the true role of discipline.	
Consistently grateful to God.	
2. Character change	**Comments:**
Understands security in Christ, and how actions should be empowered by God, not self-effort.	
Knows how to worship God in all ways, and with enthusiasm.	
Understands the process of spiritual growth verses quick fixes.	
Knows and practices the means of growth as a lifestyle.	
Able to withstand suffering with an attitude of faith.	

Obeys God much of the time.	
Victory over discrediting sin.	
Loyal to God over materialistic goals.	
Possesses an eternal value system.	
Convinced that self-giving love is the key to fulfillment.	
3. Interpreting the Bible	**Comments**
Able to articulate and defend biblical authority, inspiration, and canon.	
Knows and can use grammatical historical biblical interpretation.	
Knows how to do inductive study.	
Knows how to use Bible study tools.	
Familiar with typical lines of attack on conservative biblical interpretation.	
Knows how to harmonize and resolve most problem passages.	
Understands salvation history.	
4. Understanding God	**Comments**
Knows how God's attributes apply to personal trust, ministry, and prayer.	
Able to articulate and defend the Trinity.	
Understands how God's image is reflected in humans.	
Able to correct common misconceptions about God and the Bible.	

5. Satan	Comments
Knows who Satan is and understands the angelic realm.	
Discerning about aberrant teaching on demons.	
Knows how to recognize, bind, and fight demonic attacks in self and others.	
Understands the "world system" and the proper response to it.	

6. Evangelism	Comments
Able to share own testimony.	
Able to witness and actively witnesses.	
Has learned sensitivity to others' decision-making process.	
Has won people to Christ, or at least brought people to church services or a small group who received Christ.	
Conversant with the main world views opposing Christ in culture and has at least some defenses for each.	
Understands and can effectively refute common misconceptions about Christianity.	
Understands and participates in world evangelism.	

7. The church and ministry	Comments
Active in body life at all needed levels (large and small meetings). Knows and embraces the importance of ministry.	

Understands what the church is and can distinguish it from the Old Testament covenant.	
Understands spiritual gifts, church offices, church discipline, and church finance.	
Has established a personal ministry within, and perhaps outside, the home church.	
Is a consistent giver.	
Has won another person into personal discipleship.	
8. Personal relationships	**Comments**
Understands biblical love and is able to maintain lasting friendships.	
Able to handle and resolve interpersonal conflict.	
Practices sexual self-control.	
If married, has adjusted to marriage and fulfills role as spouse and parent.	
Has developed relationship-related character qualities (patience, kindness, initiative, honesty, etc.), so that he/she is known as a loving person both inside and outside the church.	
9. Teaching on the Holy Spirit and Jesus	**Comments**
Knows what the ministries of the Spirit are and regularly depends on the power of the Spirit for living and ministry. Knows the difference between the role of the Spirit in the OT & NT.	

Ready to answer aberrant teaching on the Holy Spirit.	
Looks for where the Spirit is leading and responds accordingly.	
Knows scriptures and can articulate the uniqueness of Christ, his dual natures, his deity, his work, and his return.	

Detailed Explanation of the Nine Areas Above

1. God's grace

Your disciples need to understand the central biblical themes of Law and Grace. God works with us through grace—meaning a free and undeserved gift. Both personal salvation and spiritual growth are to be accomplished through drawing on God's grace, rather than through humanistic self-improvement.

A disciple who understands grace knows how to confess sin and claim God's forgiveness and acceptance. How freeing it is to admit our failures to one another because we understand God's forgiveness in our lives! Teach your disciples how to avoid alienation from God when they fall into sin. Knowing grace also means your disciples are able to set spiritual goals and pursue them under grace rather than in a legalistic way. Understanding grace will also enable them to shake off failure in their lives or ministry and carry on. Grace gives us the courage to fail, at the same time it gives us the power to succeed.

Understanding grace also means they need to know about God's part in ministry—that he alone can empower us to win others and see lives change. Healthy disciples depend on God's power to come through for them when they go out to serve him.

Help your disciples develop reasonable ethical priorities, in the sense that they know the difference between serious sin and minor sin. Help them focus on the main issues in spiritual growth rather than "straining out the gnat and swallowing the camel," like the Pharisees did. When holding a legalistic mentality, people want to focus on minor, external issues in order to distract attention from their failures in major areas. Teach them that grace gives us the ability to be honest about where we're failing in our growth—and be sure to show them grace when they confess! You may need to focus on sins of omission (like failing to love others, to serve, to pray, etc.) because these are important but are often ignored.

Disciples need a theology of law and the role it has played in salvation history and in becoming our tutor to lead us to Christ. Until your disciples recognize legalism in themselves and in others they will be unable to escape Satan's accusations.

2. Character change

We pray our disciples will see their lives changed, and their character conformed to the image of Christ. So, we teach them how to live in their identity in Christ, rather than their feelings about reality, or their performance for God. Seeing real progress in character development is very slow and difficult. Negative habits may stand as key barriers to spiritual growth. Your disciples may have a habit involving sexual wrongdoing, over-eating, drugs, pornography, compulsive gambling, fits of rage, constant suspicion of others, lack of forgiveness, self-righteousness, or a host of other problems. A a discipler, you must uncover the problems, and help them apprehend the power of God for change. Any of these or many other habits may completely block spiritual growth if left unresolved.

A key sticking point here is learning how to initiate and develop good relationships based on mature Christian love. Jesus taught that loving others is just as key to spiritual growth as loving God

(Mat. 22:36-40). But people come to Christ as selfish relators with many false conceptions about how relationships should work. You have your work cut out if you hope to help a young Christian change from being a selfish love-demander or alienated non-relater to a warm-hearted, loving Christian who forms lasting, quality relationships. Here is a typical area where only first-hand knowledge based on actually seeing how someone relates to others can you hope to make a difference. Modeling is key. When younger believers see their discipler loving others, they come to realize what real love is. In this area, the superiority of personal discipleship is evident compared to other forms of instruction.

Character transformation means not only loving other people, but loving God. A successful disciple learns how to worship God in all the ways named in scripture. This includes fully committing her life to Christ (Rom. 12:1), serving him in ministry (Rom. 15:), giving generously (Phil. 4: Heb. 13) as well as praising him consistently (Heb. 13). All of these passages use the language of worship. People need help seeing how reasonable, biblical, and pleasurable worshiping God can be.

You must convince your disciples that being conformed to the image of Christ is a process of growth, not a quick fix or shortcut. Many in the Christian world today advance miraculous shortcut approaches to sanctification that are actually pointless distractions.

If you want to help your disciples see change in their characters, you must teach them to take advantage of key means of growth presented in scripture. They must learn the importance of regular times in the word of God, deep involvement in body life and fellowship, a consistent prayer life, and ministry, or service to others. God uses all these to transform lives, and missing any one of them will eventually block spiritual growth.

They must also develop the ability to withstand suffering with an attitude of faith and even thanksgiving if they are to move on to full maturity.

Eventually, growing disciples need to reach the point where they enjoy obeying God much of the time. You shouldn't expect they will ever obey him all the time, but should hope to see them living a life generally centered in Christ, following his will, and free from discrediting sin habits.

Especially important in the American culture is that mature disciples are loyal to God over materialistic goals. They will experience many trials where the world demands that they earn and enjoy money and possessions. These demands will often conflict with God's goals for their lives. To be victorious here, they must develop an eternal value system—a value system that sees how eternal things are much more important than passing pleasures. People with an eternal value system also draw their sense of security from their future with God rather than from laying up treasure on earth.

3. Interpreting the Bible

You must equip your disciples to use their Bibles. Paul tells his disciple, Timothy, "Be diligent to present yourself approved to God as a workman who does not need to be ashamed, accurately handling the word of truth" (2 Tim. 2:15 NASB). You should study why Christians believe the Bible is inspired, and why the books in the Bible are there. By the time you're done, your disciples will hopefully be able to articulate and defend biblical authority, inspiration, and canon, because these issues come up often for anyone trying to witness or lead a Bible study.

They must also be equipped to interpret the text fairly. They should know how to do basic inductive Bible study. Furthermore, they should be familiar with Bible study tools such as Bible dictionaries, concordances, word study books, background commentaries, etc. In more advanced disciples, they should be familiar with typical lines of attack on grammatical-historical hermeneutics (especially reader-centered or postmodern schools of interpretation, but also allegorical and literalistic approaches) and have basic responses ready (See Appendix 4).

You will typically have to spend time showing your disciples how to harmonize and resolve most key problem passages, because their future disciples are going to ask questions about these, and they should be ready.

Finally, to "handle the Bible accurately," disciples must understand salvation history, and how progressive revelation affects the interpretation of the text in the New and Old Testaments. Hopefully, you will have them reading through the Bible, and most of these questions will come up in the course of their reading. A good discipler can excite disciples about the plan of God for the ages, and how that plan works out down to our present day, and into the future.

4. Understanding God

Your disciples need to understand who God is, and his attributes. This area of theology has great impact in every area of life and biblical interpretation. The fact that we can trust God, how we do ministry, and how we pray, are all based on the attributes of God as revealed in scripture. Your disciples should be able to correct people's common misconceptions about God.

They also need to understand the trinity and be able to defend biblical teaching on this key area against the many cult-based and New Age attacks they will encounter. Understanding God's personality and his moral attributes are also crucial for a correct understanding of humans created in God's image.

5. Satan

Do your disciples know about Satan? Unless they understand who he is and how he works, they will be poorly equipped to wage effective spiritual war. They will need knowledge about the angelic realm in order to resist unbiblical teaching on angels and demons. Unless they know how to recognize and resist demonic temptation, accusation, and deception, they will continually be confused. They should understand the key area of New Testament teaching on the world system and how to respond to it.

6. Witnessing

Teach your disciples how to share their faith. Although some young Christians seem to have natural ability in this area, most do not. But we firmly believe their Christian walk will be impoverished unless they have the opportunity to lead others to Christ. Christians who never lead others to Christ turn inward, and an inward version of Christianity will be a self-centered version. If inward believers later lead groups, they will have difficulty leading those groups into victorious evangelism unless they have some success here themselves. Go out with your disciples to meet their friends and show them how to share their faith. Or, you may have opportunities to do this when they bring friends to meetings and you visit with them afterward.

Your disciples must possess the ability to share their own testimony, to share the gospel message in a living way, and to be good listeners. Most important, they must be actively witnessing on a regular basis. They need to understand how people make decisions, and be patient about leading people to Christ in friendship evangelism. To consider disciples "mature," we like to see that they have led someone to Christ, or at least brought people to church or Bible study who later received Christ.

Equip your disciples with appropriate responses to the main

worldviews opposed to Christianity in their cultural setting. Relativism, New Age spirituality, and naturalism (or practical agnosticism/atheism) are world view they will frequently confront in their efforts to share their faith. They should also be ready to respond to common misconceptions about Christianity.

Finally, we firmly believe God wants disciples to have a heart for world missions. You should try to inspire your disciples to participate in world evangelization, and have a general understanding of what missions are all about.

7. *The Body of Christ*

The seventh area has to do with the church and related truths. Disciples need to understand what the body of Christ is, and how they fit into that picture (1 Cor. 12-14; Rom. 12; Eph. 4:1-16). The last thing you want to do is develop individualistic disciples who don't understand that Christian growth is a corporate activity that cannot be attained in isolation. They should be active in body life at all needed levels—worship, group study, and small group fellowship— because only in small groups will they be able to develop relationships and use their spiritual gifts.

Aside from knowing about the church, they need to specifically understand principles of Christian ministry. Until your disciples understand the importance of developing their own ministries, they will never grow to maturity. We find that when our disciples become ministry-minded, their growth accelerates noticeably. Help your disciples develop a fruitful ministry of their own, including discipling others. Only when your disciples have developed a defined ministry, and have served under your guidance and coaching for a good period of time should you consider them advanced enough to go out on their own.

Aside from these crucial areas, it would also be valuable to make your disciples aware of the main issues in church history including the early church, the medieval church, the reformation, the evangelical awakening, the rise of theological liberalism, and recent movements. Questions about these issues come up with some regularity, so the more you equip them here, the better; although this is probably one area you could skip if you must.

Disciples certainly need some training in biblical issues like spiritual gifts, church offices, church discipline, and church finance.

At Xenos, we do not feel our job is complete until our disciples become consistent givers. Paul warns that leaders should not be "fond of sordid gain" (1 Tim. 3:3). A Christian who is enslaved to material-istic avarice is ill-suited to serve God. Jesus warned that unless we are faithful in insignificant areas like the use of our money, God will not entrust us with the greater riches of the church, such as caring for other people's lives (Luke 16:10, 11). In our experience, disciples who won't give in a disciplined way usually make poor leaders. The failure to give, especially in a culture as affluent as ours, signals much bigger problems.

8. Special Relationships

Special relationships are a crucial area. They include dating, marriage, and family life. Although we mentioned relationships earlier, this area is so central that it should be discussed further. In addition to under-standing biblical love and being able to maintain lasting friendships, good disciples must develop several additional specific skills.

The sexual drive is powerful. We have found that many would-be disciples are lost to Christian service because they cannot control their sexual desires. Others are lost because they marry someone who has no desire to follow the Lord. Some people come to Christ already in a marriage where they may be "unequally yoked," because their spouses do not share their zeal for God. These cases clearly show why you need to get involved helping your disciples win in this crucial area.

With singles, we find ourselves counseling and teaching Christian principles of sexuality. Singles won from the world today are very likely to have profound dysfunctionality when it comes to forming a lasting, self-giving marriage. Most have very distorted views of sexuality that only slowly yield to a godly view.

With married couples, we offer detailed counseling related to improving marriages that may be very distressed. Some married people are faced with the need to try to win their unbelieving spouses. Others may be married to Christians, but have often damaged their marriage in significant ways. Reconstruction could take years. We've seen amazing and beautiful transformations of nasty, seemingly hopeless situations, but not without a struggle. Teach your disciples how to handle and resolve interpersonal conflict with loved ones.

As part of the character transformation in this area, help your disciples develop relationship-related character qualities such as patience, kindness, empathy, firmness in discipline, loyalty, forgiveness, etc. How wonderful it is to raise up a disciple who is known as a loving person both inside and outside the church!

9. The Holy Spirit and Jesus

Finally, teach your disciples key theological truths in the areas of the Holy Spirit and Jesus Christ. Good disciples know what the ministries of the Holy Spirit are, and they know how to regularly depend on the power of the Spirit for living and ministry. Prepare them to refute unbiblical teaching on the Holy Spirit. Mature disciples look for the Spirit's leading and respond accordingly.

When it comes to Jesus, your disciples should have a basic knowledge of the uniqueness of Christ, his dual natures, his kenosis, or emptying of Himself (Phil. 2:7), his deity, his work, and his return. You should remember that cult groups always attack and deny biblical Christology, so this area is very important.

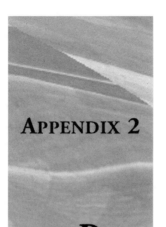

APPENDIX 2

VERBAL PLENARY
INSPIRATION OF THE BIBLE

See http://www.xenos.org/disciple

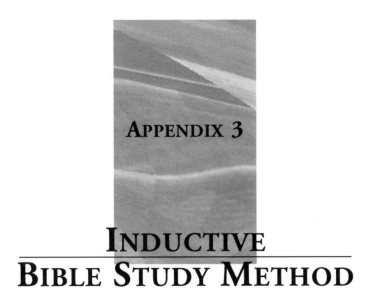

APPENDIX 3

INDUCTIVE
BIBLE STUDY METHOD

See http://www.xenos.org/disciple

GRAMMATICAL-HISTORICAL HERMENEUTICS FOR LAY LEADERS

See http://www.xenos.org/disciple

ASSURANCE OF
SALVATION

See http://www.xenos.org/disciple

APPENDIX 6

WHAT IS GOD LIKE?

See http://www.xenos.org/disciple

FIVE THINGS THAT HELP PEOPLE GROW SPIRITUALLY

Teaching new Christians about the so-called "means of growth" is urgent. Their spiritual survival may depend on learning about these in the first weeks of their Christian walks. We suggest going over outlines like this, reading the verses together and discussing what each passage contributes to our understanding of that area.

The Bible

Reading and learning from the word of God is like spiritual food: with it we grow stronger, without it our spirituality suffers. Go over each of the following passages and discuss what each teaches or implies about God's word and its role in spiritual growth:

John 8:31,32; Col. 3:16; John 17:17; 2 Tim. 2:15; Acts 20:32
2 Tim. 3:16; Rom. 10:17; Heb. 5:11-14; Rom. 15:4; 1 Pet. 2:2

Prayer

Prayer is talking to God. We can't develop a good personal relationship with Christ without communicating with him regularly, intimately, and honestly. Also, in some cases God waits until we ask before he acts (James 4:2). Go over the following verses and try to determine what each teaches or implies about prayer:

Mat. 6:5-7; Rom. 15:30; Mat. 18:19; 1 Cor. 14:15; Luke 18:1-8
Eph 6:18; John 15:7; Phil. 4:6; Acts 2:42; Col. 4:2; Acts 12:5
1 Thess. 5:17; Rom. 8:26,27; 1 Pet. 5:6; Rom. 12:12
1 John 5:14,15

Fellowship

Because we are a part (and not the whole) of the Body of Christ, we need what the other parts of the Body supply (1 Cor. 12:21, 22). Going to Bible studies is important, but we will grow even more spiritually if we build good relationships with the Christians we know. Involvement in the body of Christ makes God's love for us and our love for God more concrete (1 John 4:20). Study each of the following passages and try to distill what they teach about fellowship:

Acts 2:42; Eph 4:11-16; Col. 3:12-17; James 5:16; Rom. 12:4-16
Eph. 5:18-21; 1 Thess. 5:14; 1 Cor. 12:14-27; Phil. 2:1-5
Heb. 3:13; Gal 6:2; Col. 2:19; Heb. 10:24,25

Serving Love

Helping other people will help us to grow spiritually more than any other thing, because it motivates us to read more, pray more, and fellowship more. "Love covers over a multitude of sins" (1 Pet. 4:8).

Loving others will help us see life as it was meant to be lived. Study these passages about serving love and determine what they teach or imply about the role of serving love in spiritual growth:

John 4:34; Eph 4:11-13; John 6:1-13; John 13:12-17,34,35
Col. 2:19; Phil. 2:1-4; Acts 20:35; 1 Thess. 5:14,15; Rom. 12:10-13
Heb. 10:24,25; 1 Cor. 12,13; 1 John 3:16-18

Suffering

Sometimes we go through suffering and this suffering can help us grow spiritually. Often, God lovingly brings discipline into our lives. At other times, the suffering we experience is not from God, but he allows us to suffer as part of the fallen world in which we live. Even suffering from the fallen world, however, can help us to grow spiritually if we let God teach us something through it. Decide to receive discipline as a sign of God's love for you. Actively seek to learn what God wants to teach through this experience of suffering (James 1:2-5). Study the following passages in context and discuss what conclusions you can reach from each about the role of suffering in the Christian life:

Mat. 18:15-17; 2 Cor. 7:8-10; Luke 9:23,24; Phil. 1:29,30
John 12:24-26; Heb. 12:1-13; 1 Cor. 10:12,13; James 1:2-5
1 Cor. 11:30-32; 1 Pet. 1:6,7; 2 Cor. 1:3-9; 1 Pet. 2:19-21
2 Cor. 4:7-13; 1 Pet. 4:12-19; 2 Cor. 7:8-10

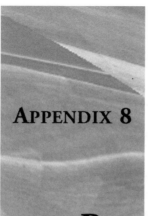

WHEN TO REFER TO
PROFESSIONAL COUNSELING

RECOGNIZING EMOTIONAL DISORDERS
Amy Merker, M.D. Psychiatry

[The following are notes from a lecture given by Dr. Amy Merker to a group of disciple-makers on when they should refer people to professional counseling.]

Introduction

The goal of this discussion is to help you learn to recognize symptoms of emotional disorders which could indicate that someone needs professional help. Hopefully, by the end of tonight you'll be able to identify individuals who need referred to a psychiatrist, or a mental health clinic.

I don't expect you all to become diagnosticians tonight, but it is helpful to be able to think of symptoms in clusters which make up a diagnosis. In the field of psychiatry, we have the Diagnostic and Statistical Manual of Mental Disorders or DSM IV. This is the Bible of Psychiatry and includes descriptive classifications of symptoms or clinical features of emotional disorders. It does not, however include any information on etiology or treatment.

Tonight we're going to discuss six diagnostic categories and how to recognize if someone has an emotional disorder:
• Affective disorders (Unipolar and Bipolar)
• Schizophrenia (psychosis)
• Anxiety disorders (Panic disorder, Agoraphobia, O.C.D.)
• Personality disorders
• Substance abuse disorders
• Eating disorders
• Affective disorders

There are a number of different types of affective disorders, or mood disorders. There are two major affective disorders:
• Major depression
• Bipolar disorder

These are called "major" because of their severity.

Major Depression
In order to merit this diagnosis, a person must have at least five of the following symptoms nearly every day for at least two weeks:

Sad mood; Tearfulness; Psychomotor retardation; Decreased energy; Diminished interest or pleasure; Insomnia; Poor appetite; Weight loss; Poor concentration; Feelings of worthlessness; Hopelessness or excessive guilt; Suicidal urges

This is the most common type of major depression. However, there is also an atypical type of major depression in which an individual experiences increased sleep and appetite, rather than decreased.

Dysthymic Disorder

If a person has experienced a depressed mood more days than not for the past two years and has at least two of the previously mentioned symptoms, they likely have what is called a dysthymic disorder.

This is a chronic low-level depression and is not considered a Major Affective disorder, and yet people with a dysthymic disorder may benefit from anti-depressant medication.

Both of the above disorders are considered Unipolar mood disorders because there is only one direction the mood tends to swing to.

Bipolar Disorder

The other type of major affective disorder is called bipolar disorder because the person's mood tends to swing in two directions.

Major depression and bipolar disorder are differentiated by whether or not an individual has ever had a manic episode. The person with a major depressive illness has recurrent depressive episodes through out their life, whereas the Bipolar patient (or manic depressive as they once were called) have periodic depressive episodes and have had at least one manic episode in their lifetime.

How does one determine if someone is currently having, or has previously had, a manic episode?

Definition of a Manic Episode: One or more distinct periods, (few days-weeks), with a predominately elevated, explosive, or irritable mood, and at least three of the following symptoms:

• Increase in activity or physical restlessness
• More talkative—difficult to interrupt
• Jumping from one topic to another very rapidly (flight of ideas or loose associations)

- Inflated self-esteem, (delusions of grandeur)
- Decreased need for sleep, (can stay up for 3-4 nights cleaning etc.)
- Easily distracted
- Excessive involvement in activities with a high potential for painful consequences—like buying sprees, foolish business investments, or sexual indiscretions, etc.

These individuals may even become psychotic during a manic episode. In other words, they may lose touch with reality. They may hallucinate, or experience delusions.

Definition of a delusion: a "fixed false belief which no amount of objective evidence will change."

Schizophrenic Disorders

These individuals are usually quite ill. This is considered a psychotic disorder--they are out of touch with reality. They experience delusions and or hallucinations. We have already discussed delusions.

Definition of a Hallucination: a false sensory perception in the absence of any external stimuli, not merely a misinterpretation of something that is really there, (i.e. not an illusion).

The most common type of hallucination is an auditory hallucination. My first patient came to the hospital with newspaper stuck in her ears in an attempt to lessen the voices she was hearing. To be considered true auditory hallucinations, these voices must be experienced as coming from out in the room, not just from inside one's head.

In addition to delusions or hallucinations, these individuals (with schizophrenic disorders) are typified by disorders of thinking. Their thinking is often not linear – it doesn't follow a logical flow.

Someone once said that being schizophrenic is like dreaming while you're awake. In a dream you may be on the way to the airport and you end up at the zoo and you run into a friend from work, who you later realize is actually your sister. There is no logical flow to their thought pattern.

In talking with someone who is actively schizophrenic, you may find it very hard to follow them and you may end up thinking "Either they are crazy or I am." This is called derailment—where their thinking gets off track. They exhibit what is called loose associations or flight of ideas.

Anxiety Disorders

The predominant symptom in this group of disorders is obviously anxiety. These folks are considered neurotic, not psychotic because they are in touch with reality.

This category includes panic disorders with or without agoraphobia, obsessive-compulsive disorder, social phobia, P.T.S.D., and generalized anxiety disorder.

Panic disorders consist of sudden distinct episodes of extreme anxiety which include four or more of the following symptoms:

• Shortness of breath, heart palpitations, chest pain, dizziness, sweating , shaking, or a fear of losing control or dying

• These individuals may also have agoraphobia and are afraid to leave their homes. Agoraphobia is a fear of open spaces. These people often find it very difficult to be in a crowd. For example, they may get overwhelmed and experience a panic attack in a grocery store.

Obsessive compulsive disorder (O.C.D.) is characterized by recurrent obsessions or intrusive, unwanted thoughts, or compulsions, which are repetitive behaviors or mental acts in which the person feels driven or obsessed to perform in response with a certain set of rules or rituals.

The individual realizes these thoughts or actions are abnormal or excessive, but is unable to control them. They are a significant source of distress to the individual or interfere with social functioning. In other words, these are more than merely excessive worries about real life problems.

Examples of O.C.D. include people who are obsessed with contamination and therefore feel compelled to wash their hands 50 times a day, or shower 2 or 3 times daily. Jack Nicholson did an excellent job of portraying O.C.D. in the movie, *As Good As It Gets*.

People with O.C.D. may be obsessed with symmetry, like the main character in "Sleeping with the Enemy." They tend to organize their spices, socks, etc. and feel the need to keep the towels perfectly straight.

Some folks with O.C.D. feel compelled to count, hoard, or check things over, and over, and over again.

Generalized anxiety disorder is the most common anxiety disorder. Symptoms include excessive worry that interferes with daily functioning, and at least 3 of the following:
• muscle tension
• insomnia
• poor concentration
• feeling restless or keyed-up
• irritability, or fatigue

This disorder is more common in women and often occurs in people who also suffer from depression.

Personality Disorders
We all have certain personality traits that we have developed over the years. These are enduring, ingrained patterns of perceiving and relating to the environment and ourselves. When these personality traits become inflexible and maladaptive and cause either significant impairment in social or occupational functioning, they constitute a personality disorder.

Examples include: narcissistic, paranoid, avoidant, dependent, anti-social, histrionic, schizoid, passive-aggressive, and Borderline personality disorder.

These people are very difficult to relate to and can be highly abrasive human beings. They often alienate people and become caught in a cycle of fragile relationships, which they periodically shatter because of their behavior. They often do not view themselves as being at fault, and therefore don't consider that they themselves need to change. They often have very rigid strategies for coping with people or situations, and therefore have difficulty assimilating healthy, biblical methods of responding to situations.

They may be so fearful of rejection that they cling on so tightly to a person that they end up pushing the person away. They set themselves up over and over again in relationship after relationship with the same self-defeating paradigm.

They also often misconstrue essentially benign events. For example, if you bring a friend to a party at their house, they assume it was because you didn't want to talk to them. They are supersensitive to rejection or being slighted in any way.

Substance Abuse

The important point here is to determine if a person abusing drugs or alcohol merely needs to be admonished in order to overcome their problem, or if their abuse is serious enough to merit treatment in a chemical dependency program of some sort.

It is important to determine the severity of their abuse, because abruptly stopping the drug or alcohol could cause withdrawal seizures. Some individuals require inpatient detox or a 30-day inpatient drug rehab program in order to safely come off the substance they were abusing.

A pattern of pathologic use involves intoxication throughout the day, the inability to stop or cut down, or blackouts.

The difference between alcohol or substance abuse verses dependence is that someone has become dependent if he has developed tolerance or withdrawal symptoms. Tolerance is the need for markedly increased amounts of the substance to achieve intoxication. Withdrawal symptoms include tremor, nausea, agitation, and seizures.

It is also important to determine if he has had to miss work because of his abuse, and if he has had any legal problems, such as an O.M.V.I. (Operating a Motor Vehicle Intoxicated or D.W.I.).

Eating Disorders
Anorexia
- Intense fear of getting fat
- Disturbance of body image—think they are fat even when thin
- Weight loss of at least 25% of original body weight
- Refusal to maintain body weight over a minimal normal weight for age and height
- No known physical illness that would account for weight loss
- Amenorrhea—loss of menstrual cycle

Bulimia
- Recurrent episodes of binge eating—rapid consumption of large amounts of food in a discrete period of time, and a sense of lack of control over-eating, or often eat in secret.
- Recurrent inappropriate compensatory behavior in order to prevent weight gain, such as self-induced vomiting, misuse of laxatives, fasting or excessive exercise.
- The binge eating and compensatory behavior both occur at least twice a week for 3 months.
- Preoccupation with weight and shape.
- Not due to any physical disorder
  For example, if you're living in a ministry house and you notice

food continues to disappear, you may have a bulimic living among you. You will need to directly confront them about their binging and purging, since secrecy is paramount to the bulimic and openness is key to their recovery.

Attention Deficit Disorder (ADD)

This disorder has a number of symptoms which overlap with bipolar disorder, but the symptoms are not episodic in A.D.D., but are consistent from day to day.

Symptoms include: poor concentration, distractibility, tendency not to finish projects, easily bored, impatience, tendency toward addictive behavior, poor listening, and the tendency to drift away in the middle of a page or conversation.

In addition to A.D.D., there is also Attention Deficit Disorder with Hyperactivity which includes hyperactivity as a core symptom. In order to be diagnosed with ADD, the symptoms must have begun in childhood. This disorder does not begin in adulthood.

WHEN TO REFER

The *red flags* to look for in discerning if someone needs professional help are:
- suicidal urges…
- Out of touch with reality (psychosis)
- O.C.D. (obsessive-compulsive disorder)
- Severe depression with changes in sleep, energy, appetite, and motivation
- Addiction to (dependence on) substances (drugs or alcohol)
- Physical causes of depression or anxiety which require an evaluation by an internist

Let's look at some of these in more detail . . .

Suicidal Urges

You should ask directly if you suspect someone may have thoughts about hurting themselves. It's important to get them to verbalize these thoughts, since they are less likely to act on them if they talk about it. Ask them if they have thought of a plan. Also ask them if they've ever had these thoughts before or ever made a suicide attempt in the past.

If they say "I wish I were dead," this is not taken nearly as seriously as if they say "I'm thinking about taking an overdose, and I have some pills." If they have a plan it must be taken seriously and you should take them to a mental health facility or hospital.

Need for Medication

If an individual is psychotic, significantly depressed, or experiencing O.C.D., they ought to be referred for an evaluation by a psychiatrist in order to determine if they need medication. Individuals with symptoms of Major Depression, Bipolar Disorder, and in some cases Dysthymic Disorder will likely need anti-depressant medication.

Also people with O.C.D., Panic Disorder with or without agoraphobia, or other anxiety disorders such as trichotillomania (hair pulling), may benefit from an anti-depressant or an anti-anxiety medication.

Obviously those with a schizophrenic illness will need an antipsychotic drug.

Recent evidence suggests that eating disorders may benefit from medication, but group therapy can also be quite helpful for these folks. If someone with an eating disorder also has a mood disorder they may benefit from an anti-depressant.

Unfortunately, medication doesn't seem to help people with a personality disorder. However if someone with a personality disorder also happens to be depressed, then an anti-depressant may be helpful. They used to say the only effective treatment for someone with a borderline personality disorder was weekly psychotherapy for a minimum of 5 years. I think therapy can help these individuals but personal sanctification, or spiritual growth is probably their best bet.

Many people are reluctant to take medication because of the cultural stigma attached to it. They fear it will imply that they are "crazy." However, if someone has gotten depressed, medication can correct an imbalance in their neurochemistry and restore normal functioning.

Medication alone is not always sufficient, but individual and/or marital therapy in combination with medication is very often helpful. Most research shows that the combination of medication and therapy provides the best chance for recovery.

People often need to have their thinking or perspective brought in line with God's truth in order to help prevent future recurrence of problems.

Need for Hospitalization

If people are suicidal or homicidal they need to be admitted to a hospital. These days, having a severe problem like these is about the only way to get someone admitted to the hospital. If they are psychotic and unable to care for themselves then they may also be admitted.

Need for Detox

If they are dependent on drugs or alcohol they may need to be hospitalized in order to be detoxed. This is because if someone who is dependent on alcohol stops drinking cold turkey they are at risk for withdrawal seizures. In the hospital their vital signs can be monitored closely and they can be administered medication which can prevent withdrawal seizures.

Need for Specific Psychotherapy

I believe that the most Biblical type of psychotherapy is probably cognitive behavioral therapy. This type of therapy attempts to identify wrong thinking and replace it with the truth. This is particularly good therapy for OCD, social anxiety disorder and phobias.

Need for a Referral to an Internist

It is always important to rule out any physical causes for depression or anxiety. If someone is fatigued and unmotivated they may actually be anemic, or hypothyroid. If someone's thyroid is too high they may appear anxious. Blood work can identify these physical causes.

Conclusion

In conclusion, it is helpful to look at hurting people in terms of these types of symptoms. If you suspect someone is depressed, for example, you may want to inquire about their sleep and eating patterns. It is also crucial that you directly ask if they have had any thoughts about hurting themselves. If so, do they have a plan?

If someone becomes delusional or begins hearing voices, you would want them evaluated as soon as possible. Particularly if they are experiencing command hallucinations which are telling them to hurt themselves or others.

In my opinion, it is always better to err on the safe side. In other words, I take it seriously when someone mentions suicide and will try and draw them out and find out what they are thinking. If they have a plan, I think it is best to get them in to see a professional right away. Professionals have been trained to determine lethality, and it should be up to them to decide if someone needs to be hospitalized, not you. You should also give a written report to the Xenos office of the event and what you did in response.

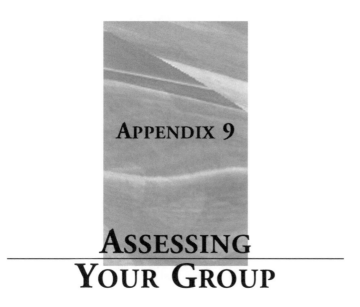

APPENDIX 9

ASSESSING
YOUR GROUP

See http://www.xenos.org/disciple

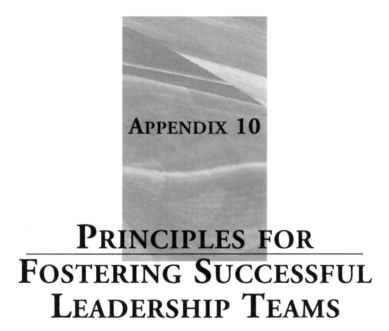

PRINCIPLES FOR FOSTERING SUCCESSFUL LEADERSHIP TEAMS

Encouraging fellow leaders

- Can you name personal characteristics you admire in each of your fellow leaders? If not, you need to spend time with God pleading for a more realistic and fair assessment of your colleagues.
- For each leader, can you name ministry accomplishments you appreciate? Again, pray for your eyes to be opened, and for the humility to admit others' value to the ministry.
- Have you articulated any of these points to your fellow leaders in person during the past two months? If not, you are tardy in your encouraging role. They will find criticisms and advice hard to accept from you if you are weak in encouragement.
- Pray for vision for each of your fellow leaders. Ask God to show you why their unique contribution is important. Then look for an opportunity to express your vision to each in a non-showy and realistic fashion.

- Pray together for each other. Make your prayer times opportunities to review what God has bestowed on the church through each of your leaders, not just a time for fretting and problem solving.

Resolving Personal Conflicts

- Take time to spell out and resolve conflicts as they arise. Help each other resolve personal problems by helping them communicate their concerns and interests. A peacemaking influencer can help people understand each other's positions.
- If leaders have taken offense or feel hurt, the conflict has moved out to the issues-oriented category into an affective, or feelings-based conflict. These affective conflicts are more dangerous, and require special attention. Review the section on counseling interpersonal conflict for ideas on how to resolve conflicts in a biblical way (Chapter 9, Counseling).
- Encouragement is especially important during times of conflict. Controversy needs to be balanced with encouragement, kindness, and approval.
- Take time for positive social relating with other leaders. Spending time with your fellow leaders should be a priority. Leaders who become relationally disengaged become far more likely to misunderstand and become suspicious of each other.
- If an irresolvable problem arises, seek help from outside. Your church leadership should be able to mediate any difficult disputes.
- Leaders should agree on a realistic, hard-working standard for group leadership. Leaders who are not living by such a standard should be criticized to their face, rather than behind their back, and challenged to step up.
- If you feel you must offer criticism to a fellow leader, your perception of any shortcomings on the part of other leaders

should be objective, and serious. Avoid picking at each other for unimportant issues, which leads to a critical atmosphere.

Observing the Principle of the "Man on the Spot"

- You should exercise extreme caution when you encounter negative thoughts regarding another leader's ministry work, especially if that work is carried on where you can't personally observe it. This is because the man (or woman) on the spot is the one who is usually best able to judge what is happening.
- The value of other leaders in this situation is mainly that of questioning the situation, rather than defining it. In other words, by a questioning process, the other leaders should bring out any doubts they have about the ministry of the one on the spot. However, if the answers given are sensible and correspond with objective fact, they should be believed. Also, if a leader contradicts an account given by a member, we should be disposed to believe the leader over the member, according to 1 Timothy 5:19. Even though this passage is specifically about elders, the principle seems to be that we should attribute high credibility to leaders' accounts.
- It will often be necessary to reassess your impression after talking to the one on the spot. If doubt lingers, you should usually keep it to yourself until the situation is completely clarified.
- Leaders should be very wary of tendencies found in most people to second-guess other workers, and to feel that "I know best." We should be very reluctant to meddle in other leaders' decision-making process beyond questioning those leaders.
- All leaders should however, submit to questioning of their ministry by other leaders—even questioning of a close nature. Only by being questioned do we re-examine our own position, and thus benefit from other leaders.
- A leader who refuses to be questioned, or who takes offense at being

questioned, is displaying an immature attitude that contradicts team leadership. Such refusal becomes an issue in itself, and must be resolved before a reasonable level of cooperation can be expected. While any leader may react defensively at first, you have no excuse for continuing in such a posture.

- Don't withdraw from a leader who flares up when questioned. This problem won't go away, and must be resolved at any cost. Get help from higher church leadership if needed.

Commitment to Success

- Each group leader should commit him or herself to the goal of seeing real success in the work of all of the other leaders. Unless you can honestly affirm that this is your goal, nothing you say is reliable because you are not working from a motive of trying to help. If you have competition or contempt in your heart, your views will be biased and unloving.

Communicating Respect

- Other leaders should be viewed as colleagues, and treated with all due respect. View fellow leaders in a way that assumes their basic competence. Communicate this in the demeanor and the words used in a leaders' meeting. Think about how respect is communicated. Leaders who talk down to colleagues or insult them are not being respectful.

Focusing the Ministry

- Unless the leaders are all focusing the majority of their attention and efforts on work that is needed and effective, frustration and negativity will inevitably result. Good leadership teams are proactive. Ascertain whether the bulk of leaders' and workers' time and effort are being used to focus on problems, or on positive, strategically sound ministry.

• Follow the principle of focusing on the responsive field. Jesus taught his followers to focus on towns that were willing to listen rather than on those that refused the message (Luke 10:8-11). Within each ministry sphere, identify the most promising and responsive people at this particular time. Avoid the three most common errors in this area:

    a) Trying to force-feed a believer (or non-Christian) who does not want it.

    b) Ignoring good, growing Christians because "they're doing alright."

    c) "Greasing the squeaky wheel"—expending all of the work of the church (and all of the discussion time in leader's meeting) on people who demand and complain the loudest, without considering others who may demand less, but who are more promising. Unless you resist this tendency, you will actually reinforce fleshly and neurotic behavior— people begin to sense that the best way to get attention is to have a crisis of faith, or an emotional breakdown.

Dealing with Negativity

Every leadership team and every leader must deal with negativity and defeatism from time to time. These attitudes are extremely damaging to the morale of the group and of fellow-leaders. When dealing with negativity, remember the following:

1. Distinguish between negativity and realism. Admit authentic problems so they can be resolved. However, you should appraise every problem area without exaggeration, and admit God's power to work through the situation.

2. Leaders need to remind each other that Christian work, like all war, is full of reversals and unexpected misfortune. Yet there are unexpected victories as well! The setbacks you see today should be

seen in the light of the overall history of God's work with the group. You can usually see that there have been periodic reversals, but overall progress is taking place.

3. Negativity regarding other leaders' ministries is particularly suspicious (see above regarding the man on the spot).

4. Verbally balance negative facts with positive ones in leaders' meeting. What a terrible mistake it would be to have most of the people in your group earnestly seeking growth, but focus on the few who are uninterested, or in defeat.

5. A leader who is projecting negativity and defeatism in the leaders meeting should be reminded to express faith in God.

6. When real problems arise, are the leaders only bemoaning the situation, or are they also creating steps to correct the situation? If no steps are possible, it is usually unwise to spend much time discussing that particular situation.

Appendix 11

Leadership
Responsibilities

See http://www.xenos.org/disciple

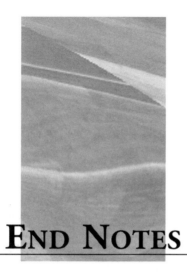

END NOTES

Introduction

[1] "Nationwide, less than 20% of all church growth comes through conversion..." George Barna, *Grow Your Church From the Outside In:* (Ventura CA: Regal Books, 2002) 132. Author Ken Sidey agrees: "Perhaps church growth's greatest challenge in North America comes from research that shows that more than 80 percent of all the growth taking place in growing churches comes through transfer, not conversion. Ken Sidey, "Church Growth Fine Tunes its Formulas," *Christianity Today*, (June 24, 1991), 46. At Xenos, we suspect that the American church's strategy of outreach based on central worship services rather than on individual duplication may have something to do with these unwelcome findings. The Xenos numbers come from a church-wide survey of home church members completed in April, 2005.

[2] Greg Ogden, *Transforming Discipleship*, (Downers Grove Ill: InterVarsity Press, 2003) 190.

[3] For more information on Xenos Fellowship, visit our extensive website at http://www.xenos.org

Chapter 1

[1] See Richard Longenecker, *Patterns of Discipleship in the New Testament* (Grand Rapids, MI: William B. Eerdmans Publishing Co., 1996), p.3. The fact that everyone in the gospels speaks about discipleship in a way that needed no definition indicates they were working from a commonly accepted understanding already in place.

[2] The Apocryphal book of Ben Sirach (Ecclesiasticus) talks about discipleship. Ben Sirach

exhorts the prospective student to find a wise teacher. The pupil is to "attach" himself to his teacher (6:34) and virtually live in his house (6:36). First century disciples needed their wives' permission to leave for more than 30 days at a time to study with their rabbi. (Mishnah, Ketubot 5:6). See a good description of rabbinic disciple-making in Günter Krallmann, *Mentoring for Mission*, (Waynesboro, GA: Authentic Media, 2002) 31-34.

[3] New Testament authors Luke and John often use the term "disciples" to refer to all Christians or followers of Jesus regardless of their level of commitment or proximity to him. In the book of Acts the term "disciples" is used several times as a synonym for "Christians" (see 9:19; 9:26; 9:38; 11:26; 11:29; 13:52; 14:20,21,22, 28; 15:10; 18:23, 27; 19:9,30; 20:1; 20:30; 21:4,16). Thus Luke, mainly in the book of Acts, refers to all followers of Jesus as disciples, although even he distinguishes between disciples of Jesus and those of Paul (9:25) and of John the Baptist (19:1).

We think the word *disciple* is used by Luke in a way different from the majority usage in the New Testament. The term is used 10 times more frequently referring to students in the more intimate sense described above (over 260 uses in the New Testament). On one level, all Christians can be called disciples of Christ. But that does not erase the usual meaning of the term (in the New Testament and in contemporary Jewish and Greco-Roman sources) as a trainee following a particular teacher. "Disciple" may not always have a particular technical definition, and the meaning depends on the context. In this book we are talking about the process of personal mentoring that was clearly practiced in the early church as the main means of raising up new leadership. No one disputes that this was the main means of developing leadership during the apostolic period. Even those who don't use the word discipleship (like Paul) clearly envision this process of personal mentoring. For a contrary view, see James Montgomery Boice, *Christ's Call to Discipleship*, (Chicago: Moody Press, 1986) 16, or Michael J. Wilkins, *Following the Master: A Biblical Theology of Discipleship*, (Grand Rapids MI: Zondervan Publishing House, 1992), p. 24-47.

[4] For instance, the *World Christian Encyclopedia*, estimates that by A.D. 100 there were 1 million Christians in the Roman Empire out of a population of 181 million. David B. Barrett, ed., *World Christian Encyclopedia. A Comparative Study of Churches and Religions in the Modern World A.D. 1900-2000* (Oxford: Oxford University Press, 1982), p. 3. Recently, Rodney Stark has written a book offering an entirely implausible estimate of only 8000 Christians by the end of the first century. We would join most historians in rejecting this estimate. In the first place, we can account for 8000 Christians within the first few chapters of Acts, unless these narratives are completely discounted. Secondly, his estimate is based on a straight mathematical formula assuming 40% growth per decade for 300 years, ending in six million Christians by the time of Constantine. But this is not how Christianity grew. The growth was far better during the early years and slowed thereafter. Rodney Stark, *The Rise of Christianity*, (Princeton: The Princeton University Press, 1996). For a more responsible account see Latourette: "Our records, unsatisfactory though they are, suffice to show that by A.D. 180 Christians were in all the provinces of the Empire and in Mesopotamia." Kenneth Scott Latourette, *A History of the Expansion of Christianity*, Vol. 1, (Grand Rapids, MI. Zondervan Publishing House, 1970), p. 85. He also observes, "Never in the history of the race has this record ever quite been equaled. Never in so short a time has any other religious faith, or, for that matter, any other set of ideas, religious political, or economic, without the aid of physical force or of social or cultural prestige, achieved so commanding a position in such an important culture.", p. 112. Of course, Islam and Communism spread fast, but both used military force. Notice that Tacitus refers to the "huge multitude" of Christians captured

during Nero's persecution Tacitus, *Anal.* XV., p. 44. Shortly after the first century, anti-Christian governor Pliny says that in his province Christians were so numerous that temples were empty, and they couldn't sell sacrificial animals or fodder. (*Pliny*, 10.96.1-2)

[5] If the same rate of growth had continued, everyone on earth would have been a Christian before the end of the second century. Only in our own day do we see a comparable level of growth in some parts of the world, unfortunately not including Europe or the U.S. See Martin Robinson and Dwight Smith, *Invading Secular Space: Strategies for Tomorrow's Church*, (Grand Rapids, MI: Monarch Books, 2003) Chapter 1. Also see David Garrison, *Church Planting Movements*, (Midlothian, VA: WIGTake Resources, 2004).

[6] On the nature of movements, see Max Weber, *On Charisma and Institution Building*, (Chicago: The University of Chicago Press, 1968), Max Weber, *The Sociology of Religion*, Translated by Ephraim Fischoff, (Boston: Beacon Press, 1963). Jay Conger, *The Charismatic Leader: Behind the Mystique of Exceptional Leadership*, (San Francisco, CA: Jossey-Bass Publishers, 1989).

[7] Personal mentoring still happened during this period, but they no longer viewed it primarily as a way to raise up leadership in the church. For instance, the monastic movement had mentors, but their goal became personal holiness and transcendence. In second and third century churches, lay people were trained in the basics of Christianity by catechumens, who taught small classes for the purpose. Priests and bishops were increasingly developed in schools like they still are today. The mentors, or older priests, assigned to students were more like personal counselors and spiritual guides during their stay in school than field trainers in ministry, like Paul. Even though some priests and bishops were trained through an apprentice process, the overwhelming majority of church members never received any personal mentoring. See a good survey of this period in Kenneth Scott Latourette, *A History of the Expansion of Christianity*, Vol. 1.

[8] As William Pauck explains the reformers' perspective, "All Christian believers, therefore, are ministers, servants, priests, by virtue of their faith in the word of God, but not every one of them can or should assume the function of preaching, teaching, and counseling. For the sake of order, certain ones must be set apart from the group of believers to undertake the office of the preacher… 'We are all priests,' wrote Luther, 'insofar as we are Christians, but those whom we call priests are ministers [*Diener*] selected from our midst to act in our name, and their priesthood is our ministry.'" Wilhelm Pauck, "The Ministry in the Time of the Continental Reformation," in *The Ministry in Historical Perspectives*, H. Richard Niebuhr and Daniel D. Williams, Ed. (New York: Harper & Rowe, Publishers, Inc. 1956, 1983) p. 112. Calvin says, "Neither the light and heat of the sun, nor any meat or drink, are so necessary to the nourishment and sustenance of the present life, as the apostolic and pastoral office is to the preservation of the Church in the world." p. 115.

[9] For instance, the medieval underground movement known as the Waldensians practiced discipleship widely. Georgio Tourn cites Catholic descriptions at the time as saying, "Everyone of them, old and young, men and women, by day and by night, do not stop their learning and teaching of others." And the Waldensians themselves said, "In our home, women teach as well as men, and one who has been a student for a week teaches another." Giorgio Tourn, *The Waldensians: The First 800 Years (1174-1974)*, Translated from the Italian by Camillo P. Merlino, Charles W. Arbuthnot, Editor (Torino, Italy: Claudiana Editrice, 1980), p. 6,21,39. Another description says, ". . .men and women, great and lesser, day and night do not cease to learn and teach; the workman who labors all day teaches or learns at night… When someone has been a student seven days, he seeks someone else to teach, as one curtain

pulls another. Whoever excuses himself, saying that he is not able to learn, they say to him, 'Learn but one word [verse of scripture] each day, and after a year you will know three hundred, and you will progress.'" "The Passau Anonymous: On the origins of Heresy and the Sect of the Waldensians," in Edward Peters, *Heresy and Authority in Medieval Europe*, (Philadelphia, PA: The Penn Press, 1980) p. 150-153. German pietism, under the leadership of Jacob Spener advanced the use of home groups with lay leaders. See Dennis McCallum, "Philip Jacob Spener's Contribution to the Protestant Doctrine of the Church" http://www.xenos.org/essays/spen_a.htm. The early Wesleyan movement and the house church movement in China also depended almost exclusively on personal discipleship for leadership training. See Dennis McCallum, "Watchman Nee and the House Church Movement in China" http://www.xenos.org/essays/nee1.htm and Howard Snyder, *The Radical Wesley & Patterns For Church Renewal*, (Downers Grove, Ill.: Inter-Varsity, 1980).

[10] Robert Coleman, *The Master Plan of Evangelism*, (Grand Rapids, MI: Fleming H. Revell, 1963).

[11] Howard & William Hendricks, *As Iron Sharpens Iron*, (Chicago, Moody Press, 1999); Leroy Eims, *The Lost Art of Disciple Making*, (Grand Rapids, MI: Zondervan Publishing Co., 1979); Waylon B. Moore, *Multiplying Disciples: The New Testament Method of Church Growth*, (Colorado Springs, CO: NavPress, 1981). Jim Peterson, *Lifestyle Discipleship* (Colorado Springs: NavPress, 1993); Walter A. Henrichsen, *Disciples Are Made, Not Born* (Wheaton: Victor, 1974); Bill Hull, *The Disciple Making Pastor* (Old Tappan, NJ: Revell, 1988). See our bibliography for more titles.

[12] See David Garrison, *Church Planting Movements*. We have had opportunity to observe explosive discipling-based church planting movements in Cambodia and India. The cell church movement has resulted in huge movements on several continents. See Joel Comiskey, *Home Cell Group Explosion: How Your Small Group Can Grow and Multiply*, (Houston: Cell Group Resources, 2002).

[13] George Barna, *Growing True Disciples*, (Ventura, CA: Issachar Resources, 2000), Chapter 3, "The State of Discipleship." He also cites some notable exceptions.

[14] George Barna, Barna Update, http://www.barna.org/FlexPage.aspx?Page=BarnaUpdateNarrow&BarnaUpdateID=182

[15] George Barna, *Growing True Disciples*, Chapters 6, 7. Even by his extremely liberal definition (where discipleship might be participating in an online spiritual chat group) only a minority of American evangelicals have been discipled. By the stricter standard where discipleship would entail a weekly meeting with a mentor, his figures appear to show that as few as 3% of American evangelicals report being discipled.

Chapter 2

[1] Thomas M. Graham, Ph. D., "Leadership Development: An Empowerment Model," (La Habra, CA: The Center for Organizational and Ministry Development, 1995) p. 2.

[2] In Xenos, deacons are not viewed primarily as servants engaged in practical ministry, like waiting on tables. We see deacons as leaders working under the oversight of elders. See the argument for this approach at http://www.xenos.org/classes/um2.htm

Chapter 3

[1] Robert Coleman, *The Master Plan of Evangelism*, 50ff.

[2] See George Barna, *The Power of Vision*, (Ventura, CA: Regal Books, 1992).

Chapter 5

[1] Adapted from Albert Bandura, *Social Learning Theory*, (Englewood Cliffs, N. J.: Prentice-Hall, Inc., 1977).

[2] From Albert Bandura and R.H. Walters, *Social Learning and Personality Development*, (New York: Holt, Rinehart, and Winston, 1963), p. 10-11, 50, 84, 94-100.

[3] We rarely agree with cross-gender discipleship. Exceptions might include elderly women discipling younger men, or fathers discipling their daughters or other close relatives.

[4] Gene Getz, *Real Prosperity: Biblical Principles of Material Possessions*, (Chicago, IL: Moody Press, 1990).

Chapter 6

[1] We believe J. P. Moreland's book, *Love God With All Your Mind: The Role of Reason in the Life of the Soul*, (Colorado Springs: Navpress, 1997) is essential reading today, especially for gen-Xers and Yers.

[2] Notice David also teaches this in his classic Psalm extolling the wonders of God's word: "I gain understanding from your precepts; therefore I hate every wrong path" (Ps. 119:104), and "Your word I have treasured in my heart, that I may not sin against you" (Ps.119:11).

[3] See also Prov. 2:6: "The Lord gives wisdom, and from his mouth come knowledge and understanding" and Prov. 3:13: "Blessed is the man who finds wisdom, the man who gains understanding."

[4] Legalistic teachers think that focusing too much on grace will lead to apathy or slackness in Christian living. But Paul said grace had the opposite effect on him: "By the grace of God I am what I am, and his grace to me was not without effect. No, I worked harder than all of them—yet not I, but the grace of God that was with me" (1 Cor. 15:10). He also pointed out that what matters is not our strength to do the things of God, but dependence on him to work through us. "[God] said to me, 'My grace is sufficient for you, for my power is made perfect in weakness.' Therefore I will boast all the more gladly about my weaknesses, so that Christ's power may rest on me" (2 Cor. 12:9). When your disciples steep their minds in scripture, they will be far more likely to "be strong in the grace that is in Christ Jesus" (2 Tim. 2:1)

[5] Our favorite is R. Laird Harris, *The Inspiration and Canonicity of the Bible*, (Greenville, SC: A Press, 1995). See also, Norman Geisler, From God to Us, (Chicago, IL: Moody Publishers, 1974).

[6] See http://www.xenos.org/books/index.htm for a good overview of the Bible in Martha McCallum and Keith McCallum, *The Scarlet Thread: Tracing God's Incredible Plan*, (Columbus OH.: Xenos Christian Fellowship, 2005)

[7] Paul Little, *Know What You Believe*, (Downers Grove Ill.: Intervarsity Press, 1988) or see the free outlines at http://www.xenos.org/classes/principles/index.htm.

[8] See http://www.xenos.org/disciple

[9] See our preferred outline for studying this at http://www.xenos.org/disciple. Also, see related books such as, Roy B. Zuck, *Basic Bible Interpretation*, (Wheaton Ill: SP Publications Inc. 1991), Howard Hendrix, *Living by the Book*, (Chicago: Moody Press, 1991) Robertson McQuilken, *Understanding and Applying the Bible*, (Chicago: Moody Press, 1983) Gordon Fee and Douglas Stuart, *How to Read the Bible for All It's Worth: A Guide to Understanding the Bible*, (Grand Rapids, MI: Zondervan Publishing House, 1982).

Chapter 7

[1] This is the "opening of the eyes of our hearts" that Paul prays for: "I pray that the eyes of your heart may be enlightened, so that you will know what is the hope of His calling, what are the riches of the glory of His inheritance in the saints, and what is the surpassing greatness of His power toward us who believe" (Eph. 1:18,19). This enlightening of the eyes of our hearts doesn't usually come to us out of the blue. It comes as we move toward God in thanksgiving and acknowledgement of what we already see. Then, God shows us more.

Chapter 8

[1] James makes it clear that God will not answer all prayers, particularly if we "ask amiss." "When you ask, you do not receive, because you ask with wrong motives, that you may spend what you get on your pleasures" (James 4:3). Of course, no believer who knows God would ever want any prayer answered that was not according to his will. He alone knows what is best for us and others.

[2] This is also what Peter means when he says, "Be of sober spirit, be on the alert. Your adversary, the devil, prowls around like a roaring lion, seeking someone to devour. But resist him, *standing firm in your faith...*" (1 Pet. 5:8,9 NASB, emphasis ours).

Chapter 9

[1] Larry Crabb, *The Silence of Adam*, 35.

[2] The use of these words is summarized in the following chart:

Biblical words related to counseling are addressed to all Christians:
Parakaleo (107 times in New Testament): encourage, comfort, exhort 1 Thessalonians 5:11 "Therefore encourage one another and build up one another, just as you also are doing. Hebrews 10:25 "...let us encourage one another—and all the more as you see the Day approaching."
Didasko (97 times in New Testament) teach, instruct (formally or informally) Colossians 3:16 "Let the word of Christ dwell in you richly as you teach and admonish one another with all wisdom..."
Noutheteo (11 times in New Testament): admonish; counsel Romans 15:14 "And concerning you, my brethren, I myself also am convinced that you yourselves are full of goodness, filled with all knowledge and able also to admonish one another."
Elencho (17 times in New Testament): reprove, expose, convict, refute 2 Timothy 4:2 "preach the word; be ready in season and out of season; reprove, rebuke, exhort, with great patience and instruction."
Epitaimao (33 times in New Testament) rebuke, warn, tell sternly 2 Timothy 4:2 see above

[3] Donald E. Bossart, *Creative Conflict in Religious Education and Church Administration*, (Birmingham: Religious Education Press, 1980) 38. Bossart goes through a number of ways in which conflict can actually enhance groups.

[4] Ken Sande, *The Peacemaker*, (Grand Rapids, MI: Baker Books, 1991,1997).

[5] Ken Sande, *The Peacemaker*, p. 22.

[6] Many conflicts are a combination of affective and material discord. Affective conflict is when people's feelings have been hurt, or they are personally offended by something the other did (e.g. feeling disrespected, insulted, discounted, etc.). Material conflicts center on actual issues, like where to go for vacation or how to run a Bible study group.

We should teach disciples to deal with the affective part of any conflict first. People won't negotiate positively on material issues when they are struggling with hard feelings toward their opponents. But if we deal with the hard feelings, we should be able to move on to the skills needed in good negotiation. Begin with prayer, asking God to reveal what the opponents' position means, and why they hold it. Look for underlying interests that could be met another way. Next be sure your disciples get the facts. They should study the situation being careful not to jump to conclusions. Teach them to identify their own interests, including where they can give way, or defer to their opponents, and where they feel they must stand their ground. They should work on new options that may be acceptable to both sides, and be ready to show their opponents why these new options will benefit them, and satisfy their underlying interests. You will have to coach your disciples through how to meet with their opponents, how to begin negotiations with some positive reflections that affirm relationships, how to invite brainstorming, how to give in on less important issues, and how to persuade opponents to accept important points. You may need to go with your disciple to a meeting as a mediator and show him in person how to use these skills. See also Sande's excellent section on negotiation.

[7] See Dennis McCallum and Gary DeLashmutt, *Spiritual Relationships that Last*, (Columbus OH: Xenos Christian Fellowship, 2002).

[8] Titles we have found helpful include Neil S. Jacobson and Gayla Margolin, *Marital therapy: Strategies based on social learning and behavior exchange principles* (New York: Brunner/Mazel,1979); John M. Gottman, Nan Silver, *The Seven Principles for Making Marriage Work*, (New York, NY: Three Rivers Press, 1999); Leslie Vernick, *How to Act Right When Your Spouse Acts Wrong*, (Colorado Springs, CO: WaterBrook Press, 2001); John Gottman, *A Couple's Guide to Communication*, (IL: Research Press, 1979); Kerry Patterson, Joseph Grenny, Ron McMillan, Al Switzler, *Crucial Confrontations*, (New York, NY: McGraw-Hill, 2004); Douglas Stone, Bruce Patton, Sheila Heen, *Difficult Conversations: How to Discuss What Matters Most*, (New York, NY: Penguin Books, 1999).

[9] See Dennis McCallum, *Walking in Victory*, (Navpress, Xenos 1992, 2003) www.xenos.org\books\wiv.htm

[10] Erickson, speaking in the context of education, says, "Basic and applied research on reinforcement confirms the dominance of reward over punishment. This reminder is relevant to instruction because it is so easy to make comments that are critical, negative, caustic, and threatening about what a student believes, says, and does. A direct or implied put-down to a student can quickly undo the tenuous allegiance and feelings of identification toward the teacher and the area of knowledge he or she represents." Stanford C. Ericksen, *The Essence of Good Teaching*, (San Francisco: Jossey-Bass Publishers, 1984), pp. 44,46.

[11] See also Romans 12:8 where Paul mentions the spiritual gift of encouragement, and urges those with the gift to use it. Paul often says he is sending one of his guys to a local church

so he can encourage them (Eph. 6:22; Col. 4:8; 1 Thess. 3:2). He urges the Thessalonians "Therefore encourage one another and build each other up, just as in fact you are doing" (1 Thess. 5:11; also 5:14). When writing to his disciples, he repeatedly urges them to encourage their people (2 Tim. 4:2; Titus 2:6,15).

[12] Erickson explains: "…a significant finding is the holding power of being reinforced only once in a while—the slot-machine or patient fisherman phenomenon. For reasons that are still a matter of theoretical debate, material learned under conditions of aperiodic [intermittent and irregular] reinforcement remains in memory better than if it were learned under constant or regular reinforcement." Stanford C. Ericksen, *The Essence of Good Teaching*, p. 45.

Chapter 10

[1] J. Oswald Sanders, *Spiritual Leadership*, (Chicago: Moody Press, 1994) p. 36.

Chapter 11

[1] See a good discussion on how leaders can use tension to motivate people in Bruce Powers, *Christian Leadership*, (Nashville, TN: Broadman Press, 1979) p. 34ff.

Chapter 13

[1] Elton Trueblood, *The Best of Trueblood: An Anthology*, (Nashville: Impact Books, 1979), p. 140.

[2] See also 2 Tim. 2:5, 1 Tim. 4:7-8, Eph. 5:15-16, 2 Cor. 5:9, Lk. 13:32.

[3] In order to avoid attaining our goals by human effort (Gal.3:3), we should be careful to place our goals under the sovereignty of God in faith. (James 4:13-15). James wasn't against setting goals. He just wanted us to set goals in a way that is contingent on the will of God.

Chapter 17

[1] Waylon B. Moore, *Multiplying Disciples: The New Testament Method of Church Growth*, p. 14ff.

[2] A number of pastors have asked me (Dennis) where I get the time to put so much focus on discipling and equipping. The answer is that I have been released from many of the functions that typically take up pastors' time. In our church, most ministry is delegated to home churches. When someone gets sick or injured or has a baby, their own home church leaders and members handle the visitation. We have also empowered our home church leaders to marry and bury people. As the senior pastor, I only agree to marry people in my own home church. Home church leaders also counsel their own members, or refer them to our staff counselors or outside pros. I don't counsel people, except those in my own home church, or leaders I'm coaching. We have also hired an adequate administrative staff under a management team. These competent people run the church, freeing our senior leadership to focus on working with people. We also have a deep bench of quality preachers and teachers who can substitute for us if we need to miss a weekend sermon or a class. Our elders' team shares the conviction that nothing our senior leaders do with their time is more valuable to the church than raising up new leaders. They periodically check on me to see if I'm getting too caught up in non-essential work that others could do. The result is that I and the other top leadership are free to focus on bringing up the next generation of leaders. I find that more than anything else, lack of free time to disciple and train are the result of pastors' own lack of priority for this area. Too many pastors are reluctant to delegate time-consuming

traditional functions to others, or to teach their fellow leaders why they should focus on equipping the saints.

[3] Some of our part-time coaches become full-time employees by serving in other capacities such as teaching classes or administration to make up the balance of their time. Others are able to work in a part time capacity because they have other profitable vocations (e.g. medical doctors, or salesmen) or because they are housewives with a second income.

[4] You can read more about the Servant Team and Servant Covenant at: http://www.xenos.org/admin/steam.htm

RECOMMENDED
READING

For a complete, annotated bibliography, see:
http://www.xenos.org\disciple

Adsit, Christopher — *Personal Disciple Making: A Step by Step Guide for Leading a Christian from New Birth to Maturity.* Nashville: Thomas Nelson Publishers, 1988.

Barna, George — *Growing True Disciples: New Strategies for Producing Genuine Followers of Christ.* Colorado Springs: WaterBrook Press, 2001.

Bruce, A. B. — *The Training of the Twelve.* Grand Rapids: Kregel, 1971.

Coleman, Robert E. — *The Master Plan of Evangelism.* Grand Rapids: Baker Book House Company, 1963.

Comiskey, Joel — *Home Cell Group Explosion: How Your Small Group Can Grow and Multiply.* Houston: Cell Group Resources, 2002. 1-800-735-5865

Comiskey, Joel — *Cell Church Solutions: Transforming the Church in North America.* Moreno Valley, CA: CCS Publishing, 2005.

Eims, Leroy — *The Lost Art of Disciple Making.* Colorado Springs: Navpress, 1978.

Forman, Rowland, Jeff Jones, and Bruce Miller. The Leadership Baton: An Intentional Strategy For Developing Leaders In Your Church. Grand Rapids, MI.: Zondervan, 2004.

Fryling, Alice — *Disciplmakers' Handbook: Helping People Grow in Christ.* Downers Grove Ill: InterVarsity Press, 1989.

Hendrichsen, Walter A — *Disciples are Made, Not Born.* Colorado Springs: Cook Communications, 1974.

Hull, Bill — *The Disciple Making Pastor.* Grand Rapids: Baker Book House Co., 1988.

Hull, Bill — *Jesus Christ disciple-maker.* Grand Rapids: Baker Books, 1984, 2004 (20th Anniversary Edition).

Kuhne, Gary W. — *The Dynamics of Discipleship Training: Being and Producing Spiritual Leaders.* Grand Rapids: Zondervan Publishing House, 1978.

Moore, Waylon B. — *Multiplying Disciples: The New Testament Method for Church Growth.* Tampa: Missions Unlimited, 1981.

Ogden, Greg — *Transforming Discipleship: Making Disciples a Few at a Time.* Downers Grove: InterVarsity Press, 2003.

Petersen, Jim — Lifestyle Discipleship: *The Challenge of Following Jesus in Today's World.* Colorado Springs: Navpress, 1993.

Robinson, Martin, and Dwight Smith — *Invading Secular Space: Strategies for Tomorrow's Church.* Grand Rapids, MI: Monarch Books, 2003.